THE DIVE SITES OF
MALAYSIA AND
SINGAPORE

JACK JACKSON

Series Consultant: Nick Hanna

Jack Jackson is a highly regarded photo-journalist who has published a number of books on adventure travel and skippered a dive boat for twelve years. A Fellow of the Royal Photographic Society and a Fellow of the Royal Geographical Society, he lectures widely and writes for many publications.

First published in 1995 by
New Holland (Publishers) Ltd
London • Cape Town • Sydney • Singapore

24 Nutford Place	P.O. Box 1144	3/2 Aquatic Drive
London W1H 6DQ	Cape Town 8000	Frenchs Forest, NSW 2086
UK	South Africa	Australia

ISBN 1 85368 475 9

Project development: Charlotte Parry-Crooke
Series editors: Charlotte Fox/Paul Barnett
Design concept: Philip Mann, ACE Ltd
Design/cartography: ML Design, London
Index: Alex Corrin

Typeset by ML Design, London
Reproduction by Unifoto, Cape Town
Printed and bound in Singapore by Tien Wah Press (Pte) Ltd

Photographic acknowledgements
All photographs by Jack Jackson with the exception of the following:

Gerald Cubitt 10, 36, 46, 73, 90, 92, 111, 122, 129; Footprints 43, 121 (Nick Hanna), 162 top right (Paul Naylor), 13, 98, 105 (Philip Waldock); Jill Gocher 15; R. Mod Noh 8, 15; Linda Pitkin title page 25, 83; Planet Earth 162 bottom left (Peter Scoones); Travel Ink 150 (Ronald Badkin); Lawson Wood 132.

Photography
The author's photographs were taken using Nikonos III, Nikonos V, Nikon F-801s and Nikon F-90 cameras. The Nikonos cameras were used with 15mm and 28mm Underwater Nikkor lenses. The Nikon F-801s cameras were housed in either of two waterproof aluminium housings and used with 14mm, 24mm, 55mm macro and 105mm macro lenses. One of these housings was manufactured by the Austrian company Subal and the other by the Swiss company Hugyfot.

  All the photographs were taken with the addition of electronic flash to replace the colour filtered out by the water. An Oceanic 2001 Strobe was used with the Nikonos III and either a Nikon SB-24 Speedlight in a Subal housing or a Hugyfot/Subtronic Hugystrobe HST300 Professional was used with the other cameras. The film stock used was, variously, Fujichrome Velvia, Fujichrome RDP and the new Kodak Ektachrome Elite/Panther.

AUTHOR'S ACKNOWLEDGEMENTS
Writing a guide book of this nature requires the help and goodwill of local experts, dive operators and divemasters who contribute their time and knowledge. Of the many people who helped me with my diving and research in Malaysia and Singapore, I would like to give special thanks and appreciation to:

- Clement Lee, Randy Davis and Ron Holland, Directors of Borneo Divers, who organized my diving at Labuan and Sangalakki
- Neil Antrum and Jon Rees for their guiding on these dives
- Veronica Lee and Danny Chin, of Pulau Sipadan Resort, who patiently endured the requests of a photographer who considers his photography before anything else!
- Andrew Chong, for showing me the diving in Tunku Abdul Rahman Marine Park and Pulau Tiga Park and for sharing his wealth of knowledge on Layang-Layang
- Daniel D'Orville, for masterminding my diving in Peninsular Malaysia and introducing me to other kindred spirits there
- Lawrence Lee, who, with the help of T.H. Foo of Redang Pelangi Resort, handled the logistics and collected together diving equipment, transport, a boat, fuel and crew so that he could show me the diving around Pulau Redang
- Ramli Chik and Stephen Ng of Perhentian Island Resort, for helping me discover the diving around Pulau Perhentian
- William and Ruby Ong, Directors of Pro Diving Services, Singapore, for their infectious enthusiasm for diving and conservation in Singaporean waters
- Michael Lim, Director of Sharkeys Dive & Adventure, for further information on Singapore diving
- Chan Chee Sing and Azman Sulaiman, for helping me with the diving around Pulau Tioman
- Raja Iskandar, Assistant Director of the Malaysian Tourism Promotion Board in London, for his help with the project; Malaysian Airlines, for flying me out to and around Malaysia
- Susan Abraham, Sarala Aikanathan and Junaidi Payne, of WWF Malaysia, for answering my many awkward questions
- Captain Sim Yong Wah, for his knowledge of some areas that are rarely dived
- And, last but not least, Michael Wong, Paul Street and Paul Etgart, for goading me into making my first visit to Malaysia's underwater paradise

PUBLISHERS' ACKNOWLEDGEMENTS
The publishers gratefully acknowledge the generous assistance during the compilation of this book of the following:

Nick Hanna for his involvement in developing the series and consulting throughout and Dr Elizabeth M. Wood for acting as Marine Consultant and contributing to The Marine Environment.

CONTENTS

How to Use this Book

THE REGIONS
The dive sites included in the book are arranged within eight main geographical regions: Peninsular Malaysia's west coast, Peninsular Malaysia's east coast, Sarawak, the Spratlys, Sabah's north-west coast, Sabah's east/northeast coast, Sangalakki (part of Indonesia but accessed from Sabah), and Singapore. Regional introductions describe the key characteristics and features of these main areas.

THE SUB-REGIONS
The larger geographical regions are divided into smaller sub-regions, ordered from north-west to southeast - west-east bands. Sub-regional introductions provide background information on climate, the environment, points of interest, and advantages and disadvantages of diving in the locality.

THE MAPS
A map is included near the front of each regional or subregional section. The prime purpose of the maps is to identify the location of the dive sites described and to provide other useful information for divers and snorkellers. Though reefs are indicated, the maps do not set out to provide detailed nautical information such as exact reef contours or water depths. In general the maps show: the locations of the dive sites, indicated by white numbers in red boxes corresponding to those placed at the start of the individual dive site descriptions; the locations of key access points to the sites (ports, marinas, beach resorts and so on); reefs, wrecks and lighthouses and travel information. *(NB: the border around maps is not a scale bar)*

MAP LEGEND

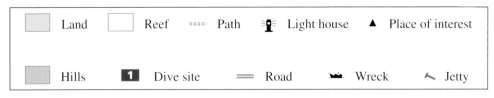

| Land | Reef | ::::: Path | Light house | ▲ Place of interest |
| Hills | 1 Dive site | = Road | Wreck | Jetty |

THE DIVE SITE DESCRIPTIONS
Placed within the geographical sections, and ordered again according to the northwest - southeast - west - east scheme, are the descriptions of each region's premier dive sites. Each site description starts with a number (to enable the site to be located on the relevant map), a star rating (see below), and a selection of symbols indicating key information (see below). Crucial practical details (on location, access, conditions, and average and maximum depths)

precede the description of the site, its marine life and special points of interest.

THE STAR RATING SYSTEM

Each site has been awarded a star rating, with a maximum of five red stars for diving and five blue stars for snorkelling.

Diving		Snorkelling	
★★★★★	**first class**	★★★★★	**first class**
★★★★	**highly recommended**	★★★★	**highly recommended**
★★★	**good**	★★★	**good**
★★	**average**	★★	**average**
★	**poor**	★	**poor**

THE SYMBOLS

 Can be done by diving (applies to all sites except those that are good purely for snorkelling)

 Can be reached by swimming from the nearest shore (even if in order to get to the shore, you need to take a boat)

 Can be reached by local boat

Can be done by snorkelling

Can be reached by live-aboard boat

Suitable for all levels of diver

THE REGIONAL DIRECTORIES

A 'regional directory', which will help you plan and make the most of your trip, is included at the end of each regional or sub-regional section. Here you will find, where relevant, practical information on how to get to an area, where to stay and eat, dive facilities, film processing and hospitals. Local 'non-diving' highlights are also described, with suggestions for sightseeing and excursions.

OTHER FEATURES

At the start of the book you will find practical details and tips about travelling to and in Malaysia and Singapore, as well as a general introduction to the countries themselves. Also provided is a wealth of information about the general principles and conditions of diving in the area, together with advice on learning to dive and snorkel. Here, too, are the contact details of agents for Borneo Divers, the region's premier dive operator. Throughout the book, double-page features and small fact panels on topics of interest to divers and snorkellers are included. As the end of the book are sections on the marine environment (including coverage of marine life, conservation and codes of practice) and underwater photography and video. Also to be found here is information on health, safety and first aid.

INTRODUCTION TO MALAYSIA AND SINGAPORE

Malaysia

Malaysia has everything: friendly people, long empty beaches, coral reefs, beautiful scenery, islands, mountains and hill resorts, and nowadays hundreds of golf courses. The weather is marvellous too; with very few exceptions, temperatures are always about 28°C (82°F). The nation is a confederation of thirteen states plus two federal territories: Wilayah (around Kuala Lumpur) and Pulau Labuan. Nine of the eleven Peninsular states have sultans, and every five years the sultans elect one of their number to reign as King of Malaysia. The states of Sabah and Sarawak in East Malaysia (North Borneo) were not part of the nation when Malaya (as it then was) became independent in 1957, joining the new-formed Federation of Malaysia in 1963 along with Singapore. Singapore left the federation in 1965; Sabah and Sarawak remain within it but retain a greater degree of local administration than the eleven Peninsular states.

In 1981 the government of Prime Minister Dato' Seri Mahathir bin Mohammad came to power, ushering in an era of stability, industrialization and economic growth. Dr Mahathir's policies have attracted foreign investors, and Malaysia is now one of the most stable, prosperous and progressive countries in Southeast Asia. Richly endowed with natural resources, it has the world's largest tin deposits, extensive oil and gas reserves and rainforests full of valuable tropical hardwoods. Until fairly recently the economy was heavily dependent on these resources and on plantation crops: rubber, pepper, cocoa and oil palm. However, dwindling world prices hit the value of plantation crops hard. The best prices are now commanded by oil palm, although the AIDS pandemic in other countries has caused an increase in demand for natural rubber, the main constituent of surgical rubber gloves and condoms.

All modern communications are available: even the remotest island resort has a mobile telephone, and elsewhere virtually every businessman carries a mobile or hand telephone at all times. The rapidly growing tourist industry is now, after manufacturing and oil, the economy's third-largest earner of foreign income.

Opposite: *The modern high-rise city of Kuala Lumpur by night.*
Above: *View across the bay to Singapore from Sentosa Island.*

The logging industry has earned the country notoriety among environmentalists, but much of Malaysia's land area is still forested – although not necessarily with primary rainforest – and the government has been enthusiastically promoting ecotourism. There are several beautiful National Parks, and in Sarawak the cultures of several forest tribes have remained remarkably intact.

THE LAND

Malaysia consists of two distinct regions separated by a 500km (310-mile) stretch of the South China Sea. Peninsular or West Malaysia is a finger of land below Thailand, extending 800km (500 miles) from north to south, with Singapore at its southern tip. East Malaysia is most of the northern part of the island of Borneo.

Most of Peninsular Malaysia is covered in tropical rainforest, especially its northern half, where there are also high mountains. The western side of the peninsula has long fertile plains descending to the sea. The mountains descend more steeply on the

The island of Pulau Tioman, off the east coast of Peninsular Malaysia, is a tropical paradise of golden sand and blue sea.

eastern side, and there are many more beaches there. The central area is sparsely populated.

East Malaysia is divided into Sabah and Sarawak, the latter surrounding the two small enclaves that are the Sultanate of Brunei. Both states are covered in dense tropical rainforest and, particularly Sarawak, have large river systems. Mount Kinabalu (4094m; 13,432ft), in Sabah, is the highest mountain in that part of Southeast Asia lying between the Himalayas and New Guinea.

Geologically, both the peninsula and Borneo are part of the Sunda shelf, although the mountains of the peninsula are older than those of Borneo. The granite pluton that is Mount Kinabalu began pushing up through the sedimentary rocks of the Crocker Range about two million years ago.

FLORA AND FAUNA

The core areas of tropical rainforest in Peninsular Malaysia, Borneo and New Guinea are possibly the most diverse of the world's terrestrial ecosystems; by way of example, in a mere 1ha (2½ acres) of Malaysian rainforest there may be as many as 176 species of tree of bole-diameter over 10cm (4in). This rainforest, dating back some 130 million years, has been cited as the oldest in the world, but this statement has to be qualified: it and its vegetation must have undergone radical change many times during its history in accordance with prevailing geological processes, climate and sea-levels. Peninsular Malaysia has more than 8000 species of flowering plants while the island of Borneo has more than 11,000, most of which – including the world's largest flower, *Rafflesia* – occur in Sabah and Sarawak.

There are some 200 species of mammals, including the Asiatic Elephant, Sumatran Rhinoceros, leopards and clouded leopards. Peninsular Malaysia has a few tigers left and

Borneo has orangutans. More than 450 species of birds, 250 species of reptile and 15,000 varieties of insects are found in Malaysia.

CLIMATE

The climate is tropical, warm and humid all year round. Except on high ground, temperatures rarely drop below 20°C (68°F), even at night, and they are usually somewhere in the range 26–30°C (80–86°F) during the day.

Although the monsoon winds affect the climate, strong winds are uncommon, and typhoons miss the country by several hundred kilometres – indeed, Borneo is often referred to as 'the land below the wind'. In fact, most of the country is not very much affected by the monsoon seasons: only in the northern section of the east coast of Peninsular Malaysia is it deemed necessary to close down offshore tourism and fishing during the monsoon period.

Rain tends to be short and heavy, and usually falls in the late afternoon. In the wetter season it may rain every day.

THE PEOPLE

Malaysia has a population of about 18 million, of whom 85% live in Peninsular Malaysia. Today's people come from many different ethnic groups:

- The **Malays**, originally from Southern China, are the most populous indigenous people of the region; they succeeded the aboriginal people in about 2000BC, and converted to Islam about 400 years ago. Although Malays account for only 50% of the population in Peninsular Malaysia and 20% in East Malaysia, they control the state's politics and determine its religion.
- The **Chinese** originally came seeking trade, some in the 15th century but most in the 19th century. The majority originated in the southern provinces of China, but belonged to a diversity of dialect groups; still today their descendants sometimes have to use English as the language of communication. The Chinese comprise 35% of the population in Peninsular Malaysia, 30% in Sarawak and 20% in Sabah. Many are merchant traders, and so this ethnic group has a large influence on the economy.
- The **Indians**, mainly Tamils, were brought in by the British to provide labour on the plantations. They account for 12% of the population of Peninsular Malaysia, concentrated mainly in the large towns of the west coast.
- The Orang Asli, descendants of the aboriginal people of the area, are scattered around Peninsular Malaysia. Most have been absorbed into modern Malay society, but a few small groups still live in the forests.
- Sarawak has several smaller indigenous tribal groups, best known of whom are the **Iban**, formerly fierce headhunters.
- Sabah has several localized tribal groups including: the **Kadazans**, agriculturists and longhouse dwellers, who live mainly in the west of the state; the **Bajaus**, formerly Sulu Sea pirates (referred to as 'Sea Gypsies' in the Philippines), who live mainly in the northwest of the state and around Semporna in the southeast (where they are known as 'Bajau cowboys' when they ride ponies to round up cattle); and the **Murut**, agriculturists who live in the southwest, in the Tenom area.
- There are also many **Filipino** and **Indonesian** refugees/immigrants in the eastern towns of Semporna, Lahad Datu and Sandakan.

The official language of Malaysia is Bahasa Malaysia, but English is widely understood. Although the state religion is Islam, the Chinese are variously Christians, Taoists, Confucians and Buddhists and the Indians are Hindus, while some of the tribes still retain animist beliefs. Remarkably, this pot-pourri of races and religions now lives together in harmony as a warm friendly people with a rich tapestry of culture.

Singapore

The Republic of Singapore, situated just north of the equator, is a state comprising the island of Singapore – almost completely filled by the city of Singapore – plus 58 islets. The island was a prosperous commercial centre during medieval times, but had so fallen in prestige that, when Sir Thomas Stamford Raffles established a British East India Company base here in 1819, it was largely uninhabited. In 1824 it became part of the British colony called the Straits Settlements, which included also Penang, Malacca and Labuan; in 1858 it came under direct British rule. The Japanese occupied the island from 1942 until ejected by British forces in 1945, and in 1959 Singapore achieved its independence with Lee Kuan Yew as first Prime Minister. Only four years later, however, in 1963, it joined the new Federation of Malaysia – a decision reversed very swiftly, for Singapore broke away again in 1965, having become disillusioned with Malaysia's government. Recent years have seen the conservative party become entrenched in what is seen by the opposition as an increasingly authoritarian government. Lee Kuan Yew finally stepped down from office as recently as 1990.

What was once a pirate haunt, a land covered by malaria-infested rainforest and mangrove swamps where fierce tigers roamed, is now a busy, sanitized city-state with the third-highest per capita income (after Japan and Brunei) in the region. Claimed to be the world's busiest port, it has the world's third-largest oil-refining facilities and acts as a clearing house for the surrounding area's raw materials, including tin, rubber, coconut oil, palm oil, rice, timber, jute, spices and coffee. It is also a major financial centre, and is becoming an increasingly popular tourist stopover.

The climate is hot and humid throughout the year. It is at its wettest and coolest from November to January, when the Northeast Monsoon blows. The hottest months are from March to July.

Singapore itself is a small island – a mere 30km (19 miles) by 42km (26 miles), with a land area of 633km^2 (244 sq miles), although this is slowly increasing as more and more land is reclaimed from the sea. The island is connected to Peninsular Malaysia by a 1200m (1310yd) causeway.

THE PEOPLE
The population is about 3 million, of whom some 76% are Chinese, most originally from the southern provinces of China. The Chinese are the powerhouse of the economy. Other elements of the population are

• The **Malays** (15.1%), the original inhabitants of the area, converted to Islam by the early Arab traders
• **Indians** (6.5%), mostly Tamils plus a smaller number of Malayalam-speaking peoples from Kerala, whose ancestors were brought in as indented labourers and built many of Singapore's fine public buildings

• **Eurasians** descended from the former Portuguese colonists of Malacca in Malaysia and Goa in India
• **Arabs** descended from the early Arab traders
• **Armenians** (it was the Armenian Sarkies brothers who established the famous Raffles Hotel)
• **Jews**, who in the mid-19th century were prominent in business, law and medicine

There is also a proportionately large professional expatriate community, representing multinational companies based in the area.

There are four official languages: Mandarin Chinese, Bahasa Malaysia, Tamil and English. English is the prime language of business and administration, and serves also as the common language between the various ethnic groups.

TIME	
Throughout Malaysia and Singapore local time is:	
GMT	+ 8hr
Australia	+ 2hr
Canada	-16hr
New Zealand	+ 4hr
USA (EST)	- 16hr
USA (WST)	- 13hr

The busy harbour of Singapore bustles with commercial ships and private yachts.

TRAVELLING TO AND IN MALAYSIA AND SINGAPORE

Getting to Malaysia and Singapore and travelling around once there is generally straight-forward unless you are heading for a very remote destination. Transport and communications are efficient and travel information is readily available. This section provides a summary of useful travel details to help you plan your trip; for more specific information check the Regional Directory at the end of each regional section in the book or contact your nearest tourist office.

HEALTH

A certificate of vaccination against yellow fever is necessary for visitors coming from endemic zones. Immunizations against hepatitis-A, tetanus, typhoid and polio are recommended. Malaysia and Singapore are clean countries: the tap water in towns and resorts is safe to drink, and freshly cooked food and peeled fruit are safe to eat. Food cooked in front of you at roadside stalls and small restaurants can be safer to eat than that in luxury hotels, where it is often cooked earlier and then reheated. The risk of AIDS is present, although less so than in some neighbouring countries. Malaria is prevalent in Southeast Asia, so do not neglect to take sensible precautions.

Medical insurance
Malaysia and Singapore have modern medical facilities, but you cannot expect to find them in remote areas. It is always wise to buy a travel and medical insurance policy that includes repatriation by Air Ambulance in case of a serious accident or illness. If you do not have a specialist diving insurance policy, make sure that you pay the extra premium on your travel and medical insurance to cover diving activities.
Recompression (Hyperbaric) Chambers
For information on recompression chambers in Malaysia and Singapore see *Diving and Snorkelling in Malaysia and Singapore* (page 33).

Opposite: *Kuala Lumpur's Moorish railway station, built by the British in 1910.*
Above: *View from the high-speed ferry on its way to Batam Island off Singapore.*

Malaysia

ARRIVING
By air: Peninsular Malaysia's main gateway, served by 27 international airlines, is Subang International Airport, 24km (15 miles) north of Kuala Lumpur. Scheduled flights are also available to Langkawi, Pulau Pinang and Kota Kinabalu. **By rail:** Trains from Bangkok run down the main Malaysian west-coast line via Butterworth (for Pulau Pinang) to Kuala Lumpur. **By road:** Long-distance express buses link major towns and cities in Malaysia with Singapore and destinations in Thailand. **By sea:** High-speed catamarans operate scheduled services linking Pulau Pinang and Langkawi on Malaysia's west coast with Medan in Sumatra and Phuket in Thailand.

ENTRY FORMALITIES
Your passport should be valid for at least six months from your date of entry into Malaysia.

Visas
Visas are not required for UK protected persons, Commonwealth citizens (except Indians) or citizens of the Republic of Ireland, Liechtenstein, the Netherlands, San Marino and Switzerland. Citizens of Belgium, Denmark, Finland, France, Germany, Iceland, Italy, Luxembourg, Norway, Sweden and the USA may stay up to three months without a visa, so long as they are not working. Citizens of ASEAN countries do not require visas for visits

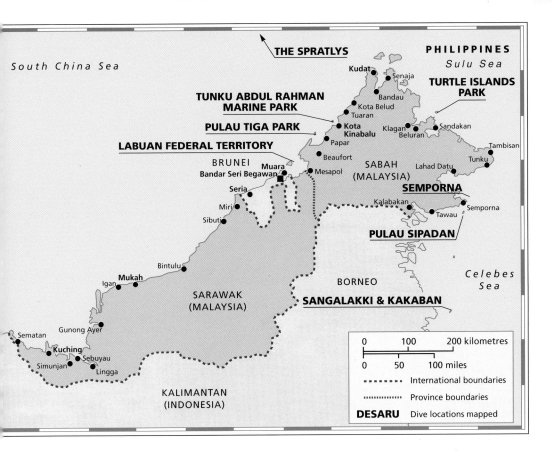

not exceeding one month. Citizens of most other countries may visit for up to 14 days without a visa, except for those of Cambodia, Eastern Europe, the Commonwealth of Independent States, Laos and Vietnam, who must obtain visas in advance of their arrival from their nearest Malaysian Diplomatic Mission or from the British Consular Representative in countries where there are no Malaysian representatives. On arrival visitors receive a one-month visitor's permit; Commonwealth citizens can get a two-month permit if required. You must keep this with you until you leave. Visitors' permits issued on entry to Peninsular Malaysia are not automatically valid for entry into Sabah and Sarawak. Visitors have to go through immigration again, even though the flight is an internal one. There is a similar check on exit from Labuan. To visit any national park, or to take an up-river trip in Sarawak, you require a permit from the national or state parks office.

LOCAL TRAVEL AGENTS IN KUALA LUMPUR

All hotels will act as agents for city tours. For tours around Malaysia:

Adventures Malaysia 1 Bangunan Bakti, Jalan Dang Wangi; tel 03—2924403

Iten Tours & Travel Sdn Bhd 3rd Floor, 7 Jalan Barat, 46200 Petaling Jaya, Selangor; tel 03—7563328/fax 03—7563613

Overland Discovery Tours Unit 15, 1st Podium Floor, Shangri-La Hotel; tel 03—2302942

Reliance Travel Agencies 3rd Floor, Sungei Wang Plaza; tel 03—2486022

Customs
The duty-free allowances are 200 cigarettes, 50 cigars or 250 grams of tobacco, perfume not exceeding 200 ringgits in value, and 1 litre of liquor or wine. There is no limit on still cameras, but visitors bringing in video equipment may have to pay a refundable deposit for temporary importation. You are not allowed to bring in weapons or pornography. The trafficking of illegal drugs carries the death penalty. Export permits are required for arms, ammunition, explosives, animals and plants, platinum, precious stones and jewellery (except for reasonable personal effects), antiques, poisons, drugs and vehicles. Visitors may import up to 10,000 ringgits and export up to 5000 ringgits.

Airline concession
Malaysian Airlines used to offer an airline concession, available on request, of 30kg (66 pounds) extra baggage allowance for divers. This was cancelled in 1993.

MONEY

The Malaysian unit of currency is the ringgit (= 100 sen), although local people always refer to it as the `dollar' and write it as $ (or M$). Most credit cards are widely accepted; credit-card fraud occurs as in any other country. Travellers' cheques are likewise widely accepted, as are cash notes of the world's major trading currencies — especially the US dollar. Banks with currency-exchange facilities can be hard to find and transactions there are generally very slow; legal money changers are usually easier and quicker to use and offer the same rates of exchange as the banks for travellers' cheques — often better rates for large-denomination cash notes. A government directive states that only foreign unmarked cash notes in perfect condition are acceptable, so if you are planning to take currency of your country of domicile ask your bank for clean, unmarked notes.

ACCOMMODATION

A wide range of accommodation to suit all tastes and budgets is on offer in Malaysia, though facilities are limited at some of the remoter dive locations. Suggestions for where to stay are given in the Regional Directory at the end of each regional section. If you need to stay in Kuala Lumpur, refer to the fact panel above.

ELECTRICITY

The electricity supply is 220-240 volts/50 cycles, as used in Europe. Most electrical sockets are of the three-square-pin type used in the UK. Many hotels now have a system whereby the electricity can be switched on only if you have inserted a plastic token, permanently attached to the room key, into a slot in your room. This is obviously a nuisance if you wish to charge batteries or keep the air conditioning going while you are out! However, many of these systems can be kept switched on by putting a piece of stiff cardboard or plastic into the relevant slot.

WHERE TO STAY IN KUALA LUMPUR

Kuala Lumpur has horrific traffic jams during the rush hours, so try to find accommodation within walking distance of the centre. There are countless hotels and restaurants; here are just a few:

Upper Price Range
Kuala Lumpur Hilton Jalan Sultan Ismail, PO Box 10577, 50718 Kuala Lumpur; tel 03–2422222/fax 03–2438069

Shangri-La 11 Jalan Sultan Ismail, 50250 Kuala Lumpur; tel 03–2322388/fax 03–2301414

Medium Price Range
Hotel Orkid 300 Jalan Pudu, 55100 Kuala Lumpur; tel 03–2486222/fax 03–2485177

Agora Hotel 106–110 Jalan Bukit Bintang, 55100 Kuala Lumpur; tel 03–2428133/fax 03–2427815

Lower Price Range
Cheng Traveller Lodge Jalan Utara, off Jalan Imbi; tel 03–9823960. Dormitory-style accommodation.

Meridien International Youth Hostel 38 Jalan Hang Kasturi; tel 03–2321428

GETTING AROUND

Peninsular Malaysia has a good road system, a railway that runs its length from Thailand to Singapore and a good internal air-transport system. All are easy to use and relatively cheap. Some areas have rickshaws, but taxis are inexpensive, and better if you have a lot of luggage; if you take a taxi between towns you will be expected to pay as if it had a full complement of four passengers. There are good, cheap long-distance bus services, though those marked 'express' in fact stop for a meal every two hours and wait an hour or more at major bus stations. I have found long-distance bus drivers and taxi drivers remarkably helpful; bus drivers often drop me at a taxi rank near where I want to go, rather than taking me to the central bus station and taxi drivers often help me organize the next part of my journey.
Kuala Lumpur's traffic comes to a standstill during the rush hours, so try to avoid those periods. There are regular ferry services to **Pulau Tioman** and **Pulau Perhentian** from the Peninsular mainland. If you do not have much luggage, air transport can save a lot of time. Most flights have the standard 20kg (44 pounds) checked baggage limit, although for flights on small aircraft to the islands the limit is only 10kg (22 pounds). On all flights there is a departure tax of five ringgits for domestic flights and 20 ringgits for international flights. In **Sabah** the road system is not as good as in Peninsular Malaysia, and in some areas it is better to fly; here again the cost of flying is relatively modest. There are regular ferry services to **Labuan. Sarawak** is rather different: most internal transport is by river. It is, however, now possible to fly to the cave systems commonly visited by tourists.

FILM PROCESSING IN KUALA LUMPUR

KL has numerous mini-labs that process print film but E6-transparency processing is limited. Most listed below also handle E6 processing for photo-shops in the provinces.

Bakway Translide Sdn Bhd 1A Jalan 19/1, 46300 Petaling Jaya Selangor; tel 03-7574140/fax 03-7579325

Kemajuan Professional Lab (M) Sdn Bhd 14 Jalan 19/3, 46300 Petaling Jaya Selangor; tel 03-7554979/fax 03-7554106

Advert Studio 22/23B Lrz Rahim Kajai, 13 Taman Tun Dr Ismail, 60000 Kuala Lumpur; tel 03-7186133/fax 03-7182321

PP Foto Sdn Bhd Lot 122, First Floor, City Point, Dayabumi Complex, Jalan Sultan Hissammuddin, 50050 Kuala Lumpur; tel 03-2744942

MALAYSIA TOURIST OFFICES

The Malaysia Tourism Promotion Board (MTPB) has offices all over Malaysia and in many different countries of the world. For further details contact the Head Office (address below).

Head Office
24th–27th Floor, Menara Dato Onn, Putra World Trade Centre, 45 Jalan Tun Ismail 50480 Kuala Lumpur tel 03-2935188 fax 03-2935884

Sabah
Ground Floor, Wisma Wing Onn Life, No 1, Jalan Sagunting 88000 Kota Kinabalu tel 088-248698 fax 088-241764

Sarawak
2nd Floor, AIA Building Bukit Mata Kuching Jalan Song Thian Cheok 93100 Kuching tel 082-246575 fax 082-248442

Australia
Tourist Development Corporation Malaysia, 65 York Street, Sydney, NSW 2000, Australia tel 672-2994441 fax 672-2622026

Germany
Tourist Development Corporation Malaysia, Rossmark 11, 6000 Frankfurt Am Main, Germany tel 069-283782 fax 069-285215

Singapore
Tourist Development Corporation Malaysia, 10 Collyer Quay #01–03, Ocean Building Singapore 0104 tel 5326351 fax 5366650

UK
Tourist Development Corporation Malaysia, 57 Trafalgar Square London WC2N 5DU United Kingdom tel 0171-9307932 fax 0171-9309015

USA
Malaysia Tourist Information Centre, 818 Suite 804, West Seventh Street, Los Angeles, CA 90017, USA tel 213-6899702 fax 213-6891530

Singapore

By air: Singapore's Changi International Airport – 20km (12$^{1}/_{2}$ miles) from the city centre – is a major international and regional hub and is served by about 45 airlines. There are also air connections to the more popular tourist islands off Peninsular Malaysia. Airport tax is S$5 for flights to Malaysia and S$12 for international flights. **By rail:** Trains from Bangkok run down the main Malaysian west-coast line to reach Singapore. **By road:** Long-distance express buses link Singapore with major towns and cities in Malaysia. **By sea:** There are regular ferries between Singapore and Indonesia's Riau archipelago. There are cruise-ship connections from Singapore to other nations.

ENTRY FORMALITIES

Your passport should be valid for at least six months from your date of entry into Singapore.

Visas

Visas are not required for citizens of Commonwealth countries, the USA and Western Europe. Citizens of these countries arriving by air receive a one-month visitors' permit on entry; those arriving by sea or from Peninsular Malaysia via the causeway receive a two-week visitors' permit. Citizens of most other countries do not require a visa for a stay of up to 14 days so long as they have confirmed onward reservations. However, citizens of China, the Commonwealth of Independent States and India must obtain a visa before arrival. If in any doubt, check with the nearest Singapore Embassy before departure.

Customs

Singapore is a free port. There is an allowance of 1 litre of liquor and 1 litre of wine. Cosmetics do not attract duty, but there is no duty-free allowance for tobacco. There are no limits on the import or export of currency. However, export permits are required for arms, ammunition, explosives, animals and plants, gold, platinum, precious stones, jewellery, poisons and drugs. You are not allowed to bring in weapons or pornography, and since 1992 the importation and sale of chewing gum has been banned. Trafficking in illegal drugs carries the death penalty. There is no duty-free allowance for goods brought in from Malaysia, and you are not entitled to duty-free goods if you have been out of Singapore for less than 48hrs.

MONEY

The unit of Singaporean currency is the Singapore dollar, usually written as $. There are 100 cents to the Singapore dollar. The Singapore dollar is directly interchangeable with the Brunei dollar and used to be so with the Malaysian ringgit, but is now worth more. When I was here in 1993 I found I could get a relatively better rate of exchange for pounds sterling than for US dollars. All major credit cards are accepted. Despite Singapore's reputation as a place for cheap shopping – the camera shops tend to be full of Japanese tourists buying Japanese cameras – in general it is much more expensive than Malaysia. As for those consumer goods, I found that most of the items I looked at were not particularly cheap, although hard bargaining could be used to reduce prices a bit.

ACCOMMODATION

Singapore has numerous hotels ranging from luxury establishments, including some of the world's best hotels, through to low-budget guest houses. For suggestions on where to stay, refer to the Singapore Regional Directory on page 154.

ELECTRICITY

The electricity supply is 220-240 volts/50 cycles, as used in Europe, and the electrical sockets are almost always of the UK three-square-pin type, only some of the older buildings still having the two-round-pin variety. The 'token' system for governing the use of electricity in hotel rooms, as employed in Malaysia, operates here in Singapore as well.

GETTING AROUND

Singapore has an excellent internal road system. Traffic jams are kept to a minimum by strict control over car ownership and by traffic no-go areas. These inconveniences are compensated for by cheap, efficient public transport. Double- and single-decker buses charge a low fixed price. Taxis are relatively inexpensive, too, even to and from the airport, and the MRT (Mass Rapid Transport – a light railway system of which about one-third is underground) is both cheap and easy to use. In fact, if you find accommodation in the central area of the city, most of the sights of interest and the main shopping area are within walking distance.

SINGAPORE TOURIST OFFICES		
For further details on other offices contact the Head Office (address below)	Germany Poststrasse 2–4 D-6000 Frankfurt/Main tel 069–231456	UK 1st Floor, Carrington House 126–130 Regent Street London W1R 5FE tel 0171–4370033
Head Office 36–04 Raffles City Tower 250 North Bridge Road tel 3396622	Hong Kong 1–3, D'Aguilar St Central Hong Kong tel 5–224052	USA NBR 12th Floor 590 Fifth Ave New York, NY 10036
Australia Suite 1604, Level 16, Westpac Plaza 60 Margaret Street Sydney 2000 tel 02–2413771	New Zealand c/o Walshes World 2nd Floor, Dingwall Building 87 Queens Street Auckland 1 tel 9–793708	tel 212–3024861 and Suite 510,8484 Wilshire Blvd Beverly Hills CA 90211 tel 213–8521901

DIVING AND SNORKELLING IN MALAYSIA AND SINGAPORE

ocal and expatriate sports divers living in Malaysia, Brunei and Singapore have been diving the east coast of Peninsular Malaysia and the west coast of Sabah, in East Malaysia, since scuba-diving equipment first became available, but it was only in the late 1980s, with the discovery of the delights of the island of Sipadan, off the east coast of Sabah, that Malaysia became a truly international diving destination. Since then, divers have been arriving in droves from all over the world.

Apart from the Layang-Layang area (see page 93), Malaysian and Singaporean diving is generally easy and relaxed. There is something for divers and snorkellers of all levels. All the dive operations I came across had instructors trained under the US PADI, NAUI or SSI systems, with a few of them trained under the BSAC system. Some operators were quite small and laid-back, but all had well maintained modern diving equipment plus oxygen equipment for emergencies.

THE EAST COAST OF PENINSULAR MALAYSIA

By comparison with Pulau Sipadan, the diving around Pulau Tioman (see page 74) and Pulau Perhentian (see page 48) is not well known outside Malaysia and Singapore, and the attractions of Pulau Redang (see page 58), Pulau Aur (see page 84) and Pulau Tenggol (see page 68) are even less well publicized. Among these, only the Pulau Tioman and Pulau Perhentian areas are properly organized for diving as yet, but Pulau Redang, Pulau Tenggol and Pulau Aur have considerable potential and are likely to become mainstream international diving destinations in the near future.

The marine life and its rate of growth are prolific around Pulau Tioman and Pulau Perhentian; this may be largely a consequence of the great amount of plankton often to be found in the water. The Pulau Redang region has larger areas of stony corals and less sand,

Opposite: *This feather star (Comanthus bennetti), like most crinoids, can walk on short jointed legs.*
Above: *Divers returning to the Pulau Sipadan resort after a boat dive.*

and possibly for this reason the visibility is often better here. Similar conditions prevail at Pulau Aur and Pulau Tenggol.

The waters around all these islands are shallow. The terrain generally consists of large boulders jumbled on top of one another leading down to sand. These boulders are carpeted with stony corals, soft corals, sponges and, in the deeper water, gorgonian sea fans, large *Dendronephthya* soft-tree corals, harp corals and black corals. Down on the sand there are also patches of stony corals and barrel sponges. Among the boulders are short tunnels that you can swim through and small caves; these latter harbour the coral and sponge growths normally associated with underwater caverns and offer shelter to shoals of fish.

Some of these jumbles of boulders break the surface, in which case they are often referred to as `islands', an appellation they hardly deserve. Those assemblages that remain entirely underwater are usually buoyed to reduce anchor damage. The dives are suitable for all standards of divers and, where the rocks and reefs come near to the surface, provide good snorkelling.

THE SPRATLYS
One of the newest frontiers for Malaysian diving is offered by the Spratlys (see page 93), a huge area of reefs, shoals and islands spread across the South China Sea from Borneo to Vietnam. The Layang-Layang area of the Spratlys offers mostly wall diving, often with strong currents. There are lots of exciting large pelagic species, although these are often found only at depths too great for all but very experienced divers.

SABAH
The famous shipwrecks at Labuan (see page 115), off the Borneo coast, are another major attraction. Shipwrecks anywhere are a haven for fish life, sponges and corals, and Labuan's are no exception.

Like cave penetration, swimming into wrecks is serious stuff, and can be dangerous; US training agencies treat these subjects as separate training modules. Only advanced divers, those already trained in wreck or cave diving, or those being trained and accompanied by an instructor should penetrate wrecks or caverns. Advanced divers still have much to explore and discover here. But this is not to say that novice divers will not find plenty to interest them on the wrecks: there is much to be seen even without penetrating the hulls.

Elsewhere in Sabah, the coral reefs around the islands of Tunku Abdul Rahman Park (see page 100) and Tiga Park (see page 110) are at shallow depths and are ideally suited to snorkelling and to the training of novices. The slightest amount of rough weather lowers underwater visibility in this area.

SIPADAN
Pulau Sipadan (see page 130) has just about everything. You can take your pick from the easiest of diving and snorkelling in shallow water above coral, drifting with the currents on the more exposed sites, diving as deep as safety allows down the walls, or penetrating the renowned Turtle Cavern.

The deep walls have exciting pelagic species, huge barrel sponges, large gorgonian sea fans and *Dendronephthya* soft corals. The shallower walls have hanging gardens of sponges, smaller gorgonian sea fans, *Dendronephthya* and *Dendrophyllia* corals, nudibranchs, reef fish, crabs, lobsters, shoals of jacks, barracuda and Rainbow Runners, while the shallow reef crest has fields of colourful stony corals, soft corals and sponges, in excellent condition, together with most of the Indo-Pacific reef-fish species. There are turtles everywhere.

Shore and night diving could not be easier or more reward-ing. All dives from boats are drift dives, but novices should be quite happy on these if they stay with the divemaster.

SANGALAKKI

Neighbouring Pulau Sangalakki (see page 143) offers the same sort of variety as Sipadan, but is especially good for Manta Rays; it also has a remarkable number of giant *Tridacna* clams, rare elsewhere. Currents are the rule rather than the exception. Shore dives are not possible, and night dives need to be carefully thought out beforehand. The wall diving on offer here is in fact at nearby Pulau Kakaban, which also has a remarkable jellyfish lake.

As at Pulau Sipadan, all dives from boats are drift dives, but novices should be quite happy on these if they stay with the divemaster.

SARAWAK

Although Sarawak is not considered a top-notch diving des-tination at the moment, there are reports of possible diving resort development in the future. The area is, however, noted for its turtle sanctuaries, some of which may be visit-ed with permission from the Office of the Director of the Sarawak Museum.

SPEARFISHING

It is not without reason that divers detest the practice of spearfishing.

• Spearfishing does not have a bal-anced effect on the local ecology since generally only the larger speci-mens – often the healthiest breeding males – are taken.

• Other fish learn to associate divers with predation, and keep well clear. This seriously mars our enjoyment of the underwater world.

With rod and line fishing, by contrast, the individual fish are caught at random (although the bait and technique may affect which species is preferentially caught) and the surviving fish have no cause to assume divers are predators.

A majestic Green Turtle (Chelonia mydas) passes by divers in the clear waters of Pulau Sipadan.

THE WEST COAST OF PENINSULAR MALAYSIA

The diving areas off the west coast of Peninsular Malaysia have prolific marine life, but the visibility is generally poor – even for snorkelling. The big resorts are highly organized and have diving operations and equipment, but this is not an area you would visit specifically for its diving; rather, you might go for a holiday at one of its luxurious resorts and try out the diving while there. The Payar Marine Park (see page 38) is the focus of the west coast's diving, but it hardly bears comparison with what is on offer elsewhere in Malaysia.

SINGAPORE

The diving around Singapore (see page 151) is much the same. This is the world's busiest port, and shipping movements and construction work never cease. This is certainly a good area for learning to dive but, once you are qualified, you are more likely to take a weekend's break and travel to Pulau Tioman or one of the nearer Indonesian islands, while the rest of Malaysian and Indonesian diving and even Palau are within relatively easy reach.

Big Fish

The fish you are likely to encounter in this region are discussed on pages 157-164, but the bigger species make their own headlines! Before talking about them, though, we should make some mention of the turtles. These are one of the big attractions of Malaysian diving. At Pulau Sipadan and Pulau Sangalakki they are everywhere and in large numbers, but you can expect to see them while diving in most of the other areas as well.

Manta Rays are likewise common. Large numbers of them are permanently at Pulau Sangalakki, but they are found in most other areas whenever the plankton is close to the surface. Also frequently encountered are Whale Sharks. As with Manta Rays, the occasional individual can appear almost anywhere at any time of year, particularly off Pulau Tioman and Pulau Aur and occasionally off Pulau Sipadan. You are certain to see them off the west coast of Sabah between January and April, when they arrive in large numbers pursuing krill that feed on the plankton.

Other sharks are less frequently seen. Timid Whitetip Reef, Nurse and Leopard (Variegated) sharks can be found at Pulau Sipadan, while Grey Reef and Hammerhead sharks may be discovered on wall dives anywhere. Silvertip Sharks have been seen at Layang-Layang. Dawn and dusk are the best times to dive if you want to look at sharks.

In fact, you may see them without having to dive at all! If you walk around the beaches of Pulau Sipadan, Pulau Sangalakki, Pulau Tioman or Pulau Perhentian at dawn you are very likely to spot small Whitetip Reef and Blacktip Reef sharks patrolling close inshore, probably hoping to find some turtle hatchlings for breakfast.

Diving Conditions

WEATHER

As in other regions of Southeast Asia, it is advisable to check climatic conditions carefully when planning your dive trip. In Malaysia each area has two main seasons: the drier season and the so-called 'monsoon' season (which in this country could more accurately be called the wetter season!). In the past few years these seasonal distinctions have become blurred, as global weather patterns have been unusual; there have even been drought-induced forest fires in some parts of the rainforest. The start and finish of a season can vary by a few weeks either way in any particular year, so it is best to try to avoid the periods of overlap.

Here are some guidelines for the different regions of Malaysia:

• In general, the western side of Peninsular Malaysia enjoys its drier season between November and March and its wetter season, due to the southwest monsoon, between April and October.

• The eastern coast of Peninsular Malaysia has the drier season from April to October and its wetter season, due to the northeast monsoon, from November to March. The eastern coast's rainy season is wetter than that on the western coast.

• Sabah's eastern coast, Pulau Sipadan and Pulau Sangalakki can be dived comfortably all year round. There may be days of heavier rain than usual when typhoons are hitting the northern Philippines, China or Japan, but not enough to stop you diving.

• The western coast of Sabah has its drier weather from January to May and its wetter season from June to September.

• Layang-Layang can have bad weather at any time, but it has its best from April to September.

UNDERWATER VISIBILITY

The clarity of the waters in which you dive is very variable, depending on a number of factors.

• Mid-ocean waters can have visibilities up to 100m (110yd), but coastal waters are affected by rain, run-off, decaying organic matter, disturbed bottom sediment, industrial and domestic pollution, landfill, quarrying, volcanic eruptions and plankton blooms.

• Local mineral deposits and/or mining activities on the nearby landmass can affect the colour of the water, a phenomenon usually first noticed by photographers.

• Heavy rain can affect the visibility, even in open water, if wind or bad weather causes the fresh and salt water – which have different densities – to mix.

• Heavy rain can also initiate a plankton bloom, particularly near sites of domestic and agricultural run-off. Such run-offs nowadays tend to be rich in phosphates from fertilizers.

• Visibility is obviously better in general over deep water or a rocky or coral bottom, since it is less affected by particles drifting up from the sea floor. If you take care over your buoyancy you will be less likely to disturb the bottom and thereby impair the visibility.

• Ebb tides carry sand from beaches and sediment from the tops of reefs, so visibility is usually better on the flood tide.

VISIBILITY

In Malaysia, as in most areas of the world, underwater visibility drops after rain. Apart from at Layang-Layang and Sipadan – where the visibility rarely drops below 30m (100ft) – Malaysian diving is over the shallow sandy bottoms of the continental shelf, which has the advantage that the water is always warm but the disadvantage that any period of wind or rain (and even heavy shipping movements) lowers visibility. The tide is another factor.

• Due to agricultural run-off, the muddy bottom and the heavy shipping traffic in the area, the west coast of Peninsular Malaysia never has clear seas, and often the visibility is downright awful.

• Heavy shipping traffic and construction work spoil the clarity off Singapore. Here a visibility of 3m (10ft) is likely to be considered good at any time!

• The visibility at Pulau Tioman and Pulau Perhentian can vary anywhere between 3m (10ft) and 30m (100ft); divemasters on these islands told me that local visibility can be very good just before the start of the wetter season, but unfortunately this was not evident when I visited in October 1993. Many of the divemasters here do not pay enough attention to the time of day and the tide tables, thus missing the opportunity to maximize the chances of diving when the visibility is good. Among additional factors, illicit overnight bottom-trawling by Thai fishing boats can affect the clarity at Pulau Perhentian, and naval exercises can diminish it at Pulau Tioman.

• When I dived Pulau Redang, Pulau Tioman and Pulau Perhentian were suffering murky waters but the waters here were clear. Redang commonly enjoys a visibility in the region of 30–60m (100–200ft).

• The diving around the islands off the west coast of Sabah is so shallow that any construction work on the nearby mainland or any windy weather lowers the visibility, which is normally around 3–15m (10–50ft). In January to April, the time when the Whale Sharks are here, there is a lot of plankton in the water, and this obviously has the effect of reducing visibility.

DRIFT-DIVING TIPS

Drift-diving may be a matter of being carried effortlessly along a wall in a gentle current. But it may involve high-voltage rushes along walls and gullies with the aim of spotting large pelagic species. Aside from the possibility of colliding with something, the main hazards concern boat cover and separation from the rest of your group.

• If you are not using surface marker buoys, carry a high-visibility orange rescue tube or a collapsible flag. Either can be raised above the swell to make you more visible to the boat crew.
• Always carry a whistle. Power whistles are better than ordinary mouth whistles.
• Buddies – and preferably the whole group – should enter the water together so as not to get separated at the outset. Thereafter you should do your best to stick together.
• Stopping to inspect or photograph something is a common way of getting separated from the rest of your group. It helps if photographers operate in pairs.
• If a pair or group lose contact with the boat cover, they should tie a buddy line between each other, inflate their buoyancy-compensator devices (stabilizing jackets) and conserve air, in case they later have to make a difficult exit through surf or foaming breakers. It is usually best to retain your weight belt unless buoyancy is a problem; in some circumstances it may be better to jettison your cylinders.
• If you want to try to fin ashore, it is usually less tiring to fin on your back.
• On approaching the shore, untie the buddy line before you try to swim through surf or breakers.

• The reefs off Labuan are affected by the outflows from Sarawak's rivers, by heavy shipping traffic and by the current major construction work for the new marina. The wrecks are quite a long way out, but even so the visibility is in general not good, though it may be better on the sheltered side of a wreck in a current. A visibility of 3–15m (15–50ft) is normal but, as with all wreck sites, the 'atmosphere' is more important than the clarity of the water.

TEMPERATURES
The waters around Malaysia and Singapore are warm, and most divers will be quite happy with just a lycra skin-suit for protection. Snorkellers, for protection against sunburn, would be wise to wear either a lycra skin-suit or an old shirt and trousers. Photographers, who do not fin around very much, will be well served by a 3–4mm (1/6in) wetsuit, although when making five dives per day I found I began to feel the cold during night dives.

Right: Large soft coral Sarcophyton trochelio-phorum colonies which grow to more than a metre (40in) across are very common. They appear smooth and leathery when the polyps are retracted.

Equipment

Although you can hire snorkelling equipment almost anywhere, it's preferable to have your own. Apart from the fact that you save money in the long term, rented equipment can sometimes be in poor condition or a poor fit. There's nothing worse than a mask that leaks.

Masks

Make sure the mask you choose fits properly. Most masks now have frames made from silicone rubber; these are pleasanter to wear and last longer. The mask should form a good seal against your face and feel comfortable. To check for the correct fit, first fold the strap over the faceplate, so that it is out of the way, and press the mask onto your face while looking at the ceiling. Then breathe in through your nose and look downwards. The mask should stay firmly on your face as long as you continue to inhale. Roll your eyes both vertically and horizontally to make sure the field of view is good.

Snorkels

Snorkels are used not only by snorkellers: divers always have one in order to save air supplies while at the surface or in case of a long swim back to the boat or shore. A good snorkel allows you to breathe comfortably while cruising on the surface with your face in the water.

Ideally your snorkel should have a short, wide barrel; these are easier to breathe through than long, thin barrels. The mouthpiece should be soft and pliable, and feel comfortable in your mouth. Many snorkels now have swivelling mouthpieces, or mouthpieces that mould themselves to your mouth-shape for greater comfort. You can also obtain snorkels that have

built-in self-draining valves at the base of the tube, so that the snorkel is automatically cleared of water when you surface. These valves have become much more reliable in recent years; even so, purists consider them unnecessary. The choice is yours.

The snorkel can be kept in position by slipping it under the mask strap. Alternatively, you can use a snorkel-keeper – a retaining ring, perhaps with a quick-release device, that attaches to the strap. Whatever you choose, always carry a spare mask strap with you in case the one you're using breaks – as usually happens sooner or later.

FINS

Fins provide fast and easy propulsion through the water. Spare fin straps should always be carried as they break easily. There are basically two types:

- **Full-foot fins** have a built-in foot pocket, so that your foot is embraced from toes to heel. They are usually smaller and less powerful than the more widely used open-heel fins.

- **Open-heel fins** cover only the front part of your foot, and are usually worn with bootees; an adjustable strap goes round the back of your heel to help keep the fin in place. This combination of bootee and fin has considerable advantages over the full-foot system; for example, you can walk on land wearing just the bootees and then put the fins on once you're in the water.

OTHER DIVE GEAR

- Many divers prefer to carry their own regulator and depth gauge. If you coil this assemblage around your other belongings it doesn't take up too much room in your luggage. If you have your own dive watch and depth gauge you can be confident of their reliability.
- You can often hire a BCD (Buoyancy Control Device) on the spot but many divers prefer to have their own.
- Most divers now use computers, these and depth guages should be packed as carry on baggage as low pressure in aircraft holds can damage them.
- A 4mm (0.2in) wetsuit is ideal for the tropics. Given the right water temperatures, however, you can make do with a Lycra skin, which takes up much less room in your luggage.
- What further bits of equipment you carry is a matter of choice, but they could include an underwater torch and a knife is essential for cutting monofilament fishing line or nets.

UNDERSTANDING THE TIDES

You should try to gain some understanding of the tides so that you can pick the best time to dive: neap tides and slack water are better for wreck diving or photography; spring tides and full flow are better if you want to optimize your chances of seeing pelagic species. It is surprising how many divemasters have little knowledge of or pay little attention to the state of the tides.

The exact mechanism of tides is extremely complex, but in essence they are a result of gravitational interactions between the earth and the moon and, to a lesser extent, between the earth and the sun, and of the centrifugal forces involved in both these systems.

The cycle of a single tide – from one high water to the next – takes 12hr. Under certain circumstances in the pacific, depending on the relative dominance of the sun and the moon, a tide cycle may seem to take 24hr. Conversely, around some islands and reefs you may effectively experience four tides in 24hr.

- Spring tides, those of maximum range and strength, occur twice a month, around the full and new moon. At these times, because of the relative positions of the sun and moon, their gravitational effects bolster each other.
- Equinoctial spring tides, which typically have the greatest range of all, occur twice a year, in March and September (i.e., at the equinoxes) at, or near, the time of the new and full moon.
- Neap tides, those of minimum range and least strength, occur twice a month around the first and last quarters of the moon. At these times, because of the relative positions of the sun and moon, their gravitational effects tend to counter each other. Local tide tables enable you to calculate flood and ebb tides and fast and slack water.

Right: *A stunning marine garden of mixed corals and sponges.*

Learning to Dive

Anyone who is reasonably fit can learn to dive, and there is no better place to do it than in the tropics, where the waters are warm and where, of course, the beauty of the underwater world is likely instantly to make you a devotee for life! There are plenty of facilities offering courses in Malaysia and Singapore.

It's perfectly feasible to walk up to a beach-front dive-shop in nothing but your swimsuit and start on a diving course: everything you need can be supplied. However, as previously mentioned, many people like to buy their own kit – mask, snorkel and fins – which they can take with them anywhere. A wetsuit is another handy item to own since, although in the warm waters of the tropics you don't always need one for comfort, your wetsuit protects you from cuts and grazes and from the stings of marine organisms. If you hope to operate from a live-aboard in a remote area you will probably need to possess everything except tanks and weight belts; make sure to check with the boat operator beforehand.

The main training agencies to look for are PADI (Professional Association of Diving Instructors), BSAC (British Sub-Aqua Club), whose branches in other parts of the world include several in Malaysia, CMAS (World Underwater Federation), NAUI (National Association of Underwater Instructors) and SSI (Scuba Schools International).

Steer clear of two-tank operations working out of a beach shack. If someone approaches you on the beach and suggests you go diving, check their credentials. If the person is well qualified, fine; if not, don't go. If they are unhappy about your checking their credentials, assume the worst.

QUALIFICATIONS

In some places you will be offered a 'resort course'. This does not lead to a diving qualification but it does allow you to go underwater with an instructor to see whether or not you want to take up the sport for the longer term.

The main qualification to aim for at the start is Open-Water Certification. This usually involves five or six days' intensive training – classroom work (covering the theory and practice of diving, medical and safety procedures, etc.), pool work, some shallow dives – followed by a number of qualifying dives at sea.

Some agencies (e.g., PADI) also offer what are known as 'referral courses'. These involve learning the basics in your home country – five classroom sessions, five pool sessions – and then completing your qualifying dives on arrival at your destination. The advantage of this system is that you need spend only the first two days of your holiday under instruction and are thereafter free to enjoy the rest of it simply diving.

Once you have passed your tests you will be issued with a 'C' card from one of the regulatory bodies. This is the diver's equivalent of a driving licence and permits you, anywhere in the world, to hire tanks and go diving – always, for safety reasons, with a companion (your 'buddy'). Your Open-Water Certification successfully acquired, you can train for higher qualifications: Advanced Open-Water, Rescue Diving, Divemaster and beyond. Alternatively, you might opt to aim for special certifications such as Wreck Diver or Cave Diver.

HAZARDS

Diving is a safe sport so long as divers are thoroughly trained and they follow the time and depth tables correctly.

Never contemplate taking a diving course without having had a medical check-up, either before leaving home or on arrival in the country. Among conditions that preclude your taking up diving are epilepsy, heart disease, chest complaints, bronchitis, asthma and chronic ear and sinus problems. Don't deceive yourself into thinking 'it'll probably be all right'; it quite possibly won't be.

Flying after diving carries significant hazards. Once you have surfaced after a dive it takes several hours for the residual nitrogen in your body to disperse; were you to get straight onto a plane the low pressure inside the aircraft could cause this residual nitrogen to emerge as bubbles in your bloodstream, causing decompression sickness (the bends – see page 169). Accordingly, reputable dive operators will not permit you to dive on a day on which you plan to fly. You should always leave a gap of at least 12hr between diving and flying; a 24hr interval, if practicable, is even better.

INSURANCE

Most holiday insurance policies exclude sports such as scuba diving. It is vital that you are properly insured, since a serious incident (although they rarely happen) could involve huge costs flying you to the nearest hospital or recompression chamber.

RESCUE LOCATION

When drift-diving, carry an inflatable 2m (7ft) rescue-location tube, so that the chase boat can find you more easily. These can be tricky to inflate and raise properly in choppy conditions, so practise first in calm waters. Tie a weight to the tube's base so that it stays upright in the water.

SPECIAL MASKS

- People with eyesight problems can have masks fitted with special corrective lenses. Your local dive-shop should be able to advise you on this.
- Low-volume masks are ideal for travelling. Not only do they take up less room but, in use, the lower volume of air inside them means they are more easily cleared of water.

RECOMPRESSION (HYPERBARIC) CHAMBERS

Recompression chambers are rare in this part of the world and, as elsewhere, are mostly owned and operated by the navy. There is one facility at Kuantan in Peninsular Malaysia, one in Labuan in East Malaysia (two if you count the Borneo Divers chamber), and one in Singapore. Although the emergency contact numbers of these chambers are shown below, in practice it is wise to ask the operator you are diving with to approach the chamber facility on your behalf; he or she should know the correct procedure and be able to sort out any language difficulties.

Peninsular Malaysia
Mawilla Sail Diving Team
TG Gelang
25990 Kuantan
tel 09–433330 (direct to operations room)
tel 09–433601 ext 2209 (to diving team)
This facility has a 10-person chamber and two portable one-person chambers in which patients are transferred under pressure.

East Malaysia (Borneo)
Pejabat Selam
Markas Wilayah Laut Dua
87007 Labuan Federal Territory
tel 087–412122 ext 2240 (officer in charge of diving team)
tel 087–410650/413934

The commercial section of Borneo Divers has a chamber but this is in use offshore most of the time. But you might be in luck. The contact is Randy Davis and the other details are:

Borneo Subsea Services (M) Sdn Bhd
PO Box 80650
87016 Labuan Federal Territory
tel 087–417105
tel 087–410900

Singapore
Naval Medicine Research Centre
tel 7505545 (Dr Michael Ong)
tel 7505546 (officer in charge)

Learning to Snorkel

It takes only a few minutes to learn to snorkel. Once you have mastered the basic techniques the way is open to hours of pleasure floating silently over the reefs watching the many fascinating creatures that live there.

Snorkelling is often considered an inferior alternative to scuba diving, but this is a misconception – for several reasons:

- Although scuba allows you to explore deep reefs, there is an enormous amount of colour on life on shallow reefs that can be appreciated just as well from the surface.
- Once you have bought your equipment, snorkelling costs nothing and is easy to organize. You can jump in wherever you want and as often as you like without having to hire tanks or make sure you have a buddy to dive with. Your time in the water isn't limited by your air supply, and you don't have to worry about the dangers of breathing compressed air at depth.
- You can often get closer to marine life if you aren't accompanied by a noisy stream of bubbles.
- Some people, for psychological, physiological or other reasons, just never take to scuba diving. If you're one of them, snorkelling could be the answer.

GETTING STARTED
Try out your gear in a swimming pool if you don't feel confident about plunging straight into the sea.

- Make sure stray hairs don't get caught under the fringe of your mask. Unless the edge is flush against your skin the mask will leak.
- Avoid overtightening the mask strap, it can give you a headache.
- Misting of the mask can be prevented by rubbing saliva on the inside of the faceplate and

DIVING FOR THE DISABLED

Aside from the conditions mentioned above, physical disability presents no barrier to learning to dive. In the UK the best source of information is Sub-Aqua for the Disabled, available through:

BSAC
Telford's Quay
Ellesmere Port
South Wirral
Cheshire L65 4FY
tel 0151–357 1951
fax 0151–357 1250

A new database called DOLPHIN (Diving Organizations Link with the Physically Handicapped and Instructors Network) aims to put suitably qualified instructors in touch with disabled divers and would-be divers. It can be contacted through:

Diving Diseases Research Centre
Fort Bovisand
Plymouth PL9 0AB
(No telephone enquiries.)

Also in the UK is:

Wet & Dry Diving Club
c/o 42A Gravits Lane
Bognor Regis
West Sussex
(No telephone enquiries.)
In the USA the main agency is:

Handicapped Scuba Association (HSA)
116 West El Portal, Suite 104
San Clemente
CA 92672
tel 714–498 6128

PROFESSIONAL TIPS

- All snorkelling and diving equipment should be rinsed with fresh water after use and dried off in the shade.
- Never leave equipment out in the tropical sun.
- For snorkelling or diving you can buy waterproof marine identification cards and waterproof books which will tell you what you are looking at underwater.

- A mesh bag is handy for carrying your kit around. When you've finished snorkelling you can simply dip the whole lot in a rinse tank or bath but you must not rinse a regulator in this way.
- If you get cramp in your calf muscles or instep, reach forward and grab the end of your fin with one hand and straighten your leg while pulling the fin

towards you. If the cramp is at the front of the leg, reach behind rather than forwards and pull the fin up and back.
- You don't need a weight belt for free diving unless you are wearing a wetsuit or are obese, in either of which cases your buoyancy will be greater than normal so that you find it harder to descend.

then rinsing with sea water. There are anti-misting products on the market which have the same effect, but saliva is readily available and free.
- If water gets into your mask, simply put your head above the surface and apply pressure to the top rim. The water will run out of the bottom.
- To clear the snorkel of water, put your head above the surface, tilt your head back and exhale vigorously. Always take the next breath slowly, since there may still be a little water left in the snorkel. Another strong blow and your snorkel should be clear.

MOVING THROUGH THE WATER

A lot of nonsense is written about the correct way to fin. The 'approved' method is to keep your legs straight, since this gives maximum efficiency; the 'wrong' way is to bicycle with your legs – i.e., to draw your knees in before you kick out. However, although the 'wrong' way may be slightly less efficient, what does it matter? The important things are that you are comfortable and going where you want to go.

Similarly, snorkelling manuals generally tell you not to use your hands and arms for propulsion. Although this is good advice for divers – novices are easily recognized by their flapping arms – for snorkellers it is basically irrelevant. Beneath the surface you may want to supplement straight fin-kicking with breast-stroke in order to increase your range, while the fastest way to travel on the surface is to use the crawl.

FREE DIVING

The term 'free diving' is sometimes used to describe snorkelling in general. In fact, what it means is diving beneath the surface without scuba tanks. Anyone who is fit can, with sufficient practice, reach depths of 7–9m (20–30ft) in the tropics. Local people often go to depths of 21m (70ft) when collecting pearls and the like.

The most important point to remember when free diving is to equalize the pressure in your ears as you descend. Sometimes they equalize of their own accord. Failing this, simply hold the nosepiece of your mask and blow gently through your nose; this should make your ears 'pop' themselves clear. If your ears hurt it's because they haven't cleared properly – an effect that can be exacerbated by a cold or bad sinuses. Come up and try again: do not continue to descend on the assumption that your ears will clear sooner or later.

As you go deeper you may feel pressure building up and pushing your mask into your face. To alleviate this, simply exhale gently through your nose.

The best way to go under the surface is to use a pike dive (surface dive). Bend forward at the waist and lift your legs perpendicular to the surface. The weight of your legs should now cause you to sink until your fins are below the surface. If necessary, augment the dive with a couple of breast-strokes.

In order to stay underwater longer you can – at your own risk – use hyperventilation. This involves inhaling and exhaling very deeply several times before you dive. The hazard is that hyperventilation can lead to sudden unconsciousness underwater or even after you have resurfaced and taken another breath. Snorkelling manuals counsel against it, but most snorkellers try it at one time or another and some do it all the time. Because of the dangers the practice can hardly be recommended. However, if you do try it – perhaps at the instigation of more experienced companions – take precautions to make it as safe as possible. Never exceed four hyperventilations before a dive. After the dive, rest on the surface for at least a couple of minutes before hyperventilating again. Never hyperventilate when diving on your own.

A last point about free diving which is often forgotten. As you surface, look upwards. Otherwise you might crash into a boat or someone swimming on the surface!

PENINSULAR MALAYSIA: WEST COAST

In between the central mountains and the sea, the coastal strip on the west of Peninsular Malaysia has long been the country's commercial heartland, thanks to its proximity to important trade routes since early times. It was here that many of the Peninsula's first towns and cities were built; in consequence, the west coast offers the visitor today some of Malaysia's most intriguing cultural and historical experiences. During the 19th century, rich alluvial deposits of tin were discovered on the plains adjoining the west coast, further fuelling the region's industrialization and leading to the development of roads and railways. During colonial times the British took advantage of these communications links to establish the vast rubber plantations that still characterize this part of the country. The Strait of Malacca (Selat Melaka), that lies between Malaysia's west coast and Indonesian Sumatra, is one of the world's oldest shipping lanes and is still heavily used today. Many of Malaysia's busiest beach resorts are located on islands off the west coast, such as Pulau Pinang and those in the Langkawi archipelago.

All of this is good news for the prosperity of the people living in the region, of course, but it has its effects on the marine environment, so experienced divers will more likely look to other parts of Malaysia. However, if you come to Southeast Asia looking for the holiday of a lifetime with a bit of diving thrown in, rather than just for the diving, you'll find much on the west coast to appeal to you.

LANGKAWI WILDLIFE

The 99 islands of the Langkawi archipelago, with their numerous inlets and bays, used to provide the perfect hiding place for pirates, and until the recent development of tourism they were still very much off the beaten track. The fortunate result is that much of the natural vegetation has remained intact. Zoologists have identified at least eight endemic species of amphibians, two of butterflies and five of reptiles. In addition, a delicate species of palas palm (*Liberbaileya gracilis*) that grows in just one place at the southern end of Dayang Bunting Island is found nowhere else in the world.

Opposite: *Sunset at Langkawi off the west coast of Peninsular Malaysia.*
Above: *Sea stars Fromia monilis crawl across reefs on vascular tube feet, searching for food.*

Payar Marine Park

The Payar Marine Park consists of the main island of Pulau Payar, the smaller islands of Pulau Kaca and Pulau Lembu to the east–northeast, and, to the west–southwest, the two large rock outcrops making up Pulau Segantang.

The Langkawi archipelago consists of 99 islands, of which only three are populated – and two of these very sparsely. The Government has concentrated on turning the area into a major tourist centre. Langkawi has had duty-free status since January 1987, and there are now direct international flights into its airport. The archipelago is part of the state of Kedah, and accordingly the people observe the Muslim weekend.

THE MALACCA STRAIT

The narrow and shallow Malacca Strait (Selat Melaka) drains rivers from Malaysia, Thailand and Indonesia, and is also affected by effluent (from centres of population) and agricultural run-off (from rice-growing areas) as well as by movement of heavy shipping. The strait is not easily able to clear itself, so the bottom is muddy and the visibility normally very poor – about 3m (10ft) on average. However, on occasion relatively clear conditions prevail locally, and if you find them anywhere it is most likely to be in the region of Pulau Payar, where the strait is wider than to the south.

PULAU PAYAR

Situated some 35km (22 miles) off the coast of Kedah – where the Strait of Malacca begins opening out into the Andaman Sea – Pulau Payar has one of the few coral reef areas along the Peninsular West Coast; together with the east coast's Pulau Redang it has been the main focus of WWF's marine-park studies. The marine life is prolific, but usually difficult to see due to the low visibility. The corals are diverse, particularly off the southwest end of Pulau Payar, with its colourful soft corals, and the north and northeast side of Pulau Kaca. There are 36 genera of hard corals, 92 other marine invertebrates and 45 genera of fish. Before being gazetted as a fisheries protected area in 1985, the region suffered badly from overfishing, blast-fishing and coral damage by trawling and sedimentation, a situation made even worse by logging.

Pulau Payar has no accommodation other than that for the marine-park staff, although it does have a visitor information centre, toilets and picnic facilities. You can camp on the island if you get permission from the fisheries management and protection office.

The park can be visited by boat from Kuala Perlis, Kuala Kedah or Pulau Pinang (Penang), but most people stay at the resorts on Pulau Langkawi, one hour by speedboat to the northwest. The Pulau Langkawi resorts that organize dive trips to Pulau Payar will also fix up the permits you require to visit the marine park.

PULAU PANGKOR

Further south in the Strait of Malacca, off the coast at Lumut, lies Pulau Pangkor, a popular beach-resort island. Within easy striking distance of the population centres of Ipoh and Kuala Lumpur, it gets crowded at weekends and during holiday periods. The narrow strait gives good shelter, and so the resorts are able to be kept open all year round.

Southwest of the main island is the small island of Pulau Pangkor Laut, privately owned by a company called Pangkor Laut Resort. The luxury resort is built on stilts (like a *kampung air*, or Malaysian water village) at Royal Bay. The resort offers diving among its many other recreational facilities, but the visibility in this area is generally rather poor.

SEMBILAN ISLANDS

Some 27km (17 miles) south of Pulau Pangkor lie the Sembilans, a group of nine uninhabited small islands: Pulau Agas, Pulau Buluh, Pulau Lalang (which has a beach large enough for camping), Pulau Nipis, Pulau Payong, Pulau Rumbia (the largest), Pulau Saga, Black Rock and White Rock.

The west coast of Pulau Rumbia goes down to 40m (130ft), with patches of table corals, sea anemones and pelagic fish. White Rock, which has a lighthouse, has steep walls to 40m (130ft), with groupers and snappers in crevices and overhangs and, in the open water, barracuda and jacks. The shallow channels between Pulau Rumbia and Pulau Lalang and between Pulau Buluh and Pulau Saga have stony corals and game-fish; they are popular with spear-fishermen (who can operate here freely, as the area is not a marine park).

There can be some fierce currents around the islands. However, novice divers and snorkellers can dive on the west side of Pulau Lalang, which slopes gently to 10m (33ft) and has some stony corals. Those diving locations that there are in the southern straits have very limited appeal and do not warrant separate site descriptions.

> ### KOTA BELANDA
>
> There is a wooden fort on Pulau Pangkor which was built by the Dutch in 1670. In 1745 it was abandoned and the fort became totally surrounded by dense forestation. However, in 1973 the fort was rebuilt and it is definitely worth a trip. It is situated approximately 3km south of Pangkor village at Teluk Gedong. Just beyond the fort, a huge stone bearing the coat of arms of the Dutch East India Company serves as a constant reminder of the Dutch presence on this island.

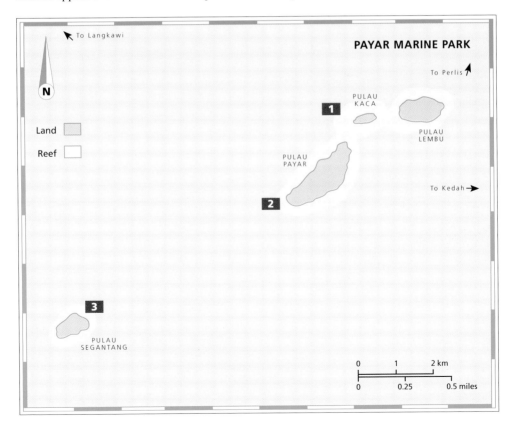

1 PULAU KACA: NORTHWEST SIDE

★★☆☆

Location: East–northeast of Pulau Payar.
Access: By boat from wherever you are based.
Conditions: Generally calm with some current; can become rough in bad weather.
Average depth: 10m (33ft)
Maximum depth: 35m (115ft)

The island can be circled, but the best reef is on the northwest side. Below 10m (33ft) there is only muddy sand, shelving off as deep as 35m (115ft), but in the 2–10m (6–33ft) range there is a good variety of colourful corals and fish life. There are lots of sea anemones with clownfish, shoals of jacks, fusiliers and snappers, many species of pufferfish, moray eels, lionfish, scorpionfish, stonefish, angelfish, butterflyfish and nudibranchs. On the sand are crabs, sea stars, sea urchins and barrel sponges.

Stony cup coral polyps (Dendrophyllia sp.) open only at night. In the day they close up and resemble twigs.

2 PULAU PAYAR: SOUTHWEST TIP

★★☆☆

Location: The southwest tip of Pulau Payar.
Access: By boat from wherever you are based.
Conditions: Generally calm; can become rough during bad weather.
Average depth: 10m (33ft)
Maximum depth: 24m (80ft)

This area, known as the Coral Garden, has rocks and steep-sided gullies carpeted with colourful *Dendronephthya* soft-tree corals and boulder corals. In deeper waters are whip corals, black corals and the dark green, branching *Tubastrea micranthus*. Further out are large barrel sponges covered with Alabaster Sea Cucumbers. There is a large resident shoal of jacks, plus smaller shoals of snappers, fusiliers, Rainbow Runners, Tuna and goatfish. Garfish swim at the surface. You can also see several species of barracuda and many of pufferfish, angelfish, butterflyfish and lionfish. If you are lucky you might see some very big Giant Groupers and occasionally a Ghost Pipefish. There are also many nudibranchs. Sea stars and sea urchins inhabit the bottom.

The shallow house-reef in front of the park's staff quarters has fine boulder corals and offers good snorkelling.

3 PULAU SEGANTANG

★★

Location: West of the southern end of Pulau Payar.
Access: By boat from wherever you are based.
Conditions: Can be rougher than the other sites in this area, so it is best to dive only when the conditions are calm.
Average depth: 20m (65ft)
Maximum depth: 30m (100ft)
Pulau Segantang comprises two steep-sided jagged rocky outcrops which join up underwater; they continue down to muddy sand at 20m (65ft).

In the deeper waters there are gorgonian sea fans growing on the walls and yellow *Tubastrea* cup corals under overhangs; soft corals swell up whenever the current plays across them. Sea anemones with attendant clownfish cluster in any relatively flat area.

The fish life is good, from shoals of juveniles to giant groupers, with many species of angelfish, butterflyfish, lionfish, scorpionfish, stonefish, jacks, rainbow runners, tuna, fusiliers, snappers, garfish, pufferfish, moray eels, whitetip reef sharks, leopard (Variegated) sharks and giant stingrays. The two outcrops also attract pelagic species, including whale sharks. Nudibranchs are common, and you can still find murex shells, ghost pipefish and spiny lobsters.

Some boats impounded for illegal fishing have been sunk off Pulau Payar. Their wrecks make good diving, although you must obtain permission from the marine-park staff.

Above: *The Yellowmask Angelfish (*Pomacanthus xanthometopon*), also known as the Blue-face Angelfish, is one of many angelfish whose juveniles have totally different colour patterns.*

Payar Marine Park

HOW TO GET THERE

Langkawi and Pulau Pinang are serviced by regular international and domestic flights. There are some ferries to Langkawi from Thailand, and ferries run three days a week from Pulau Pinang and regularly from Kuala Kedah (1hr) and Kuala Perlis (45min). You can travel by road from Kuala Lumpur to Kuala Kedah via Alor Setar (474km; 294 miles) or Kuala Perlis (524km; 323 miles). There are also rail connections from Kuala Lumpur and Singapore to Alor Setar.

Pulau Pinang has connections with Singapore, Kuala Lumpur and Thailand by rail; from Kuala Lumpur by road is 380km (234 miles). There are very frequent ferries from Butterworth (15min), or you can cross by the Penang Bridge (toll).

A boat direct from Kuala Kedah to Pulau Payar takes 1hr and a boat from Pulau Pinang to Pulau Payar takes 4hr.

There are regular ferry services from Lumut to both Pulau Pangkor and Pulau Pangkor Laut. Lumut is 170km (105 miles) south of Butterworth, 83km (52 miles) from Ipoh and 183km (114 miles) from Kuala Lumpur by road. Ipoh is serviced regularly by air and rail from Kuala Lumpur.

Permission to visit Payar Marine Park must be obtained from:

Fisheries Management Protection Office
Wisma Tani, Jalan Mahameru, 50628 Kuala Lumpur; tel 03–2982011
or
Wisma Persekutuan Jalan Kampung Bharu, 05000 Alor Setar; tel 04—725573

WHERE TO STAY

Langkawi
Upper Price Range
Pelangi Beach Resort Pantai Cenang, 07000 Langkawi; tel 04–911001 fax 04–911122

Langkawi Island Resort Jalan Pantai Dato Syed Omar, Kuah; tel 04–788209

Lower Price Range
Hotel Langkasuka Batu 3/4, A–14–15, Pokok Asam Kuah, 07000 Langkawi; tel 04–916828/fax 04–916882

Outside Kuah
Captain Resort Jalan Penarak Kuah, 07000 Langkawi; tel 04–789100

Langkawi Chalet 1 Kampung Penarak Kuah, 07000 Langkawi; tel 04–789993

Pantai Cenang
Sandy Beach Motel Pantai Cenang, 07000 Langkawi; tel 04–911308

Pantai Tengah
Delta Motel, Kampung Tanjung Mali, Temonyong; tel 04–911307

Tanjung Mali Beach Motel, Pantai Tanjung Mali, 07000 Langkawi; tel 04–911891

Pulau Pinang
Upper Price Range
Eastern & Oriental Hotel 10 Farquhar Street, Georgetown; tel 04–638322

City Bay View Hotel 25A Lebuh Farquhar, Georgetown; tel 04–633161

Ferringhi Beach Hotel 12.5km Batu Ferringhi Road, 111000 Batu Ferringhi; tel 04–805999/fax 04–805100

Lower Price Range
YMCA 211 Lorong Macalister, 10400 Pulau Pinang; tel 04–362211

New China Hotel 22 Lebuh Leith; tel 04–631601

Swiss Hotel 431F Lebuh Chulia; tel 04–620133

Tye Ann Hotel, 282 Lebuh Chulia; tel 04–614875

Pulau Pangkor Laut
Pulau Pangkor Laut Resort
tel 05–934075/fax 05–934077

DIVE FACILITIES

Dive clubs and dive training agencies sometimes organize boats to Pulau Payar from Pulau Pinang. The only permanent diving facilities are at a few resorts on Langkawi.

Pelangi Beach Resort Pantai Cenang, 07000 Langkawi; tel 04–911001 fax 04–911122
Runs fishing and diving trips to Payar Marine Park (including permits).

Pro Dive Lot 974, Pantai Cenang, 07000 Langkawi; tel 04–95, 53739 or 010–227 6876 (mobile)/fax 04–955 3475 (A branch of Pro Dive in Kuala Lumpur)

Langkawi Island Resort Jalan Pantai Dato Syed Omar, Kuah; tel 04–788209

Pangkor Laut Resort Pulau Pangkor Laut; tel 05–934075/fax 05–934077
Kuala Lumpur Address:
2nd Floor, Yeoh Tiong Lay Plaza, 55 Jalan Bukit Bintang, 55100 Kuala Lumpur; tel 03–2416564/fax 03–2448562
US$50 per tank dive, including boat and divemaster.

Boats from Pulau Pinang
Asian Overland Services, 33M Jalan Dewan Sultan Sulaiman 1 (off Jalan Tunku Abdul Rahman), 50300 Kuala Lumpur; tel 03–2925622/fax 03–2925209

Boats from Langkawi and Pulau Pinang
Pernas Oue Cruises Sdn Bhd, 8A Jalan Pandak, Mayah 6, Kuah, 07000 Langkawi

FILM PROCESSING

None is available on the islands. For Payar, the nearest processing on the mainland is offered by:

Star Colour Sdn Bhd, 24 Jalan Petani, 08000 Sungai Petani, Kedah; tel 04–425895

President Foto, 4114 Jalan Bagan Luar, Butterworth; tel 04–318601

For Pangkor and the Sembilan Islands, use Kuala Lumpur suppliers (see listing on page 19) or:

Photo Speed Corporation Sdn Bhd, 90–92 Jalan Sultan Idris Shah, 30000 Ipoh; tel 05–532006/fax 05–501217

HOSPITALS

Payar
District Hospital, Langkawi; tel 04–196422

General Hospital, Alor Setar; tel 04–723333

General Hospital, Pulau Pinang, Jalan Residensi; tel 04–373333

Pangkor and the Sembilan Islands
Ipoh District Hospital, tel 05–533333

Lumut District Hospital, tel 05–935333

Kuala Lumpur General Hospital, Jalan Pahang; tel 03–2921044

LOCAL HIGHLIGHTS

Langkawi
The resorts here have everything from golf to horse-riding, tennis and watersports, not to mention jungle and hill trekking, bird-watching and walks along which you can search out butterflies, exotic orchids and tropical flowers. Pulau Singa Besar has been turned into a wildlife sanctuary and marine reserve.
Pulau Pinang (Penang)
Pulau Pinang is the pearl of the Orient. Its lure goes beyond its palm-fringed beaches to the elegant colonial buildings and the rich variety of ethnic cultures represented here.

Among the many sights are the **Kek Lok Si Temple**, the **Pinang State Mosque** and the Moorish architecture of the **Kapitan**

Keling Mosque and the Kuan Yin Teng Temple (1800), the oldest temple in Pulau Pinang. Wat Chayamankalaram has a reclining Buddha 33m (108ft) long. Khoo Konsi Temple is Pulau Pinang's most picturesque building. The Snake Temple was built in 1850 in memory of the Buddhist priest Chor Soo Kong; it contains, as the name might suggest, a variety of snakes. The oldest Hindu temple on Pulau Pinang is the Sri Mariamman Temple (1833); the biggest is Nattukotai Chettiar Temple on Waterfall Road. Also of interest is the Bat Temple at Air Itam. Relics of the British presence include Fort Cornwallis, dating from 1804–5, and St George's Anglican Church, which was built in 1818.

There is a butterfly farm at Teluk Bahang and the orchid and hibiscus garden on Bukit Jambul is well worth a visit, as are the museum and the various art galleries. You can take a trip up Pinang Hill on the funicular railway; there are services every 30min. The Pinang Bridge is well worth seeing.

West Coast Mainland

On the mainland, a short ferry-ride away, is Kedah. This state is Malaysia's ricebowl. There are many historical buildings in and around Alor Setar, including the Zahir Mosque and, opposite the mosque, the Thai-influenced Balai Besar ('Great Hall'), built in 1898 and used for royal and state occasions. The Balai Nobat ('music hall') houses the sacred instruments of the royal orchestra.

At Langgar are the Royal Mausoleum, the Royal Boat House (facing Darulaman Stadium on the banks of the Sungai Anak

Bukit), the Di Raja State Museum and the Balai Seni Negeri (the state art gallery). Pekan Rabu Bazaar sells traditional goods and handicrafts representative of the Kedah region.

If you have the energy you could try a climb up Gunung Jerai (Kedah Peak), which is 1200m (3937ft) high; on and around the mountain are jungle paths, waterfalls and campsites.

Between Gunung Jerai in the north and Sungai Muda in the south is Lembah Bujang, Malaysia's richest archaeological area. Here there are Indian temples believed to date from the 5th century; 50 have been discovered, of which eight have so far been restored. Many artefacts from this area are now on display in the Bujang Valley Archaeological Museum in Pengkalan Bujang.

Pulau Pangkor and Pulau Pangkor Laut

Pulau Pangkor and Pulau Pangkor Laut are oriented towards beach-resort activities, notably watersports. Pulau Pangkor has Indian and Chinese temples as well as the Dutch Fort (built 1670) at Teluk Gedan.

Perak is called the 'silver state' because of the wealth it has derived from the mining of not silver but tin. It has the imposing, Moorish-style railway station at Ipoh, Buddhist cave temples, the Tambun hot springs, the Ubudiah Mosque, the Sam Poh Tong Temple, the Perak Museum, the leaning tower at Teluk Intan and the unfinished Kellie's Castle.

The Cameron Highlands are 60km (37 miles) off the Kuala Lumpur–Ipoh–Butterworth road.

The tiny, privately owned, island of Pangkor Laut boasts a luxury resort offering diving and water sports.

Night on a coral reef is a time of change. Many diurnal fish alter their colours at night. Sometimes the change is minor, but in other cases it can be total; occasionally it is similar to that used by the same fish at a cleaning station to signal it is ready for cleaning. In some instances solid colours become blotchy, while on other fish bold patterns appear; the effect in either event is to make the fish more difficult for predators to pick out against the background.

Dusk and dawn are the times when predators are at their most active, rising unseen out of the darkness to take prey silhouetted against the still light sky. One can often sit on a boat or jetty in the evening watching the water churn as shoals of small fish are attacked by jacks, tuna or barracuda. There really is no escape for the unfortunate victims: if they jump out of the water to escape the predators from beneath they are likely to be snapped up by the sea birds hovering expectantly overhead.

Bumphead Parrotfish (Bolbometopon muricatum) asleep in a cave at night. Parrotfish often change colour or encase themselves in a cocoon to discourage predators.

NIGHTLIFE

Diving at night is a fascinating experience, as one's light picks out small fishes and other creatures adopting their different stratagems to avoid the attentions of larger ones. Parrotfish and butterflyfish hide in crevices in the reef and angelfish penetrate even further, either concealing themselves completely or leaving just an eye or snout in view. Most wrasse bury themselves in the sand, as do some pufferfish, lizardfish, flounders and rays – not that this is a foolproof tactic, as many sharks have electro-receptors that can detect the hidden fish. Snappers and grunts shoal in small, closely knit groups in caves, small valleys or between gorgonians. Triggerfish flatten themselves against depressions in the coral; smaller Hawksbill and Green Turtles do likewise if they cannot find a cave or a large enough gorgonian to use for concealment. Every nook and cranny in the coral contains something of interest: shrimps, prawns, crabs, lobsters, cuttlefish, worms, octopuses ...

A BLAZE OF COLOUR

However, not all of the denizens of the reef are elusive at night. Various fish – like squirrelfish, soldierfish, bigeyes and cardinalfish – feed at night, and some less common fish can

be seen only at night. Nudibranchs, sea urchins, flat worms, cowries, conches, huge tun shells and sea cucumbers come out to graze. Overhanging roofs are turned into a blaze of colour by the feeding polyps of *Tubastrea* corals. Sea hares graze sedately, ready to eject a spurt of magenta ink if anything touches them. Moray eels dash from crevice to crevice. Clownfish, shut out because the anemones that are their daytime homes are closed for the night, lurk forlornly. Comb jellies, often too transparent to be easily noticed in daylight, show clearly in your torchlight. Young cuttlefish and shellfish hide among the long spines of spiny urchins. Meanwhile, small crabs and brittle stars feed among the arms of corals and gorgonians.

TORCHLIGHT

The shallows are the realm of basket stars, brittle stars and feather stars, which sift the current for plankton. If your light is too bright these creatures will curl up and disappear too quickly for you to see them, so keep your torchlight level low. Other reactions to torchlight differ: diurnal fishes, hiding in holes or acting sleepily over the reef at night, are often mesmerized by lights, so that you can come

> ### NIGHTLIFE
>
> Before you leave the water, turn off your light for a few minutes. At first it will be all the noise that surprises you: creatures eating, snapping and grunting. However, as your eyes get used to the dark, you will start noticing many phosphorescent creatures. Notable among these will be Flashlight Fish, *Photoblepharon*, swimming around in small shoals; a pouch beneath each eye contains bioluminescent algae, so that the area glows like a firefly. Also evident will be phosphorescent plankton: if you wave your arms about you will disturb millions of these, so that it will be as if you were in the midst of a snowstorm of light.

up very close to them; many will spread out their fins to look larger in an attempt to frighten you off, and some pufferfish will inflate. Particularly interesting are the larger parrotfish, which at night back into unlikely-looking overhangs, holes or branched corals and fall asleep. Their eyes remain open, but the fishes ignore lights and can be stroked. If you are diving very late you can find them enclosed in a cocoon of mucus, believed to act as a protection against predators and parasites.

Flat worms (Pseudoceros sp.) crawl across the reef at night and are rarely seen in the day.

PENINSULAR MALAYSIA: EAST COAST

By comparison with the hectic, industrialized, Chinese-influenced west coast, Peninsular Malaysia's east coast is a relaxed collection of fishing villages, coconut plantations, beaches, mangroves and 'get away from it all' offshore islands. To the tourist it is often described as the 'real Malaysia'.

THE TRADITIONAL EAST COAST

Part of the reason the east coast has managed to retain so much of its traditional character is that, until recently, it was relatively inaccessible, with the impenetrable jungles of the central mountains effectively cutting it off from more westerly parts. Although in rural areas the slow-paced lifestyle remains largely unchanged, there are now good transport links with the rest of the Peninsula – in particular, the east–west highway carving through the mountains near the Thai border. There is a main highway running down the east coast, and driving is much easier than on the west coast because of the lack of traffic.

LOCAL SENSIBILITIES

The east coast of Peninsular Malaysia is predominantly Muslim, so the weekend is officially Thursday afternoon and Friday – though in some places it can drag on until Sunday! Be prepared for this if you want to visit banks or government offices; also, bus timetables may be changed without warning.

Ramadan does not much affect island tourist resorts, but bus, boat and train schedules can be unpredictable, as can office hours. As a matter of courtesy you should be careful about eating and drinking while travelling during daylight hours. The sale of alcohol is likely to be curtailed. Travellers from outside Malaysia would probably be wise to avoid this period; conversely and consequently, people living in the region – or expatriates working there – may find this a good time for diving, if only because the reefs are quieter without the influx of foreign divers.

Opposite: *Coconut Palms lining the coast of Pulau Tioman.*
Above: *Red feather stars (Himerometra robustipinna) and Tubastrea cup coral.*

Pulau Perhentian (Terengganu Marine Park)

The Perhentian Islands lie some 20km (12 miles) off Kuala Besut on Peninsular Malaysia's North-eastern coast. They form the northernmost part of the Terengganu Marine Park, which also comprises a number of other islands: Pulau Lang Tengah, Pulau Redang (see page 58), Pulau Bidong Laut, Pulau Kapas, and Pulau Tenggol (see page 68) to the south.

Relaxed diving and snorkelling in an extremely idyllic and very laid-back setting is on offer at Pulau Perhentian. Excellent diving and snorkelling is also available at Pulau Redang and Pulau Tenggol, but a large, somewhat controversial, up-market resort is currently being constructed on Pulau Redang and further smaller resorts are under construction both here and on Pulau Tenggol.

THE IDYLLIC 'STOP-OVER ISLANDS'
If you are looking for unstressful but organized diving with simple but comfortable accommodation, a good licensed restaurant and friendly helpful staff, where the setting is an unspoilt tropical island with uncrowded white sandy beaches sloping gently to coral reefs, you could hardly do better than to think about the Perhentian Islands (the name means 'Stop-over Islands').

PERHENTIAN BESAR AND PERHENTIAN KECIL
The group comprises two main islands – Pulau Perhentian Besar (*besar* = 'big') and Pulau Perhentian Kecil (*kecil* = 'small') – plus several smaller islets to the northwest. These islets often have remote isolated beaches, but some are hardly more than rock outcrops emerging from the sea; the diving from these is particularly good. In the main they consist of a jumble of huge volcanic boulders tumbling down to a maximum depth of 30m (100ft), forming caves, crevices and tunnels ideal for swimming through. Below the tide-line the boulders are carpeted with soft corals and anemones, and below 7m (23ft) they are covered in large gor-

gonian sea fans, often weighed down with wing oysters (mussels). There are also many large *Tubastrea* corals and unusually large soft-tree corals (*Dendronephthya*), some as tall as 1m (40in). Harp corals are particularly common around the Perhentians.

Deeper down there are fields of stony corals, barrel sponges covered in Alabaster Sea Cucumbers, and many different species of nudibranchs, including Spanish Dancers (which together with basket stars are often seen out in daylight). Christmas-tree Worms, fan worms and stinging hydroids are common. Down at sand level there are various pelagic fish including jacks, trevallies and barracuda, and moray eels, many species of sea cucumbers and congregations of black sea urchins can be found on the sand itself.

Half of a metal landing craft sunk in 1976, fortunately after the escaping Vietnamese boat people whom it had been carrying had disembarked, lies on the sand at 24m (80ft) off Pulau Perhentian Kecil. It offers adequate diving, but no more than that – although the marine life is good. This is the only wreck site in the Perhentian region.

PERHENTIAN ISLAND RESORT

Although the main fishing village, Pasir Hantu, is on the southeast coast of Pulau Perhentian Kecil, the tourist accommodation is predominantly on Pulau Perhentian Besar. Most of it is fairly basic, but Perhentian Island Resort, managed by Ramli Chik, is comfortable, clean and friendly and has 24-hour electricity; it was here, on 7 June 1993, that Malaysia's first underwater wedding was performed. The house-reef in front of the resort is ideal for family swimming and snorkelling.

LIFE ON THE REEF

The reef fish life is prolific, with most of the smaller angelfish as well as the larger Blue-ring, Yellowmask, Six-band and Emperor Angelfish, many species of pufferfish, filefish, triggerfish, boxfish, batfish, lionfish (including Zebra Lionfish), scorpionfish, cardinalfish, hawkfish, Threadfin Bream, Pennant Coralfish, Coral Trout and garfish, plus turtles, octopus, cuttlefish and squid. Shoals of Spotted Sweetlips, Yellowtail Jacks, fusiliers and razorfish dash around. In July and August dolphins and Pilot Whales are often seen.

TERENGGANU TURTLES

In the 1960s a 20km (12-mile) stretch of Terengganu beaches centred on Rantau Abang and nearby Kuala Abang became famous because large numbers of Leatherback Turtles used them as a major nesting site each year between May and September; after a time the nesting turtles became a tourist spectacle, with a festival being held in July and August. The beaches are particularly suitable for Leatherback turtles because their deep-water approaches, heavy surf and steep slopes give the gravid creatures only a short distance to crawl up the beach to nesting areas above the high-water mark. Even so, in recent years the numbers of Leatherbacks here and on Pulau Tengah have dropped to a handful. It is tempting to blame tourist intrusion, but in fact most of the beaches were closed to tourists, the remainder being protected and having controlled turtle hatcheries.

WWF believe the increased use of fishing nets is the main cause of the depletion. All turtles, not just Leatherbacks, get caught up in trawl nets, gill nets, trammel nets, bottom longlines and fish traps. Once caught, they mostly drown – even though they can go for up to 2hr between breaths. The increased use of open-ocean drift nets, many kilometres long, has taken a heavy toll on the Leatherback Turtle. In addition, offshore arrays of fishing boats, lit up at night, can cause gravid turtles to turn back out to sea and dump their eggs in the water.

1 TELUK PAUH

★★★★

Location: This is the resort's house-reef. It is close in front and to the right (east) of the dive-shop.

Access: Straight off the beach.

Conditions: Calm, except in the monsoon season. Average visibility is only about 5m (16ft), although better in the early morning.

Average depth: 1m (40in)

Maximum depth: Less than 3m (10ft) until you get a long way out

A gentle slope, ideal for children. The site consists of mainly stony corals. There is quite a lot to be seen: immature angelfish and butterflyfish, small parrotfish, larger Bumphead Parrotfish, batfish, pufferfish, stingrays, small moray eels and the occasional sea snake. On the sand are sea stars and several varieties of sea cucumbers. The fish are tame through long-time familiarity with being fed by visitors! In the early morning, when the visibility is better, you might also see the occasional small Whitetip and Blacktip Reef Shark.

2 TIGA RUANG

★★★★★★

Location: Midway between Perhentian Island Resort and Tanjung Besi, on Pulau Perhentian Besar.

Access: By boat (10min) from the resort northeast around the first headland to the end of the beach in the next bay.

Conditions: Generally calm; can be choppy with some current. Visibility is normally about 10m (33ft).

Average depth: 8m (26ft)

Maximum depth: 12m (40ft)

The site has boulders down to coral and sand; the sand continues out to sea with occasional coral heads. There are shoals of Yellowtail Jacks, small parrotfish and fusiliers, plus many species of pufferfish, boxfish and lionfish, and the occasional turtle. On the sand are several varieties of sea cucumbers, sea stars, sea urchins, fan worms and sea anemones, together with stingrays.

3 TANJUNG BESI

★★★

Location: The northernmost point of Pulau Perhentian Besar.

Access: By boat (25min) northeast from the resort.

Conditions: Generally calm, but can be rough and choppy, with swell and current, if the weather turns bad. Average visibility about 10m (33ft).

Average depth: 12m (40ft)

Maximum depth: 24m (80ft)

This site offers caves and overhangs in a jumble of big boulders going down to sand. Because there is open sea to the north you may meet pelagic species at any time, as well as Grey Reef and Whitetip Reef Sharks. Among the reef fish you can expect to encounter are shoals of snappers, jacks, fusiliers and sweetlips, plus damselfish, rabbitfish, filefish and scorpionfish. There are lots of small soft corals and anemones as well as patches of boulder corals. Christmas-tree Worms, bubble coral, sea stars, cushion stars, sea cucumbers and sea urchins can be found on the sand, and there are moray eels and immature Whitetip Reef Sharks further out.

4 LALUAN NAGA

★★

Location: Just north of Pasir Tinggi, on the east coast of Pulau Perhentian Besar.

Access: By boat (50min) from the resort clockwise around Pulau Perhentian Besar.

Conditions: Usually calm; can be very choppy with a current after bad weather. Visibility is generally pretty poor – about 7m (23ft).

Average depth: 12m (40ft)

Maximum depth: 18m (60ft)

A jumble of large boulders descending to sand. There are some good soft corals, patches of boulder corals, most of the local species of angelfish, butterflyfish, filefish and pufferfish, and shoals of fusiliers, jacks and snappers; also in evidence are batfish, parrotfish, barracuda, groupers, Coral Trout, Spotted Sweetlips, surgeonfish and the occasional turtle. Down on the sand are stingrays, sea cucumbers, sea stars, cushion stars, sea urchins, fan worms, moray eels and cowrie and volute shells.

PULAU KAPAS

Pulau Kapas is just a couple of kilometres (30min) off the coast from Marang, so it gets crowded at weekends and on public holidays. It has some good snorkelling, although not as good as off the nearby Pulau Raja. The resort is:

Primula Kapas Island Resort
Marang Village, Terengganu, tel 09–632989
National Sales Office: Lots 1–22 & 1–23
Wisma Stephens, 88 Jalan Raja Chulan, 50250 Kuala Lumpur
tel 03–2487795 fax 03–2424877
Pulau Lang Tengah, 10km (6 miles) from Pulau Redang, is another place where you can find good snorkelling, see page 52, but divers usually go to Perhentian for serious diving.

Opposite: *Cup coral (Tubastrea micranthus),*
Red Feather stars (Himerometra robustipinna).

5 TERUMBU TIGA (TIGER ROCKS)

★★★★

Location: Just south of Pasir Tinggi, at the centre of the east coast of Pulau Perhentian Besar.
Access: By boat (55min) from the resort clockwise around Pulau Perhentian Besar.
Conditions: Can be rough, with a strong current and swell after a heavy storm; novices should dive here only in calm weather. Visibility is about 10m (33ft) on average.
Average depth: 10m (33ft)
Maximum depth: 20m (65ft)
This dive is claimed to be the best off the Perhentian Islands. I did it twice. In both instances it was as a drift-dive in bad weather, with a heavy swell and less than 2m (6ft) visibility, but I still found it very good. If the visibility had been better I would have given it five stars rather than four. The site is the usual jumble of large boulders down to sand, but is teeming with fish and, when a current is running, has some of the biggest soft corals I have seen anywhere. The shallow rocks are carpeted with leathery soft corals and purple *Dendronephthya* soft-tree corals, while down around the 9m (30ft) mark are good *Acropora* table corals, cup corals and zoanthids.

The deeper rocks have fluted oysters and lots of large white gorgonian sea fans, weighed down with wing oysters; there are also many red harp corals and green *Tubastrea micranthus* corals, some with their polyps out feeding during the day. Down on the sand are huge *Dendronephthya rubeola* soft-tree corals, some black corals, small whip corals, many varieties of sea cucumbers, sea stars, cushion stars and various shells (including cowrie and volute shells) and nudibranchs. Barrel sponges covered with Alabaster Sea Cucumbers are most noticeable.

The fish life includes barracuda, batfish, surgeonfish, lionfish, scorpionfish, filefish, angelfish, butterflyfish, parrotfish, Coral Trout (and other groupers), moray eels, snappers, sweetlips, Whitecheek Monocle Bream, Threadfin Bream, razorfish, hawkfish, Bumphead Parrotfish and shoals of jacks, parrotfish and fusiliers. There are feather stars everywhere plus the occasional turtle. Sadly, there is also a working fish-trap.

6 BATU BUTUK   7 TANJUNG TUKAS

★★★

Location: The southeast corner of Pulau Perhentian Besar.
Access: By boat (30min) from the resort anticlockwise around Pulau Perhentian Besar.
Conditions: Usually calm; can be choppy with a current in bad weather. The average visibility is about 7m (23ft).

Average depth: 12m (40ft)
Maximum depth: 18m (60ft)
A jumble of boulders descending to sand, with good stony corals but fewer soft corals than at Terumbu Tiga (Site 5). Likewise, the fish and shellfish life is similar but less prolific. Turtles are sometimes found on the west side of Tanjung Tukas.

8 TELUK DALAM

★★★★

Location: The west side of the main southern bay of Pulau Perhentian Besar.
Access: By boat (20min) from the resort anticlockwise around Pulau Perhentian Besar.
Conditions: Usually calm – good protection from the weather. Visibility only about 7m (23ft) on average.
Average depth: 9m (30ft)
Maximum depth: 15m (50ft)
A jumble of rocks going down to sand. The deeper rocks support many black corals, and these in turn support many wing oysters. On the sand you can find many sea anemones, sea cucumbers, sea urchins, sea stars, nudibranchs and shells, plus the occasional stingray.

9 GUA KAMBING

★★★★★★

Location: South of the Cempaka Chalets on the east coast of Pulau Perhentian Kecil.
Access: By boat (about 20min) from the resort southwest across the channel between the two islands.
Conditions: Generally calm, although there may be a slight current. Average visibility only about 7m (23ft).
Average depth: 9m (30ft)
Maximum depth: 15m (50ft)
Yet again, this site offers a jumble of boulders going down to a sandy bottom. Usually on view are pufferfish, filefish, surgeonfish, unicornfish and parrotfish, and there are patches of stony corals with angelfish and butterflyfish. On the sand are sea stars, cushion stars, sea cucumbers, sea anemones, moray eels and stingrays.

PULAU LANG TENGAH

This new resort can be reached by boat from Merang. Contact:
Blue Coral Island Resort Sales Office
Suite 24-4, 24th Floor,
Menara Haw Par, Jalan Sultan Ismail,
50250 Kuala Lumpur
tel 03–2380907 fax 03–2380910
Divers tend to go to Pulau Redang or Pulau Perhentian for serious diving.

10 SHIPWRECK

★★★

Location: South–southwest of the southwest corner of Pulau Perhentian Kecil.

Access: By boat (about 30min) from the resort southwest to the southern end of Pulau Perhentian Kecil, then round to the southwest end.

Conditions: Generally calm; the surface current decreases as you descend to the wreck. Surface conditions can be bad after bad weather. The visibility is not good – only about 7m (23ft).

Average depth: 22m (72ft)

Maximum depth: 24m (80ft)

This is half of a steel landing craft which originally came to Malaysia bearing Vietnamese boat people. It was being towed back to Kuala Besut for repairs when it sunk in 1976.

The whereabouts of the other half was not known to Stephen Ng and his staff of the dive centre at Perhentian Island Resort.

This is not in fact a particularly good wreck dive, though it can be penetrated, but it is a splendid haven for marine life: big *Dendronephthya* soft-tree corals and black corals covered in wing oysters and feather stars, together with all the fish you might expect in this area, including filefish, hawkfish, Pennant Coralfish and the local species of angelfish, butterflyfish, batfish, snappers, wrasse, jacks, barracuda, groupers and stingrays.

ARTIFICIAL REEFS

Constructing artificial reefs in shallow waters is, as any sea fisherman will tell you, an excellent way of enhancing fish stocks. Purpose-built artificial reefs are commonly placed either on damaged reefs or on the seabed near reefs about 1.5km (1 mile) offshore.

Artificial reefs have been laid all around Malaysia; mostly by the Department of Fisheries (31 off the east and west coasts of Johor State alone by 1994) but also by Raleigh International volunteers and by fishermen themselves. There are reef-rescue projects underway off Singapore.

Most often used for the construction are old tyres chained together, sometimes stabilized by concrete blocks. The system is cheap and highly effective, although there is a risk the tyres may release toxic pollutants as they gradually deteriorate, and the 'reef' is likely to break up when caught in a trawl net – not as uncommon an event as one might think. Concrete slabs or small pyramids chained together or linked with chain-link fencing would seem a better, if more expensive, system.

Artificial reefs need not be deliberate constructions. Shipwrecks rapidly take on the attributes of a reef, forming a good substratum for coral larvae to settle on and offering shelter for bigger fish and breeding sites for smaller fish and invertebrates.

---

11 PASIR KERANGI: PVC-PIPE ARTIFICIAL REEF

★★★★

Location: West of Pulau Perhentian Kecil, midway between Coral Bay and Mira's Place.

Access: By boat (about 45min) from the resort southwest and then around the west side of Pulau Perhentian Kecil.

Conditions: Generally slightly choppy with quite a strong surface current, which gets less as you pull down the line from the buoy. The pipe structure is open, so there is no lee. Visibility is usually only about 7m (23ft).

Average depth: 18m (60ft)

Maximum depth: 18m (60ft)

I dived this artificial reef (an open latticework of polyvinyl chloride pipes anchored down on sand in 1991) after bad weather, in a strong current and with almost zero visibility, but I was still impressed. The prolific growth on the pipes in such a short time of *Dendronephthya* soft-tree corals – up to 80cm (30in) high – and of black corals, sponges and wing oysters is quite amazing.

12 PULAU SERENGGEH: SOUTH END

★★★

Location: The southern end of Pulau Serenggeh, due west from the northern end of Perhentian Pulau Kecil.

Access: By boat (about 50min) from the resort northwest around the north coast of Pulau Perhentian Kecil, then out due west to Pulau Serenggeh.

Conditions: Usually a bit choppy with some current. Visibility, generally about 10m (33ft), is better than around the two larger Perhentians.

Average depth: 12m (40ft)

Maximum depth: 18m (60ft)

This site comprises a jumble of rocks descending to sand, with small soft corals on the rocks in the shallow water, black corals, fire corals, gorgonian sea fans and harp corals on the deeper rocks, and lots of whip corals on the sand. The fish life is good.

13 TANJUNG PANGLIMA ABU

★★★★

Location: Northwest corner of Pulau Perhentian Kecil.

Access: By boat (about 40min) northwest from the resort, then the north coast of Pulau Perhentian Kecil.

Conditions: Normally calm – it is not worth diving here if the conditions are rough or choppy. Visibility is normally only about 7m (23ft).

Average depth: 12m (40ft)
Maximum depth: 15m (50ft)
A shallow dive with some big boulder corals. Novice divers and strong snorkellers would find it attractive.

14 TANJUNG BUTUNG

★★★

Location: North of the northwest corner of Pulau Perhentian Kecil.
Access: By boat (about 40min) northwest from the resort and then around the north coast of Pulau Perhentian Kecil.
Conditions: Usually calm; it can sometimes be choppy with some current. The visibility here is generally about 10m; 33ft.
Average depth: 18m (60ft)
Maximum depth: 25m (82ft)
A jumble of rocks descending to sand at 25m (80ft). The rocks sport leathery soft corals and some quite big *Dendronephthya* soft-tree corals. A good variety of fish live at the site, including all the local species of angelfish and butterflyfish, batfish, filefish, parrotfish, groupers and moray eels, plus shoals of fusiliers, snappers, jacks and trevallies.

15 TOKONG LAUT

★★★★

Location: West–northwest of the northwest corner of Pulau Perhentian Kecil.
Access: By boat (about 50min) northwest from the resort, around the north coast of Pulau Perhentian Kecil, and then out to the west–northwest.

Conditions: Usually a bit choppy; can be rough after storms (I dived here in a heavy swell with a strong surge). These waters are nice and clear: expect visibility around 30m (100ft).
Average depth: 10m (33ft)
Maximum depth: 19m (62ft)
A jumble of large boulders going down to sand. In the rocks are caves and tunnels you can swim through. The upper rocks are liberally carpeted with leathery soft corals and small *Dendronephthya* soft-tree corals; the deeper ones are covered in black corals, gorgonian sea fans, stinging hydroids and harp corals, together with lots of sea anemones, clownfish, zoanthids, bubble corals, wing oysters and oysters. Down on the sand there are some large barrel sponges covered in Alabaster Sea Cucumbers, many species of sea stars, cushion stars, sea cucumbers, nudibranchs and congregations of black sea urchins. Parrotfish, angelfish, butterflyfish, rabbitfish, pufferfish (many varieties), lionfish, surgeonfish, unicorn-fish, damselfish, cardinalfish, lizardfish, hawkfish and stingrays may all be seen, as well as shoals of sweetlips, snappers, razorfish and fusiliers.

16 PULAU SUSU DARA BESAR: NORTH SIDE

★★★★

Location: The north side of the larger of the two Susu Dara islets, west–northwest of the northwest corner of Pulau Perhentian Kecil.
Access: By boat (about 50min) from the resort northwest around the north coast of Pulau Perhentian Kecil and

Below: *One of the many beautiful, unspoilt beaches of Pulau Perhentian Besar, fringed by coconut palms.*

A HAVEN FOR RAPID CORAL GROWTH

The growth-rates of gorgonian sea fans, black corals, soft corals and mussels in the warm shallow waters around the Perhentians are truly remarkable.

In 1991, as an experiment for the Malaysian Fisheries Department, Stephen Ng and his assistants used corkscrew anchors to lay an artificial reef, made from PVC plastic pipes, at 18m (60ft) on the sandy bottom. Just two years later, when I dived here in October 1993, these pipes had become a haven for fish life, and were covered in soft corals and mussels; I measured several *Dendronephthya* soft-tree corals that were 70–80cm (27½–31in) tall. (For more on this, see Site 11.)

---

then out west–northwest to Pulau Susu Dara Besar.
Conditions: Usually a bit choppy; can be rough after bad weather.
Average depth: 10m (33ft)
Maximum depth: 18m (60ft)
This site offers much the same as Tokong Laut (Site 15); although the fish life is just as good and plentiful, the corals are a bit less exciting. The waters are as beautifully clear as at Tokong Laut.

17 PULAU SUSU DARA KECIL: NORTH SIDE

★★★★

Location: The north side of the smaller of the two Susu Dara islets, northeast of Pulau Susu Dara Besar.
Access: By boat (about 50min) northwest from the resort around the north coast of Pulau Perhentian Kecil and out west–northwest to Pulau Susu Dara Kecil.
Conditions: Usually a bit choppy; can be rough after bad weather.
Average depth: 10m (33ft)
Maximum depth: 18m (60ft)
Much the same as Tokong Laut (Site 15), and with the same lovely clear visibility. The fish life is just as good and plentiful, the corals not quite so good.

18 TOKONG BOPENG: NORTH SIDE

★★★★

Location: The north side of Tokong Bopeng, west–northwest of the northwest corner of Pulau Perhentian Kecil, and west of Pulau Rawa.
Access: By boat (about 50min) northwest from the resort around the north coast of Pulau Perhentian Kecil and out west–northwest to Tokong Bopeng.
Conditions: Usually a bit choppy; can be rough after bad weather.

Average depth: 10m (33ft)
Maximum depth: 18m (60ft)
Much the same as Tokong Laut (Site 15), and with the same excellent visibility: fish life just as good and plentiful, corals not quite so good.

19 TOKONG BURUNG KECIL

★★★

Location: South of Tokong Bopeng.
Access: By boat (50min) northwest from the resort around the north coast of Pulau Perhentian Kecil and then out west–northwest.
Conditions: Usually calm; can be choppy after bad weather. Average visibility about 10m (33ft).
Average depth: 9m (30ft)
Maximum depth: 15m (50ft)
A jumble of boulders descends to sand. This site is quite good for corals, but the fish life is less than brilliant.

20 PULAU RAWA: SOUTHEAST CORNER

★★★

Location: West–northwest of the northeast corner of Pulau Perhentian Kecil, east of the Pulau Susu Dara islets.
Access: By boat (about 50min) northwest from the resort around the north coast of Pulau Perhentian Kecil and out west–northwest to Pulau Rawa.
Conditions: Usually choppy; can be rough after bad weather. Visibility is about 10m (33ft) on average.
Average depth: 20m (65ft)
Maximum depth: 30m (100ft)
The site comprises a jumble of big boulders forming caves and tunnels you can swim into and through. There are some soft corals, black corals and gorgonian sea fans, but the scenery and fish life are not as good as at the other sites (Sites 15–19) in the area west–northwest of Pulau Perhentian Kecil.

21 TELUK KERMA

★★★

Location: The southern end of the headland east of D. Lagoon on the east coast of Pulau Perhentian Kecil.
Access: By boat (about 30min) west–northwest from the resort.
Conditions: Usually calm with some slight current. Visibility normally about 10m (33ft).
Average depth: 13m (43ft)
Maximum depth: 13m (43ft)
Here you find, as usual for this region, a jumble of rocks

from the coast down to the sand; you can then swim along the junction of the rocks with the sand. There are a few stony corals plus many species of pufferfish, parrotfish, surgeonfish, snappers and some Bumphead Parrotfish and turtles. On the sand you can see several species of sea cucumbers, sea stars – including Crown-of-Thorns Starfish – stingrays and sea urchins.

BATU NISAN

★★★

Location: The headland north of Matahari Chalets, on the east coast of Pulau Perhentian Kecil.
Access: By boat (about 20min) just north of west from Perhentian Island Resort.
Conditions: Usually calm with some slight current. Visibility generally about 10m (33ft).
Average depth: 13m (43ft)
Maximum depth: 13m (43ft)

A jumble of rocks descends from the coast to the sand, where you are guaranteed to see stingrays, fan worms, several species of sea cucumbers and sea stars – including the Crown-of-Thorns Starfish – as well as congregations of black sea urchins. In the water over the rocks are many species, both large and small, of pufferfish, boxfish, surgeonfish, unicornfish, parrotfish, snappers, sweetlips and fusiliers.

Gorgonian Sea Fan (Subergorgia hicksoni). Sea fans usually grow on the edge of a reef where they are exposed to plankton-bearing currents. Some specimens are very large, perhaps as much as 3m (10ft) across.

HOW TO GET THERE

The cheapest way to reach Perhentian from Europe is to fly with Malaysian Airlines via Kuala Lumpur to either Kota Bharu or Kuala Terengganu; then take either a bus (very cheap) or taxi (cheap) to Kuala Besut. From Kuala Besut there are several ferries each day.

Slightly more expensive, but more direct from Europe, is to fly with Thai Airways direct to Phuket in Thailand; from here you cross the border to Kota Bharu.

Kuala Terengganu can be reached by road from Kuala Lumpur via Kuantan 455km (282 miles) and from Singapore via Johor Bahru and Kuantan 559km (347 miles). There are regular flights from Kuala Lumpur and from Singapore via Kuantan or Johor Bahru.

Ramli Chik, at Perhentian Island Resort (see address below), can organize all transport and transfers from Kuala Lumpur or Phuket.

You should avoid August, which is the local holiday and high season. The resort closes down for the monsoon season, from the end of October until the beginning of March. May to July are particularly good times for diving.

WHERE TO STAY

Medium Price Range
Perhentian Island Resort, Pulau Perhentian Besar, Daerah Besut, 22200 Besut Terengganu; tel/fax 011–345562 (resort direct, mobile) and 011–333910 (Kuala Besut office, mobile)
Kuala Lumpur Office:
25th Floor Menara Promet, Jalan Sultan Promet, 50250 Kuala Lumpur
Postal Address:
PO Box 10849, 50726 Kuala Lumpur; tel 03–2480811/fax 03–2418463
There are two standards of accommodation at Perhentian Island Resort.

The cheaper 'A' frame chalets are built on a hill and have electric light and fans but no electrical sockets for charging (you can charge equipment in the dive hut). These chalets share a separate shower/toilet block.

More expensive are the bungalows, built on level ground near the restaurant. These have en suite toilets and showers, electric lights and fans, as well as three-square-pin electrical sockets (240 volts) for charging, etc.

Lower Price Range
The island has a number of very basic huts, which can be booked through the Bonaza 1 Express Ferry Office (tel 09–970290), which you find where taxis and buses drop you off in Kuala Besut, about 50m (165ft) from the ferry jetty. In many cases you will need to take your own food, bottled water and some form of lighting, with spare batteries or gas cartridges.

Most of the cheaper accommodation does not have access to a jetty; so you may have to embark or disembark in shallow water.

Some of the huts go beyond 'basic' to revolting. You will find a reasonable standard at, among others:

Coco Huts, Pulau Perhentian Besar, 22300 Besut; tel 01–975952 (mobile)

Rosly's Chalets, Pulau Perhentian Besar, 22300 Besut; tel 09–793155

The resthouse is reserved for government officials.

WHERE TO EAT

There is little or nothing on offer by way of separate restaurants, so in general people use the restaurant attached to their accommodation.

DIVE FACILITIES

Currently Perhentian Island Resort (see address above) has the only dive centre on the islands. It is run by NAUI instructor Stephen Ng, one of the veterans of Malaysian diving. Stephen's Dive Shop (tel 011–349396, mobile) is beside the restaurant at Perhentian Island Resort.

Diving costs, if you have your own equipment, are US$70 for two dives on a one-day trip, US$40 for one dive. Full diving equipment is available for rent. Overseas bookings may be made through Perhentian Island Resort.

At the time of going to press we were advised of a new resort:
Coral Sky Sdn Bhd, PO Box 265, 15730 Kota Bharu; tel 011–977963 (mobile) and a new dive operator:
Turtle Island Dive Centre, Pasir Panjang, Pulau Perhentian, Kuala Besut, 22300 Terengganu; tel 011–337514 (mobile)/fax 03–2535280.

FILM PROCESSING

No film processing is available on the island or in Kuala Besut. Kuala Terengganu has several mini-labs for processing print film, but I could find no E6 processing.

HOSPITAL

Terengganu General Hospital, Kuala Terengganu; tel 09–633333

LOCAL HIGHLIGHTS

Pulau Perhentian Besar offers walks on its exquisite beaches and opportunities to go jungle trekking and catch glimpses of the interesting birds, monkeys, squirrels and lizards. If you want to go further afield in search of land-based experiences, your best – perhaps your only – option is the mainland, where you'll find coastal beach resorts, fishing villages and offshore islands. One highlight used to be watching the Leatherback Turtles coming ashore at Rantau Abang to lay their eggs, but sadly the number of Leatherbacks nesting here has collapsed, and what was once a spectacle is now barely worth a detour. Instead, you could take a trip to **Taman Negara National Park**, en route visiting **Lake Kenyir** – formed by the Kenyir Dam (finished 1985) – the **Sekayu waterfalls** and the **Batu Biwa caves**.

Kuala Terengganu, the major local population centre, is worth exploring: it has the **State Museum**, the **Maziah Palace**, the **Zainal Abidin Mosque** and various batik-printing, silk-weaving, songket-weaving and handicraft centres. You can see traditional-style boat-building on **Pulau Duyung Besar**, an island on the Terengganu River.

Northwards, across the state border into Kelantan, is **Kota Bharu**, with one of the largest and liveliest markets in Malaysia, as well as batik printing and local handicrafts; this is also the place to see kite-flying and top-spinning contests.

The further north you go towards the national border, the stronger becomes the Thai influence. **Wat Phothivihan**, at Tumpat, has one of the largest reclining Buddhas in Southeast Asia.

Depending on your schedule you may arrive in Kuala Terengganu or Kota Bharu too late to connect with the Perhentian ferry from Kuala Besut. If transfers prove a problem and you find you have to stay overnight, the following accommodation details may prove useful:

Upper Price Range
Primula Beach Resort, JL Persinggahan, PO Box 43, Kuala Terengganu
Tel 09–622100/fax 09–633360.

Hotel Perdana, JR Mahmud, PO Box 222, Kota Bharu Tel 09–748 5000/fax 09–744 7621.

Medium Price Range
Qurata Riverside Resort, Lot 175K Kuala Ibai, Kuala Terengganu Tel 09–675590/fax 09–675511.

Juita Inn, 60-64 JL Pintu Pong, Khota Bharu Tel 09–7446888/fax 09–744 5777.

Lower Price Range
City Hotel, 97–99 Jl Banggol, Kuala Terengganu Tel 09–744 3049.

Hotel Aman, 236 C–D Jl Tengku Besar, Kota Bharu Tel 90–744 3049.

Pulau Redang
(Terengganu Marine Park)

There are nine islands in the Pulau Redang archipelago. The largest is Pulau Redang itself, followed by the much smaller Pulau Pinang and then seven tiny islets: Pulau Ekor Tebu, Pulau Kerengga Besar, Pulau Kerengga Kecil, Pulau Lima, Pulau Ling (often called Pulau Chipor), Pulau Paku Besar and Pulau Paku Kecil.

Situated 45km (28 miles) northeast of Kuala Terengganu and 27km (17 miles) off Merang, this area probably has the best coral reefs off Peninsular Malaysia, and certainly they are the most intensively studied.

Currently a massive tourist resort is being constructed on Pulau Redang which may have adverse affects on the environment. Nevertheless, diving in September 1993 I found the underwater visibility much better here – about 30m (100ft) at all the sites – than off Pulau Perhentian (see page 48) and Pulau Tioman (see page 74).

Although rain is frequent throughout the year, the climate of the archipelago enjoys a wetter season during November to March, when the northeast monsoon is blowing.

KAMPUNG KUALA REDANG

The fishing village of Kampung Kuala Redang, built on stilts at the estuary of the Sungai Redang on Pulau Redang, is home to about 200 families who moved here from Pulau Pinang, just opposite, several years ago. The people subsist mainly on fishing, though some supplement their income by collecting edible swiftlets' nests (from the caves along the

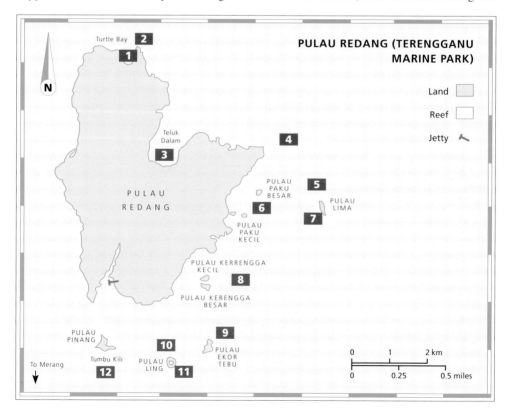

northeast coast) as well as turtles' eggs, 50% of which are – or are supposed to be – sold to the hatchery managed by the Department of Fisheries. There is some agriculture on the flat land of the Sungai Redang Valley, including fruit trees on the hillsides. You can still see remnants of the old coconut and pepper plantations.

At present the islands have no electricity, no sewage- or garbage-treatment plants and very little fresh water. Part of the plan for the new resort is to move the villagers some 3km (2 miles) inland to Kampung Ulu Redang – but this idea must surely be doomed to failure, since the people's way of life is entirely adapted to being based in a *kampung air* (water-village), like Kampung Kuala Redang.

REEF-LIFE
The beaches are sandy on the east side of Pulau Redang and stony on the island's west side. The waters separating Pulau Redang from the small islets are relatively shallow (up to 25m; 82ft). The most extensive reefs are around these islets, showing the greatest variety on the deeper north and east sides. There are shallow reef flats and coral gardens dominated by staghorn, table and boulder corals. In places where the cliffs are steep you can find soft corals, encrusting corals and sea anemones on the granite. All told, 52 genera of hard corals are reported in these waters, plus 43 genera of crustaceans, 57 species of marine algae, 36 species of marine worms and 82 species of molluscs. Hawksbill and Green Turtles nest along the west coast of Pulau Redang, and while I was diving there I saw a Leatherback Turtle. Reef fish and pelagic species are plentiful, and Manta Rays and Whale Sharks are often seen in the open waters around Pulau Redang.

FAUNA
The islands' fauna is impoverished by comparison with that of the mainland – the inland forest bird fauna, for example, includes only nine species (plus migrants). Scant as it is, the fauna has evolved in the absence of carnivorous predators, and is therefore vulnerable to introduced species, so it is worrying that the new resort has plans to establish an aviary, a butterfly farm, flower and orchid farms and a crocodile farm.

ACCOMODATION
Until the completion of the Redang Island Resort the only options for visitors seeking accommodation on the islands will remain camping on the beaches or putting up in one of the huts belonging to the few very basic resorts that are

MALAYSIA'S FIRST MARINE PARK
The marine waters surrounding the Pulau Redang archipelago to a distance of 5.6km (3 nautical miles) from the low-water marks of the shores of the islands were in 1985 designated a Marine Park — Malaysia's first. (Before that, from 1983, they were Prohibited Fisheries waters.) The Marine Park is administered by the Department of Fisheries. Most dive sites have fixed mooring buoys to stop anchor damage.

Core Zone
No fishing or shell collecting is allowed within the core zone, defined as 1 nautical mile (1.85km) from the islands' low-water marks; in the outer zone, between this limit and the 3-nautical-mile boundary, trawl-fishing, fish-traps and spear-fishing are forbidden, although resident fishermen are permitted to practise traditional non-destructive fishing and visitors can indulge in rod-and-line fishing with the requisite permit from the Department of Fisheries.

The news is not entirely good, however. Before protection was enforced by the Prohibited Fisheries status, shell life was overcollected and blast-fishing, trawling and spear-fishing were common, and it will be a while before the area recovers. Also, immediately outside the Park's boundary, night-time line and squid-fishing with lights are permitted. This almost certainly has the effect of deterring many of the turtles who would otherwise come here to nest, and also attracts some fish species out of the protected area to places where they can be legally caught. Moreover, while the designated waters might be protected, the Marine Park legislation does not extend to cover activities on the islands. This goes in the teeth of the prevailing wisdom about Marine Parks, which has it that, if they are to be at all effective, activities on the adjoining land areas must also be controlled.

MASTER BOATBUILDERS

Many of the deep-sea fishing boats you see bobbing about in these waters were built on a small island in the Terengganu estuary, Pulau Duyong ('Island of the Mermaid').

These islanders are famous for their boat-building skills, which have been handed down from generation to generation. The master craftsmen build their traditional boats using simple woodworking tools. They start off by merely sketching the design in the sand before laying the keel.

Today the islanders of Pulau Duyong also make custom-built yachts for Western clients.

TURTLE NESTING

Turtle nesting is done mainly at night and is a slow and laborious process, lasting at least an hour. The female hauls herself up the beach and with her front flippers partially clears several sites before settling on a suitable one. Using sweeping motions she digs a pit 25–45cm (10–18in) deep into which she lays her eggs. She then fills in the egg pit with sand and tries to do the same with the body cavity although it is rare that she makes a good job of concealment. The eggs are vulnerable as they are not hard-shelled but covered in a parchment-like membrane.

here. None of these enterprises have mains electricity, diving equipment, fuel or jetties where you can land your equipment, and consequently you have to arrange things in advance if you want to dive here, and bring all your own equipment and fuel with you – an expensive venture if you happen to be the only client.

The resorts I inspected made no effort to keep their lovely beaches clean of drift rubbish, and not much to dispose of garbage: monkeys, squirrels and insects attracted by this rubbish can be a nuisance – I soon learned to shut all my equipment away when I was out after we found a squirrel eating the silicone rubber off my buddy's facemask! Currently the resorts use small electrical generators at night, but I found these were not powerful enough to charge my quick-charge strobe (flash-gun) batteries (although they gave enough power for trickle charging). Spare batteries are not available on the island, so, if your strobes can use them, take your own.

At present the only jetties on the islands are at the fishing village and at the Department of Fisheries Visitor Centre on Pulau Pinang (where there are also the Marine Parks staff quarters and research station). The Visitor Centre is beautifully clean and has delightful flower gardens, turtle hatchlings, maps, information brochures and exhibits; it is well worth a visit in its own right.

SNORKELLING

You can snorkel off the turtle-nesting beaches of Pasir Mak Kapit and Pasir Mak Simpan and off the west coast of Pulau Redang, but the turtles are almost the sole interest here as the fish life is not good. The main diving and snorkelling areas are off the east coast and, in particular, off the small islets. The southwest coast of Pulau Pinang generally offers good diving in shallow water, to 18m (60ft). The northeast coast of Pulau Pinang is good for snorkelling.

Opposite: *On Pulau Pinang, a small island just off Pulau Redang, there is a fascinating Visitor Centre with flower gardens, turtle hatchlings and exhibits.*

1 TURTLE BAY
2 TANJUNG BATU TOKONG
★★★

Location: The northernmost coast of Pulau Redang and Turtle Bay.
Access: By boat.
Conditions: Sheltered in Turtle Bay; off Tanjung Batu Tokong it can be rough, with strong currents.
In calm weather you can snorkel all along the north and northeast coasts, with turtles on view in all the bays. At Turtle Bay as many as 22 turtles have been seen at one time. At Tanjung Batu Tokong the jumbles of large boulders bear soft corals and gorgonian sea fans, and there is good fish life here as well.

3 TELUK DALAM
★★★

Location: The large bay of Teluk Dalam.
Access: Either off the beaches in the bay or by boat from elsewhere.
Conditions: Sheltered outside the monsoon season.
Another bay where you can find turtles. The fish life is good, especially at the base of the rocks, which form caves and overhangs. There is a coral garden with a wide variety of hard and soft corals, including encrusting corals, table corals, mushroom and boulder corals.

4 TANJUNG GUA KAWAH
★★★

Location: The easternmost point of Pulau Redang, north of Pulau Paku Besar.
Access: By boat.
Conditions: This area tends to have strong surface and deep-water currents, so experienced divers should check the conditions before their less experienced companions enter the water.
Average depth: 15m (50ft)
Maximum depth: 20m (65ft)
A jumble of rocks descends to sand. The strong deep-water currents keep coral growth down, but as partial compensation there is abundant fish life, especially sheltering in the caves and under overhangs among the rocks. You might also see some pelagic species.

5 BIG SEAMOUNT
★★★★★

Location: Approximately 50m (165ft) north of Pulau Lima, east of Pulau Paku Besar.
Access: By boat to the buoy over the seamount.
Conditions: Normally calm; can become choppy and have a strong current after bad weather.
Average depth: 25m (82ft)
Maximum depth: Beyond 40m (130ft)
The diving all around Pulau Lima is excellent, and this oval seamount in particular is considered by many to

offer Peninsular Malaysia's most spectacular diving. It is a jumble of boulders with its longer axis oriented east–west; it rises from a depth of 30m (100ft), on the landward side, to within 10m (33ft) of the surface. The flat top is covered in hard corals, leathery soft corals, encrusting corals, mushroom corals, tunicates and sponges, gorgonian sea fans and sea anemones with attendant clownfish.

The seaward slope, which continues down to a depth of more than 40m (130ft), has a variety of whip corals and in the deeper waters, dark green *Tubastrea micranthus* branch-like cup corals, large *Dendronephthya* soft-tree corals and nudibranchs.

The fish life found here includes all the expected angelfish, butterflyfish and wrasse; there are also many species of parrotfish, pufferfish and triggerfish, plus damselfish, sergeant majors, scorpionfish, lionfish (including Zebra Lionfish), stonefish, moray eels, Blue-spotted Lagoon Rays, soldierfish, squirrelfish, batfish, groupers and barracuda. In the open water there are shoals of fusiliers, jacks and snappers, at least two varieties of jellyfish and the occasional turtle. Cardinalfish and sweepers congregate in the caves.

There are fan worms on the sand and Christmas-tree Worms in the boulder corals, and also on view are several varieties of sea cucumbers, sea stars, cushion stars and sea urchins.

6 PULAU PAKU BESAR: SOUTH SIDE

★★★★

Location: Pulau Paku Besar lies, 1/2km (1/3 mile) east of Pulau Redang.
Access: By boat.
Conditions: Normally calm, but can become choppy and have a strong current after bad weather. Snorkelling is possible in the shallow water near the cliffs.
Average depth: 15m (50ft)
Maximum depth: 21m (70ft)
Cliffs slope down at an angle of 30–40° to a level bottom where there are lots of whip, staghorn, table, lettuce and mushroom corals; the cliffs themselves are covered in leathery soft corals, small *Dendronephthya* soft corals and many feather stars. Also on view are some big Giant Clams plus several other species of shellfish and tunicates. The fish life, though not prolific, includes many species of wrasse, pufferfish and triggerfish, as well as all the expected angelfish and butterflyfish, damselfish, sergeant majors and batfish.

In the deeper water there are small gorgonian sea fans, large *Dendronephthya* soft-tree corals, some dark green *Tubastrea micranthus* cup corals and several species of nudibranchs, while in the open water you have a chance of seeing at least two species of jellyfish and shoals of jacks, fusiliers and snappers. On the bottom live

many varieties of sea cucumbers, sea stars and sea urchins, but very few sea anemones.

7 PULAU LIMA: WEST SIDE AND SOUTH END

★★★★★

Location: Pulau Lima lies 2km (1 1/4 miles) east of Pulau Paku Kecil.
Access: By boat.
Conditions: Normally calm; can become choppy and have a strong current after bad weather.
Average depth: 24m (80ft)
Maximum depth: 30m (100ft)
I dived here immediately after my arrival from Pulau Tioman (see page 74), and the clear visibility (about 30m/100ft) did wonders in raising my spirits! All of the diving around Pulau Lima is pretty spectacular. Here off Pulau Lima you find the usual jumble of boulders dropping steeply to 20m (65ft), then gently down to sand at 30m (100ft). There is the same wide variety of corals, sponges and fish life as at Big Seamount (Site 5). The west side has rather more sea anemones with clownfish and also more boulder corals with Christmas-tree Worms, plus lots of good staghorn, table, mushroom and lettuce corals. The boulders at the island's southern end offer further caves and tunnels in which you can spot cardinalfish, sweepers and invertebrates hiding.

8 MINI SEAMOUNT

★★★★★

Location: 100m (330ft) east of Pulau Kerengga Besar.
Access: By boat to the buoy over the seamount.
Conditions: Usually calm and more sheltered than Pulau Lima, but can get rough with a current after bad weather. The usual clear visibility found off these islands.
Average depth: 18m (60ft)
Maximum depth: 20m (65ft)
A small seamount consisting of a jumble of boulders down to sand at 20m (65ft). The deeper rocks are covered in leathery soft corals, with some *Dendronephthya* soft-tree corals and dark green *Tubastrea micranthus* cup corals, tunicates and encrusting corals and sponges. There are sea anemones everywhere.

The abundant marine life is similar to that at Pulau Lima (Site 7), but with more varieties of pufferfish and groupers, more turtles and fewer stony corals. On the landward side you should be able to see several species of immature fish.

On the sand there are big *Dendronephthya* soft-tree corals and many large barrel sponges covered with Alabaster Sea Cucumbers.

The channel, 15m (50ft) deep, between Pulau Kerengga Kecil and Pulau Kerengga Besar is good for snorkelling. There is a colourful coral garden with staghorn, lettuce and mushroom corals. Off the south-west side of Pulau Kerengga Besar is a large area of mushroom corals.

9 PULAU EKOR TEBU: NORTHEAST CORNER
★★★★★

Location: Pulau Ekor Tebu lies 2½ km (1½ miles) east of Pulau Pinang and northeast of Pulau Ling.
Access: By boat.
Conditions: Normally calm; can be choppy with a strong current after bad weather.
Average depth: 19m (62ft)
Maximum depth: 24m (80ft)
The northeast corner is the deepest part of the waters off Pulau Ekor Tebu: boulders extend northwards, dropping steeply to 10m (33ft) and then at a more gentle gradient to 24m (80ft).

There is an underwater cave at 20m (65ft), and some 30m out from the cave is a rock outcrop which may break the surface at low tide.

I dived this site as a drift-dive after a heavy storm. Despite the rough night the visibility was excellent. There were fish and jellyfish everywhere, but what attracted me most were the table and lettuce corals, which were of the quality more commonly associated with Pulau Sipadan (see page 130) and Pulau Sangalakki (see page 143), off Borneo, and the Tubbataha Reefs in the Philippines Sulu Sea.

There are also healthy staghorn corals, many large Giant Clams and several shells. The fish life is generally similar to if not so concentrated as that at Pulau Lima (Site 7), but I did also see here a cuttlefish, squid and an Eagle Ray.

10 BATU CHIPOR
★★★★

Location: Marked by a buoy 20m (70ft) from a tiny rock pinnacle just breaking the surface north of Pulau Ling (Pulau Chipor), east of Pulau Ekor Tebu.
Access: By boat to the buoy.
Conditions: Usually calm; can be choppy with a current after bad weather.
Average depth: 8m (26ft)
Maximum depth: 15m (50ft)
A pretty wall, covered in small colourful *Dendronephthya* soft-tree corals, leathery corals and gorgonian sea fans, goes down to a flat sandy bottom where there are lots of

---

GORGONIANS

Gorgonians, like their relatives the stony corals, are colonial animals made up of numerous anemone-like polyps sharing a common, flexible skeleton of keratin, which is similar to the material in animal horn. There are literally hundreds of different species of gorgonians and they occur in a variety of forms including whips, harps, fans and bushes that may grow to as large as 3 or 4 metres. A mature colony of gorgonians may take many years to grow but can be spectacular. They grow in abundance in tropical waters, in a variety of stunning colours and are perhaps most interesting to observe at night when the polyps are feeding.

---

staghorn, table, mushroom and lettuce corals and some boulder corals with Christmas-tree Worms.

Interestingly, there are not so many fish as there are at the other dives in the Pulau Redang group, but most of the local angelfish and butterflyfish, pufferfish, lion-fish, parrotfish, wrasse, groupers, cuttlefish and Blue-spotted Lagoon Rays are present.

At sand level there are moray eels, nudibranchs as well as a variety of species of sea cucumbers, sea stars and cushion stars.

11 PULAU LING
★★★

Location: The small islet of Pulau Ling, east of Pulau Pinang, southwest of Pulau Ekor Tebu.
Access: By boat.
Conditions: Well sheltered and therefore usually calm although bad weather from the south can adversely affect this area, but otherwise only the foulest weather will cause you any problems.
Average depth: 10m (33ft)
Maximum depth: 20m (65ft)
The main attractions of this islet are two enormous boulder corals (*Porites* species), the bigger of which is 40m (130ft) in circumference and 10m (33ft) in height, with a cave 2m (6ft) high at its base. These boulder corals are the largest known coral structures off the east coast of Peninsular Malaysia, and are estimated to be many hundreds of years old.

Also of interest in the area are the marvellous staghorn, table and lettuce corals, mushroom corals, soft corals, sponges, tunicates, sea anemones and gorgonian sea fans.

12 TUMBU KILI

★★★★★

Location: This small rock breaks the surface just off Tanjung Tumbu Kili, the southernmost point of Pulau Pinang.

Access: By boat.

Conditions: Well sheltered and therefore usually calm; bad weather from the south can adversely affect this area, but otherwise only the foulest weather will make diving difficult.

Average depth: 10m (33ft)

Maximum depth: 20m (65ft)

Below the low-tide mark, down to sand at 20m (65ft), the jumble of boulders here is carpeted with leathery and *Dendronephthya* soft corals, gorgonian sea fans and sea anemones. On the sand itself are larger *Dendronephthya* soft corals and gorgonian sea fans, whip corals, some staghorn corals, table corals, mushroom corals and boulder corals, nudibranchs, sea cucumbers, sea stars, cushion stars, Giant Clams and shells. Hundreds of long-tentacled jellyfish and many shoals of fish – including parrotfish, jacks, trevallies, snappers, fusiliers, soldierfish, sweepers and wrasse – swim out in the open water. You can also see several species of pufferfish, angelfish and butterflyfish, some barracuda, batfish and Bumphead Parrotfish. There are feather stars on all the whip corals and gorgonian sea fans. Further out on the sand barrel sponges are common.

The Zebra Lionfish (Dendrochirus zebra) is one of the most beautiful of the Scorpaenidae, with venomous spines that cause great pain if contacted.

HOW TO GET THERE

There are no regular ferries to Pulau Redang so you will have to hire a boat from Kuala Terengganu, Merang or Kuala Besut. In some situations it may be possible to hire a boat from Pulau Perhentian; a fast speedboat takes 1hr.

The shortest boat trip to Pulau Redang is from the sleepy little fishing village of Merang (not to be confused with Marang), 38km (24 miles) north of Kuala Terengganu; a fast speedboat from here takes just over 1hr. You can get to Merang (or to Kuala Besut) from Kuala Terengganu by bus or taxi. Kuala Terengganu can be reached by road from Kuala Lumpur via Kuantan, 455km (282 miles), and from Singapore via Johor Bahru and Kuantan 559km (347 miles). There are regular flights from Kuala Lumpur and from Singapore via Kuantan or Johor Bahru.

Perhentian Island Resort is looking into the possibility of setting up a resort on Pulau Redang, which could considerably improve the facilities available there.

WHERE TO STAY

T.H. Foo Redang Pelangi Resort
27 Jalan Bandar, 21210 Kuala Terengganu; tel 09–623158, 010–934158 (mobile), 011–970426 (mobile –resort direct)
Kuala Lumpur Office:
28A, Lorongo Dato Sulaiman Satu, Taman Tun Dr Ismail, 60000 Kuala Lumpur; tel 03–7182471/fax 03–7172571

E.S. Lim Redang Bay Resort Sdn Bhd
139 Jalan Bandar, 20100 Kuala Terengganu; tel 09–636048, 011–971261 (mobile)/fax 09–628190
On some weekends PADI instructor Liu Saow Hong attends this resort:
tel 010–933709 (mobile).

DIVE FACILITIES

There are as yet no permanent facilities for visiting divers in the Pulau Redang archipelago. Currently dive trips are organized by dive operators or diving clubs, mostly in Kuala Lumpur or Singapore, who bring their own equipment and either camp on a beach or organize chalet accommodation with the existing small resort operators.

There are no regular ferries so, to cut the costs of boat and personnel hire, the transport of equipment, fuel, air cylinders and the organization of a compressor, you will need to get a sizeable group together.

Lawrence Lee of Scuba Quest regularly uses Pulau Redang for his diving courses. On my behalf he brought equipment and air cylinders from Kuala Lumpur and arranged with T.H. Foo for the hire of a speedboat, crew, fuel and extra air cylinders and the use of a chalet at Mr Foo's Redang Pelangi Resort. Mr Foo also lent me a local diver, Bund, to help out. There are no jetties at either Merang or Redang Pelangi Resort, so I was more than pleased to have an extra pair of hands to carry equipment!

At the time of going to press I received information on a new dive operator:

Eco Diving
24 Tingkat Satu, Wisnia Awang Chik, Jalan Sultan Mahmud, 20400 Kuala Telengganu; tel 09–6236200/fax 09–6236300.

Lawrence Lee Scuba Quest Sdn Bhd
Lot 3–38, 2nd Floor, Wisma Central, Jalan Ampang, 50450 Kuala Lumpur; tel 03–2642697/fax 03–2636032, tel 010–226543 mobile
NAUI and PADI courses.

FILM PROCESSING

None available on the islands. Kuala Terengganu has several mini-labs for processing print film, but for the nearest E6 processing you have to go to Johor Bahru or Kuala Lumpur.

HOSPITAL

Terengganu General Hospital, Kuala Terengganu; tel 09–633333

LOCAL HIGHLIGHTS

The islands' flora and fauna are quite interesting but, at least until work on the new resort is completed, you may find the walks and views on Pulau Redang somewhat disappointing.

For details of local highlights on the mainland opposite, refer to the directory covering Pulau Perhentian (page 57).

Diver and table coral. Good-size table corals (Acropora sp.) are common off Pulau Redang.

The Crown-of-Thorns Starfish, *Acanthaster planci*, first gained notoriety in the 1960s and 1970s, when it was observed that hugely increasing populations were causing massive coral-reef destruction in the Indo-Pacific, particularly on Australia's Great Barrier Reef and the reefs of Southern Japan, and later off the islands of Micronesia (especially Guam) and to a lesser extent in the Red Sea.

ENVIRONMENTAL CONCERN

These early observations caused panic among scientists and environmentalists. Some blamed the depletion of the creature's natural predators, such as the Triton Shell, pufferfish, triggerfish and Humphead Wrasse; others pointed out that many of the worst-hit areas had been affected by blast fishing, harbour construction, dredging and pollution, with consequent decline of the smaller creatures and some corals that eat *Acanthaster planci* at the egg and larval stage (a female Crown-of-Thorns Starfish can produce 12–24 million eggs annually).

However, analysis of core samples drilled through the Great Barrier Reef suggests such population explosions have occurred regularly throughout history, and it may be just that, as scuba diving has become ever more popular, there are many more divers and marine scientists in the water to observe the changes.

DEVASTATION

The stark white skeletons of *Acropora* corals killed by aggregations of *Acanthaster planci* are a terrible sight: in some cases 80–90% coral destruction occurs. Many attempts have been made to eradicate the starfish during local population explosions, but none has been fully effective.

A FEARSOME CREATURE

About 30cm (12in) across, with up to 23 arms covered on the dorsal surface with short fat spines – 3–5cm (0.8–2in) long – *Acanthaster planci* varies in colour from orange to green/blue and purple. The spines contain a nasty venom that gives some people a severe reaction, ranging from a skin rash to nausea

and severe pain. Unlike many other predators on coral, *Acanthaster planci* does not damage the coral skeleton: only live coral tissues are eaten. It feeds on the polyps, preferably those of *Acropora* table corals, by everting its stomach over the coral so that the digestive enzymes come into direct contact with the coral tissue; thus digestion starts before the food is taken into the mouth. These enzymes may be the cause of the severe skin reaction suffered by divers who are foolish enough to pick the creatures up without gloves.

The Crown-of-Thorns Starfish regularly returns to the same coral table until that table is dead. When aggregations of these creatures occur, newcomers are attracted to the coral table. It is likely that attractant chemicals are given off during feeding.

Normally *Acanthaster planci* feeds at night, preferring to hide deep in crevices during the day. When aggregations occur, many of the individuals involved make less effort to hide during the day, often only crawling into the shade of the coral table's underside. Others can be seen before dusk moving through shady areas towards their prey.

EFFECTIVE EXTERMINATION

Damaged Crown-of-Thorns Starfish soon regenerate. Injections with formaldehyde, copper sulphate or sodium hypochlorite are expensive, slow and inefficient. The only successful way of exterminating the creatures is to bring them ashore en masse and bury them – or, better still, burn them. This was how the Malaysian Fisheries Department (with private-sector backing) combated the recent major infestation at Pulau Redang. The good news is that on a recent visit to Pulau Redang I saw few Crown-of-Thorns Starfish, and those reefs unaffected by the resort construction were regenerating well.

Crown-of-Thorns Starfish (Acanthaster planci). These voracious predators sometimes occur in large aggregations, completely decimating large areas of live stony corals.

Pulau Tenggol
(Terengganu Marine Park)

The southernmost islands of the Terengganu Marine Parks, the Pulau Tenggol group, consists of the main island of Pulau Tenggol, 29km (18 miles) east-northeast of Kuala Dungun, plus, to its north-northwest, the smaller island of Pulau Nyireh, along with the islets and rocks of Batu Tokong Kamudi, Pulau Tokong Burong and Tokong Talang (north of Pulau Nyireh) and Batu Tong Daik (south–southwest of Pulau Tenggol).

STEEP-SIDED CLIFFS

The west side of Pulau Tenggol has a beach facing a deep-water bay that offers good anchorage; but more characteristic of these islands are steep-sided cliffs descending into deep waters – deeper than along most of Peninsular Malaysia's east coast – with many underwater boulders carpeted by good mixed soft and stony corals and encrusting corals and sponges, forming a classical spur-and-groove topography. The deeper waters offer good visibility – about 30m (100ft) on average almost everywhere – but some strong currents render this not the best of areas for novices. Diving schools like Scuba Point in Kuala Lumpur use Pulau Tenggol for their advanced open-water courses.

A NEW RESORT

Until recently divers either had to hire a boat and take out all their own equipment or hire a package from the Tanjung Jara Beach Hotel, 13km (8 miles) north of Kuala Dungun; how-

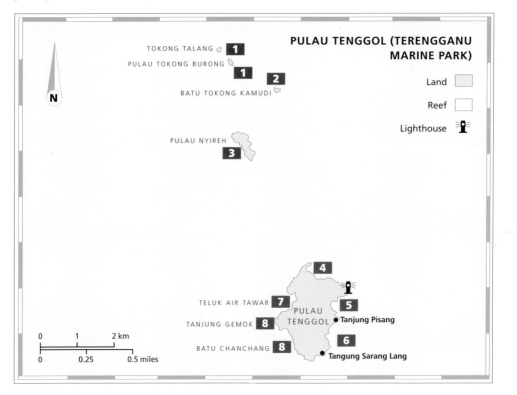

The Clown Triggerfish (Balistoides conspicillum) is one of the most conspicuous reef fish, preferring coral-rich terraces near steep slopes.

ever, there is now a chalet resort in Teluk Air Tawar (Fresh Water Bay), with another being built in the same bay. Most of the dive sites are buoyed to prevent anchor damage. The islands are easily reached, and so get busy at weekends.

These islands are attractive to nudibranch enthusiasts. Nurse Sharks, Reef Sharks, Manta Rays and Eagle Rays are often seen, as are pelagic fish like Tuna. Whale Sharks are relatively common in March/April and September/October. Before it became a marine park the area was a favourite with spear-fishermen, particularly for big groupers.

The diving season is March to September, but when currents are running you require an experienced and reliable boatman to keep track of divers.

NUDIBRANCHS

Nudibranchs are among the most colourful and interesting of the marine molluscs. 'Nudibranch' means 'naked gill', referring to the feathery gills found on the creature's back.

There are thought to be at least 2500 species of these 'snails without shells', which are part of a large group commonly referred to as sea slugs. All nudibranchs are hermaphroditic (i.e., they can become both male and female) and carnivorous.

One of the most flamboyant and spectacular is the aptly named Spanish Dancer (*Hexabranchus sanguineus*), a large bright red creature so named because the white fringe is like the twirling skirt of a flamenco dancer. The bright colour warns predators that they are poisonous.

1 TOKONG TALANG TO PULAU TOKONG BURONG

★★★★

Location: North of the northwest tip of Pulau Nyireh.
Access: By boat (30min) north–northwest from Teluk Air Tawar.
Conditions: Generally calm, with surface and deep-water currents, but can be choppy on the surface after bad weather. This dive is suitable for all levels of diver provided novices are accompanied by a divemaster.
Average depth: 24m (80ft)
Maximum depth: 30m (100ft)
When the current is right you can drift-dive at 25m (80ft) from Tokong Talang to Pulau Tokong Burong. On the sandy bottom there are large boulders covered with good soft, encrusting and stony corals (including fire coral) together with sponges, sea anemones and Christmas-tree Worms. Among the fish life found here are shoals of barracuda and many species of jacks, fusiliers and snappers, plus large tuna, good-sized groupers, nudibranchs, wrasse, batfish and all the expected angelfish and butterflyfish. On the sand are moray eels, stingrays and fan worms.

As alternatives you could either circle Tokong Talang or concentrate on the south side of Pulau Tokong Burong.

2 BATU TOKONG KAMUDI: NORTHEAST SIDE

★★★★

Location: Batu Tokong Kamudi is northeast of Pulau Nyireh, north of the west side of Pulau Tenggol.
Access: By boat (25–30min) from Teluk Air Tawar, around Tanjung Air Tawar, and then directly north.
Conditions: Generally calm with surface and deep-water currents; can be choppy on the surface after bad weather. Novices should be accompanied by a divemaster.
Average depth: 15m (50ft)
Maximum depth: 31m (100ft)
The site consists of a wall down to 30m (100ft) with, at its bottom, huge boulders on the sand. There is a good covering of soft, encrusting and stony corals, sponges and Christmas-tree Worms. In the deep water you can see some large *Dendronephthya* soft-tree corals plus many sea anemones and nudibranchs.

Fish on view include all the expected angelfish and butterflyfish, surgeonfish, triggerfish, parrotfish, batfish and wrasse, with snappers and soldierfish hiding in caves and under overhangs. In addition there are shoals of barracuda, tuna, jacks, fusiliers and snappers. On the sand are fan worms, moray eels, stingrays (and sometimes

Eagle Rays), scorpionfish, lionfish, stonefish and mushroom corals. On every high point feather stars fan out in the current.

3 PULAU NYIREH: WEST SIDE

★★★★★★★★

Location: North–northwest of Teluk Air Tawar.
Access: By boat (15min) from Teluk Air Tawar.
Conditions: Generally calm and sheltered with some current; can be choppy after bad weather.
Average depth: 15m (50ft)
Maximum depth: 30m (100ft)
Pulau Nyireh is a good area for novices and, near the shore, snorkellers. The west side of the island is one of two dive sites (the other is Site 8) referred to by local divers as the 'highway' because of the rich fish fauna that used to attract spear-fishermen before the islands were protected. There are shoals of barracuda, tuna, jacks, snappers and fusiliers, many quite large groupers, wrasse, squirrelfish, soldierfish, all the expected angelfish and butterflyfish, batfish, surgeonfish, scorpionfish, lionfish, stonefish, moray eels, Blue-spotted Lagoon Rays, triggerfish and pufferfish.

On the sand you can spot many species of sea stars, cushion stars, sea cucumbers, mushroom corals, sea urchins and fan worms. The rocks are covered in soft, encrusting and stony corals as well as sponges, sea anemones and Christmas-tree Worms. There is some fire coral as well as lots of stinging hydroids and countless feather stars.

4 PULAU TENGGOL: NORTHEASTERN BAY

★★★★★★★★

Location: The northeast bay of Pulau Tenggol, between Tanjung Nakhoda Terang and Tanjung Gua Jantong.
Access: By boat (10–15min) clockwise around the island from Teluk Air Tawar.
Conditions: Sheltered, except when bad weather comes from the east. There are some currents, and they can be strong; novices should be accompanied by a divemaster.
Average depth: 24m (80ft)
Maximum depth: 30m (100ft)
This is a popular site among training agencies offering open-water diving courses. Snorkelling is possible near the shore. There are many large boulder outcrops on sand at 25m (82ft). The boulders are well covered in stony corals with Christmas-tree Worms, feather stars, sponges and nudibranchs, colourful soft corals, encrusting corals and sea anemones. The fish life includes shoals of parrotfish, Bumphead Parrotfish, snappers, fusiliers

and jacks, all the expected angelfish and butterflyfish, wrasse, bream, batfish, hawkfish, surgeonfish, triggerfish and pufferfish. Whale Sharks, Manta Rays and Eagle Rays are sometimes seen. On the sand are moray eels, lizardfish, lionfish, scorpionfish, stonefish, Blue-spotted Lagoon Rays, stingrays, crocodilefish, sea cucumbers, sea stars (including Crown-of-Thorns Starfish), cushion stars, sea urchins and fan worms.

5 6 THE TWO BAYS ON THE EAST SIDE OF PULAU TENGGOL

★★★★

Location: On the east side of Pulau Tenggol, south of the lighthouse, between the lighthouse and Tanjung Pisang and between Tanjung Pisang and Tanjung Sarang Lang.
Access: By boat.
Conditions: You would snorkel here only in calm weather; there can be some strong currents. Visibility can reach 20m (65ft).
Average depth: 5m (16ft)
Maximum depth: Whatever you can snorkel
Both bays have sandy bottoms with rocks and coral heads harbouring sponges, sea anemones with and without clownfish, stingrays, lionfish, scorpionfish, angelfish, butterflyfish, triggerfish, pufferfish, parrotfish, surgeonfish, hawkfish, bream and fan worms.

On the sand itself are lizard fish, gobies, seastars, sea cucumbers and sea urchins. If you are lucky you may spot a turtle.

7 TELUK AIR TAWAR

★★★★ ☆☆☆☆☆

Location: The house-reef off the resorts in Teluk Air Tawar.
Access: Off the beach in front of the resorts.
Conditions: Well sheltered, except from very bad weather. The visibility, at 20m (65ft), is low for this region.
Average depth: 12m (40ft)
Maximum depth: 34m (110ft)
The house-reef slopes off to sand, where there is a colony of garden eels, at 25m (82ft), plus the usual boulder outcrops as well as fan worms. The boulders are well covered with sponges and corals, both stony and soft as well as encrusting. In deeper water are larger *Dendronephthya* soft corals as well as all the fish life generally found in the area, but in concentrations less than those prevalent off the headland to the south.

AN INTERESTING WRECK

About 1km (0.6 mile) north of Kuala Dungun and 200m (220yd) off the coast in 7m (23ft) of water lies an old steel wreck 20m (65ft) long that has good coral growth and fish life.

You may see both stony and soft corals as well as encrusting corals. There are jacks, trevallies, snappers, fusiliers, angelfish, butterflyfish, parrotfish, bream, hawkfish, batfish, wrasse and pufferfish.

If you are travelling in a private group you could take time out to dive this wreck en route to Pulau Tenggol.

---

8 DRIFTING FROM BATU CHANCHANG TO TANJUNG GEMOK

★★★★★

Location: The southwest side of the reef from Batu Chanchang through Tanjung Pasir Tingara to Tanjung Gemok.
Access: By boat (10–15min) anticlockwise around Tanjung Gemok from Teluk Air Tawar.
Conditions: Usually calm, with a current along the coast that can be strong; novices should be accompanied by a divemaster.
Average depth: 24m (80ft)
Maximum depth: 34m (110ft)
Considered by many the best dive in the area, this is, like Site 3, often referred to as the 'highway' because of the concentration of fish life seen here. The bottom is a collection of rock outcrops on sand, with good coral cover – both stony and soft as well as plenty of encrusting corals, sea anemones, sponges and nudibranchs. However, it is the fish fauna that is the main attraction. There are shoals of jacks, trevallies, snappers, fusiliers, barracuda, tuna and Bumphead Parrotfish. Then there are all the local angelfish and butterflyfish, plus surgeonfish, triggerfish, unicornfish, parrotfish, Eagle Rays, bream, hawkfish, batfish, wrasse and pufferfish. On the sand are lionfish, stonefish, scorpionfish, crocodilefish, moray eels, Blue-spotted Lagoon Rays, stingrays and lizardfish, while on every high point there are feather stars spreading themselves out in the current.

Previous page: *Feather star (Comanthus bennetti). When at rest during the daytime feather stars tuck their arms inwards.*

HOW TO GET THERE

Boats run from the little fishing village of Kuala Dungun, 73km (45 miles) south of Kuala Terengganu, which is 145km (90 miles) north of Kuantan. You can get either a taxi or a bus from Kuala Terengganu to Kuala Dungun. Alternatively, you can take a bus to Kuala Dungun from Kuantan.

There are regular bus and air services to Kuantan and Kuala Terengganu from Kuala Lumpur and, via Johor Bahru, from Singapore.

WHERE TO STAY

Pulau Tenggol
Tenggol Aqua Resort, 8 Jalan Sungai, Penaga, 2300 Kuala Dungun; tel/fax 09–844862
Mainland
Upper Price Range
Tanjung Jara Beach Hotel, Mile 8, Jalan Dungun, 23009 Dungun; tel 09–841801 fax 09–842653.

Kuala Lumpur Office:
tel 03–2542188
Lower Price Range
Rantau Abang Visitors Centre, Mile 13, Jalan Dungun, 23009 Dungun; tel 09–841533

Hotel Kasanya, 225–7 Jalan Tambun, 23000 Dungun; tel 09–841881

DIVE FACILITIES

Currently the only diving operation on the island is Tenggol Aqua Resort in Teluk Air Tawar. It is contactable c/o the Tanjung Jara Beach Hotel (address above).

Unfortunately this hotel, one of the best-known five-star beach resorts on the east coast, is lazy about replying to enquiries.

Scuba Point Sdn Bhd, 8A Jalan Desa Jaya Taman Desa, 58100 Kuala Lumpur; tel 03–7820177/fax 03–7810210
A PADI Five-Star Centre. Regularly organizes diving excursions to Pulau Tenggol.

FILM PROCESSING

None available on the island. Kuala Terengganu has several mini-labs for processing print film, but I could find no E6 processing.

HOSPITAL

Terengganu General Hospital, Kuala Terengganu; tel 09–633333

LOCAL HIGHLIGHTS

Pulau Tenggol has interesting flora and fauna. For details of local highlights on the mainland opposite, refer to the directory covering Pulau Perhentian (page 57).

Leatherback Turtle Hatchlings make for the sea. Leatherbacks are the world's largest turtle species.

Pahang Marine Parks

Pahang Marine Parks comprise the large island of Pulau Tioman and the very small islands Pulau Renggis, Pulau Sepoi, Pulau Labas, Pulau Soyah, Pulau Chebeh, Pulau Tulai (Coral Island), Pulau Sembilang and Pulau Seri Buat.

The largest and most developed of the 64 volcanic islands in the Seri Buat archipelago, Pulau Tioman has, along its west coast, good sandy beaches with coral reefs and mangroves. The island is considered one of the top 10 most beautiful islands in the world; it was chosen to be Bali Ha'i for the filming of the 1958 Hollywood classic South Pacific. It is mountainous, and most of it is covered with dense natural forest – a haven for birds, bats, Mouse Deer, lizards, squirrels and insects. Zoological expeditions are still discovering new invertebrate species here.

ACCOMODATION

Most of the accommodation is on the west side of Pulau Tioman; the best diving is around the smaller islands, 13km (8 miles) to the northwest. Pulau Tioman's east coast is too exposed to the weather for coral growth, apart from a few encrusting species and some soft corals. All the dive operators have their own house-reefs. In general these are ideal for training novices and offer quite good snorkelling. The Berjaya Imperial Beach Resort also has Renggis Island, just off the beach, but you should be careful of the boat traffic around the jetty if you decide to try snorkelling out to the island.

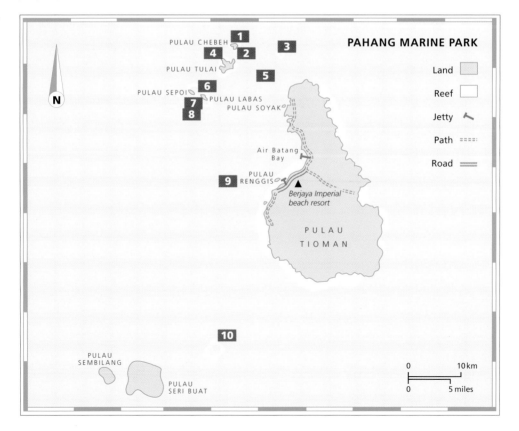

Pulau Sembilang and Pulau Seri Buat have well developed reefs, but are of much less interest than Pulau Tioman. You can organize a boat from Mersing if you wish to visit them. There is good snorkelling off Pulau Tulai, off Pulau Soyah (at Teluk Salang) and off the point by Nazri's Place at the southern end of Air Batang Bay. Pulau Tulai (advertised as Coral Island) is a favourite for travellers taking picnics and snorkelling. Most of the regular dive sites in the area are buoyed to stop any anchor damage.

PROLIFIC MARINE LIFE

The marine life is remarkably prolific. Manta Rays and Whale Sharks can be seen in March, April and May, though while I was there a Whale Shark was seen in September. Turtles and cuttlefish most commonly lay their eggs here in July and August, though despite this attraction August is best avoided: it is the local holiday high season.

The main diving season is April to October. On my visit the visibility could only be described as terrible but, to be fair, I was there not long after a large multinational naval exercise had seen 32 ships stirring up the waters.

Some of the smaller operators are frustratingly laid-back, and do not depart for dives before midday.

A CLEANER SEA

Apart from Johor, which covers the southern tip of Peninsular Malaysia, only Terengganu, which handles the industries associated with the large oil and gas installations off the northeast coast, is in any way industrialized. As a result, the South China Sea is a lot cleaner than the Strait of Malacca, the body of water off the Peninsula's west coast. A large oil-spill off Terengganu might, of course, temporarily alter this assessment: studies of ocean-current patterns predict that the Tioman group of islands and those off Johor would be at risk.

Soft white sand, lapped by clear blue sea is the order of the day at Air Batang Bay on Nazri's Beach, Pulau Tioman.

1 PULAU CHEBEH: NORTHEAST CORNER

★★★★☆

Location: The northeast corner of Pulau Chebeh, northwest of the northern end of Pulau Tioman and north of Pulau Tulai.
Access: By boat (20min) northwest from Pulau Tioman's Air Batang Bay.
Conditions: Usually calm, but can be choppy. There is often a surface current and surge, but these disappear as you get deeper. Visibility is likely to be around 8m (26ft).
Average depth: 25m (82ft)
Maximum depth: 27m (90ft)
Here you can swim in, around and through the gaps between large volcanic boulders that tumble down to a flat sandy bottom.

There are lots of big *Dendronephthya* soft corals, large white gorgonian sea fans, smaller yellow and blue gorgonian sea fans and some black coral. Many shoals of the smaller reef fish are in evidence, along with some large pufferfish, most of the local species of angelfish, butterflyfish and wrasse, moray eels, Spotted Sweetlips, gobies and lizardfish.

On the sand are patches of stony corals with Christmas-tree Worms, plus soft corals, fan worms, sea stars, cushion stars, sea cucumbers, scorpionfish and stingrays.

Although this is primarily a dive site, there is some good snorkelling by the rocks.

2 PULAU CHEBEH: SOUTHEAST SIDE

★★★☆☆☆

Location: The southeast side of Pulau Chebeh, northwest of the northern end of Pulau Tioman and north of Pulau Tulai.
Access: By boat (15–20min) northwest from Pulau Tioman's Air Batang Bay. Descend the shotline from the buoy through surface current.
Conditions: Generally calm, but can be choppy. There is usually a surface current, but this is less obvious on the bottom. Visibility is about 10m (33ft).
Average depth: 20m (65ft)
Maximum depth: 27m (90ft)
A jumble of huge volcanic boulders descends to a sandy bottom, producing clefts and tunnels that you can swim through. There are not too many fish, but this is partly compensated for by lots of large white gorgonian sea fans and smaller brown and blue gorgonian sea fans.

On the sand are patches of stony and soft corals. Shoals of fusiliers and snappers, lone triggerfish, turtles, Napoleon Wrasse, groupers and batfish can be found at

the site; most of the local species of angelfish and butterflyfish, wrasse, parrotfish, gobies and lizardfish are also around. The boulder coral has Christmas-tree Worms, and there are fan worms, stingrays and moray eels on the sand.

3 MAGICIENNE ROCK

★★★★

Location: North–northwest of the northern end of Pulau Tioman.
Access: By boat (20–25min) from Pulau Tioman's Air Batang Bay.
Conditions: Usually calm, but can be very choppy. There are strong currents at the surface, although these are less powerful on the bottom. It is best to dive here in calm weather. The visibility can be expected to be about 10m (33ft).
Average depth: 15m (50ft)
Maximum depth: 21m (70ft)
Magicienne Rock is a pinnacle that rises to 8m (26ft) below the surface. The strong currents and the fact that the site is open to the ocean mean that you can find many pelagic fish – including, on occasion, Manta Rays, Whale Sharks and Leopard (Variegated) Sharks – here among the reef fish, colourful corals and sponges.

All the local species of angelfish and butterflyfish are also present, together with shoals of jacks, Golden-striped Trevallies, fusiliers, snappers and groupers.

4 PULAU TULAI: NORTHERN END

★★★

Location: North–northwest of the northern end of Pulau Tioman.
Access: By boat (20min) from Pulau Tioman's Air Batang Bay. Pull down the shotline from the buoy.
Conditions: Mostly calm, but can be choppy. There is usually some surface current, but the current lessens as you get deeper.
Average depth: 17.5m (57ft)
Maximum depth: 17.5m (57ft)
The site offers a jumble of boulders that you can swim around and through. There are lots of soft corals, white, beige and blue gorgonian sea fans and black coral. You can find many species of sea cucumbers, sea stars and cushion stars on the sand.

All the local species of angelfish, butterflyfish and wrasse are present.

Also lurking among the rocks and corals are Blue-spotted Lagoon Rays, some Crown-of-Thorns Starfish, lots of feather stars, some soldierfish, gobies and lizardfish.

5 MALANG ROCKS

★★★★☆☆☆☆☆

Location: West of the northern end of Pulau Tioman.
Access: By boat (15min) from Pulau Tioman's Air Batang Bay.
Conditions: Usually calm, but can be choppy. Visibility is not great – about 8m (26ft) on average.
Average depth: 8m (26ft)
Maximum depth: 8m (26ft)

This very pretty shallow dive also offers good snorkelling; you can swim around and in and out among the big volcanic boulders. There are large patches of lettuce corals, sponges and some very big *Dendronephthya* soft corals (1m; 40in tall) in the caves. Also present are many stinging hydroids and some fire coral. Nudibranchs and large cuttlefish abound, and there are hundreds of anemones with attendant clownfish. There are shoals of barracuda and trevallies hanging in the open water and of Yellow-lined Snappers hiding in the caves. All the local species of angelfish and butterflyfish (including the larger Six-band and Blue-ring Angelfish) parrotfish, Blue-spotted Lagoon Rays, male and female Slingjaw Wrasse and Moon Wrasse can also be seen.

Down on the sand are many species of sea cucumbers, sea stars, cushion stars and congregations of black sea urchins, gobies, lizardfish and the occasional Leopard (Variegated) Shark.

6 GOLDEN REEF

★★★★

Location: Between Tiger Reef and Pulau Sepoi, west of the northern end of Pulau Tioman.
Access: By boat (20min) from Pulau Tioman's Air Batang Bay. Pull down the shotline from the buoy through the strong current and swell.
Conditions: Usually choppy; the strong current at the surface gets weaker as you get deeper. Average visibility is a pretty paltry 7m (23ft).
Average depth: 15m (50ft)
Maximum depth: 18m (60ft)

This underwater plateau, boasting lots of small shoaling fish and their predators, is very pretty on the bottom,

The shy Blue-ringed Angelfish (Pomacanthus annularis) hides at the approach of a diver.

with copious white, blue and beige gorgonian sea fans and a variety of colourful sponges and soft corals, littered with feather stars. Also in attendance are stingrays, scorpionfish, lionfish, stonefish, batfish, murex shells, sea cucumbers and sea stars, including the Crown-of-Thorns Starfish.

7 TIGER ROCKS

★★★★

Location: Midway between Pulau Labas and Pulau Sepoi, west of the northern end of Pulau Tioman.
Access: By boat (20min) from Pulau Tioman's Air Batang Bay. Pull down the shotline from the buoy.
Conditions: Can be very choppy on the surface. There is usually a strong current and swell, but the effects decrease the deeper you go. Visibility averages 10m (33ft).
Average depth: 25m (82ft)
Maximum depth: 30m (100ft)
This is considered the best dive off Pulau Tioman. A jumble of volcanic boulders, rising to within 10m (33ft) of the surface, teems with large shoals of fish. You can swim around these boulders and through the gaps between them, enjoying the good sponges, gorgonian sea fans, lots of nudibranchs and many species of pufferfish. Barracuda, Rainbow Runners, tuna, batfish, trevallies, snappers, Yellowtail Jacks, fusiliers and wrasse shoal in the open water, while on the sand there are sea cucumbers, sea urchins, sea stars, nudibranchs and fan worms. Among the corals are all the local species of angelfish, butterflyfish, Slingjaw Wrasse, parrotfish, damselfish, surgeonfish, triggerfish, lionfish, scorpionfish, stonefish, bream, cuttlefish, juvenile moray eels, groupers, Blue-spotted Lagoon Rays and occasionally turtles. A Whale Shark was seen near here during my visit in September 1993.

8 PULAU LABAS

★★★

Location: West of the northern end of Pulau Tioman.
Access: By boat (20min) from Pulau Tioman's Air Batang Bay.
Conditions: Usually calm but can be choppy; only a gentle current. There is no buoy here – the whole island can be circled in one dive. Visibility is poor, though – a mere 5m (16ft) on average.
Average depth: 15m (50ft)
Maximum depth: 17m (56ft)
Here you can swim in among, around and through a jumble of large volcanic rocks. The dive is much the same as Site 7 but lacks the same concentration of reef fish

and shoals. However, most of the local species of angelfish, butterflyfish and small wrasse are present, and there are good gorgonian sea fans and lots of cuttlefish, while on the sand you can find scorpionfish, stonefish, sea urchins, sea cucumbers and sea stars.

There is a small steel shipwreck on the northwest side, but only its skeleton still remains.

9 PULAU RENGGIS

★★★★

Location: A few hundred metres west of the Berjaya Imperial Beach Resort, southwest of the busy jetty.
Access: A few minutes by boat from Berjaya Imperial Beach Resort.
Conditions: There is usually calm sheltered water around this island, but the visibility is spoilt by boat movement to and from the main jetty – 5m (16ft) visibility is about what you can expect.
Average depth: 9m (30ft)
Maximum depth: 12m (40ft)
This site is good for training and night dives; the west (seaward) side is the best. Most of the local species of angelfish and butterflyfish, barracuda, batfish, triggerfish, Blue-spotted Lagoon Rays, moray eels and small Blacktip Sharks can be found here, and the west side has good gorgonian sea fans. On the sand are sea urchins, sea cucumbers, cushion stars and sea stars.

10 BAHARA ROCK (TOKONG BAHARA)

★★★

Location: Southwest of the southwest corner of Pulau Tioman.
Access: By boat (35–40min) from Berjaya Imperial Beach Resort.
Conditions: Tends to be choppy, with strong currents. Visibility is normally around 10m (33ft).
Average depth: 15m (50ft)
Maximum depth: 18m (60ft)
This is a mini drop-off with various pelagic species as well as most of the local reef fish. The area is not dived often, so on a calm day you can expect to find plenty of marine life among the corals, some of which is relatively unusual.

Opposite: *Large shoal of Caranx (Jacks) Caranx sexfasciatus. These carnivorous fish can move with impressive speed in pursuit of prey.*

HOW TO GET THERE

Pulau Tioman's short airstrip at Kampung Tekek accepts many STOL flights daily from Singapore (50min), Kuala Lumpur (1hr) and Kuantan.

What passes for an asphalt road runs from the airstrip south along the west coast to the telecommunications tower 1km (0.6 mile) south of Berjaya Imperial Beach Resort. There is also a walking path north from the airstrip to Kampung Salang, but in parts you have to climb over headlands. Transport of heavy diving luggage and underwater camera equipment along this path is not easy! I arrived from Singapore on the fast ferry and, by arrangement, was met by a small boat which ferried me to Air Batang Bay. On departure I had to enlist the help of new friends and a wheelbarrow to get my equipment to the nearest jetty!

There are daily fast ferries (air-conditioned catamarans) from the World Trade Centre in Singapore, 226km (122 nautical miles, 5hr) away, to the jetty at Berjaya Imperial Beach Resort. You can buy tickets on the ground floor of the World Trade Centre. There is a customs check and baggage search as you leave the ferry. If you are not staying at the resort, you can take a waterbus from this jetty to jetties at Kampung Air Batang, Kampung Salang, Kampung Tekek and Kampung Juara.

The ferry from Singapore is expensive and the luggage you check at the World Trade Centre will be surcharged. It is cheaper to go by bus from Singapore to Mersing and take a ferry the 56km (35 miles) from there. You can travel by road to Mersing from Kuala Lumpur, either via Kuantan (470km; 290 miles) or via Kluang (410km; 254 miles). From Singapore to Mersing via Johor Bahru is 160km (100 miles).

At Mersing you can choose between fast (2hr) air-conditioned ferries and slower ones; most stop at Berjaya Imperial Beach Resort, Kampung Air Batang, Kampung Tekek and Kampung Salang. However, due to silting of the river, ferries can arrive at and depart from Mersing only at high tide; there is also some bad feeling between local state governments over the fact that Tioman, which is in Pahang State, is serviced by ferries from Johor State. So it is possible that the ferry service may soon be altered to depart from Pahang State.

It is unwise to take any ferry that leaves Mersing after 1500 hours, because onward transport and accommodation on Pulau Tioman are difficult to find after dark. Mersing, on the mainland, is quite a small place and the accommodation situation is always in a state of flux (but see the directory covering Johor Marine Parks, page 87! If you have to stay overnight – perhaps

because you get stuck due to the tide – the local 'Mr Fixit' is Duncan Dominic (of Dive Asia – address below), who also organizes diving and snorkelling on the many other smaller islands off Mersing. In addition, he can sort out any transport you might require.

Bus and ferry tickets and other help are available from:

Golden Mal Tours Sdn Bhd, 9 Jalan Dato Mohammad Ali, 86800 Mersing Johor; tel 07–791643/fax 07–791613

'Express' buses stop at Mersing *en route* between Johor Bahru and Kuantan. During holiday periods it can be difficult to get a seat on one of these when leaving Mersing at the end of your stay, so try to book ahead.

Just across the road from Golden Mal Tours, in the goldsmith's shop on Jalan Abu Bakar, there is a licensed moneychanger where you can change cash and travellers' cheques quickly.

WHERE TO STAY

Accommodation on Pulau Tioman varies from the five-star Berjaya Imperial Beach Resort (address below) – which has all facilities from golf and horse-riding to watersports – through bungalows and chalets down to the cheapest 'A'-frame huts, some of which can only be described as grotty and come complete with bedbugs!

However, the situation is constantly changing. Medium-price resorts are being constructed and many of the cheaper lodgings are being bought out and replaced with higher-priced chalets.

The west coast of the island has a reliable 240-volt mains electricity supply and most of the accommodation has UK-type three-square-pin electrical sockets for charging. In some of the cheapest accommodation you will find electric lights but no electrical sockets.

Upper Price Range
Berjaya Imperial Beach Resort, PO Box 4, 86807 Mersing Johor; tel 09–445445/fax 09–445718
Head Office:
Level 14, Shahzan Prudential Tower, 30 Jalan Sultan Ismail, 50250 Kuala Lumpur; tel 03–2429611/fax 03–2488249
Singapore Office:
11–09/10 Orchard Towers, 400 Orchard Road, Singapore 0923; tel 02–7335488 (from within Malaysia), 65–7335488 (international)/fax 02–7335487 (from within Malaysia), 65–7335487 (international)
Worldwide:
Utell International (branches in every major city – check your telephone directory).

The resort is built on the site of the old Kampung Lalang (Elephant Village). The beach is not especially brilliant; the golf course and watersports are the main attraction.

Lower Price Range
Accommodation in this category varies from small wooden 'A'-frame chalets or longhouse blocks to what is no more than a wooden tent. Prices of these range from US$3 (with a bed and electric light but nothing else) to US$12 (includes a fan and electrical sockets, plus an *en suite* toilet and shower). Some chalets supply mosquito nets, but many do not. Mosquito nets and insect repellent are useful after rain.

Kampung Tekek, the island's administrative centre and largest village, has some well stocked 'supermarkets', many cheap chalets to the north of the boat jetty, and eating places nearby. Most of the dive operators here are to be found between Kampung Tekek and the hill north of the Berjaya Imperial Beach Resort.

Kampung Air Batang (usually referred to as ABC), north of Kampung Tekek, is the main travellers' centre. It has lots of cheap accommodation and restaurants. The beach is good but a bit rocky for swimming. The best and most popular beach here is at the southern end of the bay, where the long established and popular Nazri's Place (Sabri Bin Nazri – address below) has good accommodation and good snorkelling; its restaurant has music. There are several quieter restaurants within easy walking distance to the north.

A new medium-price resort is being constructed just south across the headland from Nazri's Place, which has its own jetty.

Sabri Bin Nazri, Kampung Air Batang, Pulau Tioman, 86800 Mersing Johor; tel 07–793244, 011–349534 (mobile)

Mokhtar's Place, Teluk Air Batang, 86800 Pulau Tioman; tel 07–376401

ABC Bungalow, Kampung Air Batang, 86800 Pulau Tioman

Kampung Salang is a small, pretty bay, at the far north of the west coast. Its limited accommodation fills up quickly. The diving here is run by Dive Asia and Ben's Diving Centre (addresses below), which have their own accommodation.

To the south, at Kampung Genting, the second largest village on the island, there is the Tropical Coral Inn, where Sharkeys run the diving:

Tropical Coral Inn, Kampung Genting, 6 Pulau Tioman

DIVE FACILITIES

Dive Operators and Training:
The two biggest diving operators, Berjaya Imperial Resort and Sharkeys Dive and Adventure, are highly organized and are costed for the international market. The many smaller dive operators on the island cost less; however, they are mainly oriented towards giving introductory courses to visiting tourists, and so serious divers may find them rather laid-back. The details of these smaller operators are always in flux as the cheaper resorts that they work from are bought out by developers for upgrading.

All the operators have dive-shops and offer dive equipment for rent.

Dive Asia Dive Shop, Tanjung Salang, Pulau Tioman, Pahang; tel 07–794098; 011–716783 (mobile)
Postal Address:
Duncan Dominic, 169 Jalan Bukit, 86800 Mersing, Johor; tel 07–794098 (office), 07–793014 (residence)/fax 07–794099
PADI and NAUI courses from Introduction up to Assistant Instructor.

Ben's Diving Centre (Zainal Ben Rahman), Kampung Salang, Pulau Tioman, 86800 Pahang; tel 011–730230 (mobile)/fax 07–791407
PADI courses.

Divers US (Jasper Bell), Kampung Tekek, Pulau Tioman, 86807 Pahang; tel 011–352776 (mobile)/fax 03–8375897
PADI courses.

Ianz Dive Shop (Azman S. Sulaiman, dive-master, and Chan Chee Sing, IDC staff instructor), c/o Mokhtar's Place, Teluk Air Batang, 86800 Pulau Tioman; tel 07–376401
or
2 Jalan Simbang 10, Taman Perling, 81200 Johor Bahru; tel 07–376401/fax 07–324210
or
Chan Chee Sing, 10 Lorong 1A/7k, 46000 Pulau Jaya Selangor; tel 07–920088
PADI courses.

Assuming you have your own equipment, the above-mentioned dive operators charge about US$45 for two dives on a one-day trip and US$30 for one dive; they will negotiate lower prices for multiple-day packages. All have equipment for hire.

Sharkeys Dive & Adventure Pte Ltd (Michael Lim/Peter Reiser), Tioman Branch, Tropical Coral Inn, Kampung Genting, 6 Pulau Tioman; tel 02–011–713465 (mobile, from within Malaysia), 65–011–713465 (mobile, international)

Head Office:
1 Park Road, #03–53/54 Peoples Park Complex, Singapore; tel 65–538733/fax 65–5386919
SSI courses at all levels
Tioman Reef Divers (Reeno C.L. Chew), c/o Babura Chalet, Kampung Tekek, Pulau Tioman, 86800 Pahang
NAUI courses.

Berjaya Imperial Beach Resort PO Box 4, 86807 Mersing Johor; tel 09–445445/fax 09–445718
Head Office:
Level 14, Shahzan Prudential Tower, 30 Jalan Sultan Ismail, 50250 Kuala Lumpur; tel 03–2429611/fax 03–2488249
Singapore Office:
11–09/10 Orchard Towers, 400 Orchard Road, Singapore 0923; tel 02–7335488 (from within Malaysia), 65–7335488 (international)/fax 02–7335487 (from within Malaysia), 65–7335487 (international)
PADI courses from Novice to Assistant Instructor.

These operators charge (assuming you have your own equipment) US$70 for two dives on a one-day trip, US$40 for one dive. They have equipment to rent, and will negotiate lower prices for multiple-day packages.

I met divers who preferred the Berjaya Imperial Beach Resort because of its superior accommodation and the fact that it has its own jetty for ferries and offers transport by road to the airport, but who booked their actual diving with the cheaper operators.

FILM PROCESSING

None is available on the island or in Mersing; the nearest is in Johor Bahru or Kuala Lumpur.

HOSPITALS

There is a very small one on the island (tel 09–445347) and a similar one in Mersing (tel 07–793333). In addition there is the main hospital in Johor Bahru:

Hospital Sultanah Aminah
tel 07–231666

However, with the STOL-aircraft service, it is just as easy to fly to Kuala Lumpur or Singapore.

LOCAL HIGHLIGHTS

Pulau Tioman is an island to relax on; most visitors go there only for the beaches and coral reefs. There are small secluded beaches all round the island. **Berjaya Imperial Beach Resort** has a first-class golf course, and offers also horse-riding and all watersports. You can walk along most of the west coast, although the path gets faint in places.

The forest is full of interesting wildlife, and the trees keep the path pleasantly shady. One popular walk traverses the island from **Kampung Tekek** (Lizard Village) to **Kampung Juara** (Catfish Village), starting beside the mosque in Kampung Tekek. The path climbs steeply through the forest, following the River Besar to its highest point; about halfway, there is a small waterfall off to the right. The slopes are more gradual on the Juara side. The whole walk takes about 3hr, and if you're tired at the end of it you can take the waterbus back.

Apart from the short climb over the headland just south of Nazri's Place, there is also a good walking path from Air Batang Bay to Kampung Tekek; this takes 30min, and you can then carry on for a further 30min along the road to reach the Berjaya Imperial Beach Resort. A poor path, faint in places, leads from here to Kampung Genting. A similar path runs from Air Batang Bay to Kampung Salang – about a 2hr walk.

The waterbus is worth at least a ride or two. As well as travelling between Kampung Salang, Kampung Air Batang, Kampung Tekek and the Berjaya Imperial Beach Resort, it runs two trips daily round the island, including stops at **Kampung Juara** and **Kampung Asah**, from where it is a 10min walk to the waterfall.

Over on the mainland is the little town of Kota Tinggi, 42km (26 miles) from Johor Bahru on the road between Mersing and Johor Bahru. Some 15km (9 miles) north-west of Kota Tinggi, on Gunung Muntahak, the Lumbong waterfalls are recommended, although they tend to be crowded at weekends. The **Endau Rompin National Park** has undisturbed rainforest and Orang Asli villages. Quite a lot further afield are the **Cameron Highlands** and **Taman Negara National Park**.

Encounters with turtles are a highlight of diving and snorkelling. There are some areas off Malaysia and Singapore where such encounters can be virtually guaranteed. Green and Hawksbill Turtles are found in large numbers off the northeastern coast of Sabah and across to the reefs of Tubbataha, in the Sulu Sea. Divers will find that Pulau Sipadan is the 'Turtle Capital of the World'.

ENDANGERED SPECIES

Of the seven oceanic turtle species – all of which are on the endangered-species list – six can be found in Malaysian waters: the Green Turtle (*Chelonia mydas*), the Hawksbill Turtle (*Eretmochelys imbricata*), the Loggerhead Turtle (*Caretta caretta*), the Leatherback Turtle (*Dermochelys coriacea*), the Pacific Olive Ridley Turtle (*Lepidochelys olivacea*) and the Flatback Turtle (*Natator depressus*). Four of these – the Green, Hawksbill, Leatherback and Pacific Olive Ridley – regularly nest on Malaysian beaches.

The two most commonly encountered are the Green and the Hawksbill. They may be difficult to distinguish underwater, where both appear a mottled dull green. However, the Green Turtle is usually larger, and has only one pair of prefrontal scales. The Hawksbill has a distinct beak; the outer edge of the latter's shell is usually jagged.

TURTLE FACTS

- Both on land and at sea, turtles often appear to be shedding tears. On land, the 'tears' are believed to prevent the eyes from becoming dehydrated and to cleanse them of sand. They possibly also help get rid of salt.

- As turtles are often observed copulating for as long as two hours, local people believe their meat and eggs have aphrodisiac properties. This hypothesis is unsupported by science.

- The bodies of marine turtles are entirely covered by a firm shell, only the head, limbs and tail protruding. Unlike their land counterparts, marine turtles cannot retract their head and limbs, so these are vulnerable to sharks and other predators. However, turtles can survive with missing limbs, and often do.

- The way that turtles swim is analogous to the flight of birds, the flippers moving up and down rather than to and fro.

THE GREEN TURTLE

The Green Turtle can reach a length of 1.2m (4ft) and weigh 135–180kg (3–400 pounds). The male is usually smaller than the female, but has a longer tail. The Green Turtle is mainly nocturnal and herbivorous, feeding on sea grasses, in daytime sleeping on the bottom, under coral heads or in caves. It nests on remote islands and lays eggs in the sand at the top of the beach, where they will be shaded by overhanging vegetation. The Loggerhead Turtle is similar to the Green but has a larger head. It feeds on fish, molluscs and crustacea.

THE HAWKSBILL TURTLE

The Hawksbill Turtle is the smallest turtle species, reaching a maximum length of 85cm (33in). In young individuals the plates of the carapace overlap; in adults they merely adjoin, and have characteristic brown and yellow markings of tortoiseshell. Hawksbills are usually carnivores, feeding on fish, molluscs, sponges and crustacea, although I have seen them eating algae. They nest by day or by night, preferring beaches along sheltered bays.

THE LEATHER BACK TURTLE

The relatively thin, heart-shaped carapace of the Leatherback Turtle has the appearance of brown leather and bears seven longitudinal ridges. It is the largest marine turtle, reaching nearly 2m (6^{1}/2ft) in length and weighing up to about 450kg (1000 pounds). The greatly reduced weight of the carapace, the more streamlined shape and the long flippers enable the Leatherback to swim at up to 10kph (6mph) and to cover huge distances – up to 5900km (3650 miles), according to the records – as it migrates after its prey, jellyfish, which are at the mercy of ocean currents.

Opposite top: *Female Green Turtle, Chelonia mydas.*
Opposite centre: *Young Hawksbill Turtle, Eretmochelys imbricata, showing the overlapping plates of the carapace.*
Opposite bottom: *The extremely rare Pacific Olive Ridley Turtle (Lepidochelys olivacea).*

Johor Marine Parks

The Marine Parks of Johor centre on the islands of Pulau Rawa, Pulau Babi Besar, Pulau Babi Hujung, Pulau Babi Tengah, Pulau Tinggi, Pulau Mentinggi and Pulau Sibu. Further out to sea, Pulau Aur and Pulau Dayang have excellent diving where you can expect regular encounters with pelagic species.

The north and east sides of many of the inner islands have rocky cliffs descending into deep water where, apart from in sheltered bays, they are too exposed to the northeast monsoon for coral growth other than a few encrusting species and some soft corals. The west and south sides have sandy beaches and fringing reefs.

VISIBILITY

Water visibility around these islands varies within the approximate range 7–15m (23–50ft), so is hardly exceptional, but off the outer islands it can reach 30m (100ft). April to June are the best months for clear, calm waters, but the season extends to September off the outer islands and October off the inner islands. The inner islands are popular with non-divers and snorkellers, so are very busy at weekends and holiday times.

DIVING OPPORTUNITIES

Dive operators can be found on Pulau Rawa, Pulau Babi Besar and Pulau Sibu. None of these islands has a regular ferry service, so you have to negotiate with agents in Mersing. These inner islands are not worth going to specifically for diving or snorkelling, rather places to go to relax and possibly dive while you are there. The outer islands are in deeper water and look set to become international diving destinations. So far, because of the cost of boat-hire, diving has been possible only in organized groups, and most of the exploratory diving has been done by clubs or dive-shop/training agencies based in Singapore and Kuala Lumpur. However, there is now one operator on Pulau Dayang.

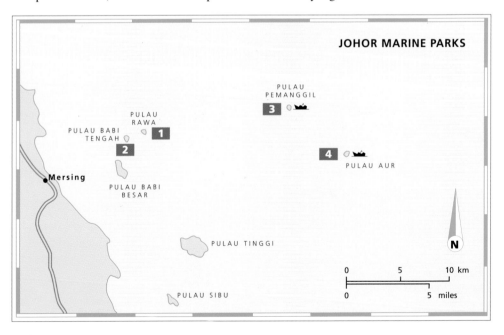

1 PULAU RAWA

★★★★★

Location: 16km (10 miles) north-northeast of Mersing.
Access: By boat from Mersing.
Conditions: You would only make this journey in calm weather. Visibility can reach 20m (65ft).
Average depth: 10m (33ft)
Maximum depth: 25m (80ft)
This is a popular island with fine beaches. Most of the coral is dead, but there is good marine life in the holes and crevices on the east side of Pulau Harimau, 30min by boat to the northwest. The diving around the two islands consists of rocks and boulders down to sand, producing crevices and swim-throughs. The coral life is poor but there are sponges, jacks, grouper, fusiliers, scorpionfish, lionfish, stonefish, moray eels, cuttlefish, stingrays, nudibranchs, sea stars and sea cucumbers, plus lots of sea urchins. Crinoids open out when the current picks up.

Pulau Babi Besar, though larger and closer to the mainland than Pulau Rawa – it is 13km (8 miles) east of Mersing – is not as developed.

2 PULAU BABI TENGAH

★★★★

Location: 14km (9 miles) northeast of Mersing.
Access: By boat from Mersing.
Conditions: You would make only this journey in calm conditions. Visibility can reach 20m (65ft).
Average depth: 15m (50ft)
Maximum depth: 25m (80ft)
Pulau Babi Tengah was once a refugee camp for Vietnamese boat people. Now it is a Marine Park protecting the Leatherback Turtles which – in dwindling numbers, alas – nest here, especially during July. Rocks and boulders on sand give caves and crevices to swim through. There are some soft corals and encrusting corals, small sponges, sea squirts, nudibranchs and flat worms on the rocks. Scorpionfish, lionfish, stonefish, cuttlefish, damselfish, Sergeant Major Fish, wrasse, soldierfish and moray eels are found in the crevices. Sea cucumbers, sea stars, sea urchins and stingrays are found on the sand.

3 PULAU PEMANGGIL

★★★★★★

Location: Some 15km (9 miles) northwest of Pulau Aur (Site 4).
Access: Usually by boat from Pulau Aur.

Conditions: Normally choppy with strong currents, but can get very rough with fierce currents. Visibility can reach 30m (100ft).
Average depth: 25m (80ft)
Maximum depth: 40m (130ft)
On the eastern side of Pulau Pemanggil are the last remains of an unknown shipwreck. The wreck attracts shoals of snappers, fusiliers and batfish and lone parrotfish, rabbitfish, sugeonfish, scorpionfish, lionfish and groupers.

4 PULAU AUR

★★★★★★★★

Location: 65km (40 miles) east of Mersing.
Access: By boat from Mersing.
Conditions: Normally choppy wth strong currents, but can be very rough with fierce currents. Novices should have an experienced divemaster with them in these conditions. Visibility can reach 30m (100ft).
Average depth: 25m (80ft)
Maximum depth: 70m (230ft)
The waters here are deeper and clearer than around the inner islands, and, because of the greater distance from the mainland, sightings of pelagic species are common. Schools of Hammerhead Sharks, lone Whale Sharks and Manta Rays can be seen, and lobsters and octopuses are still found. Pinnacles on the east side of Pulau Aur rise 30m (100ft) from the seabed to within 10m (33ft) of the surface. Teluk Meriam (Cannon Bay), on the island's southwest coast, gained its name when a cannon from the wreck of a 17th-century Chinese Junk was found here, although the wreck itself is no longer recognizable.

Nearby are the three smaller islands of Pulau Dayang, Pulau Lang and Pulau Pinang. The latter, 1km (2/3 mile) southeast of Pulau Aur, has good wall-diving down to 60m (200ft); groupers and snappers congregate in the caves and overhangs.

The beach opposite Pulau Pinang on Pulau Aur and the beaches on the north side of Pulau Dayang slope gently and have large staghorn and table corals. In the channel between Pulau Aur and Pulau Dayang lies the wreck of an aircraft thought to have come from the Australian ship HMS Melbourne.

Rayner's Rock, 200m (220 yd) northeast of Pulau Dayang, is a submerged rock 33m (108ft) high.

For very experienced divers only, there is a World War II Japanese wreck 90min by boat east of Pulau Aur. The bottom here is at 70m (230ft) and the shallowest part of the wreck at 50m (165ft).

Next page: *Christmas Tree Worms Spirobranchus giganteus and sea squirts. The colourful tentacles of the Tube-Worms retract completely into the tube when touched.*

HOW TO GET THERE

There are 'express' buses to Mersing from Johor Bahru, 135km (85 miles) to the south, and from Kuantan, 190km (120 miles) to the north. Long-distance buses from Singapore also stop here (see the directory covering Pahang Marine Parks, page 80). From where the bus drops you off it is an easy walk (10–15min) to the jetty. If you've come by car, you can leave the vehicle in the jetty's car park. Around the jetty you'll find offices representing each of the islands. It's a good idea to buy not only your boat ticket but also your accommodation here – or at one of the travel agencies in Mersing – rather than wait until you get to your destination island, since otherwise you are quite likely to find yourself with nowhere to stay. Travel times to the islands vary from about 1½hr to 4hr. If you need to change money, do so in Mersing – there is a licensed money changer in Jalan Abu Bakar, just opposite Golden Mal Tours – because the exchange rates you will be offered on the islands are exorbitant.

Since the 'express' buses stop at Mersing only en route to Johor Bahru, Kuantan or Singapore, it can be difficult during holiday periods to get a seat on one when you want to leave Mersing at the end of your stay, so it is a good idea to try to book in advance. Failing that, taxis to Johor Bahru or Kuantan are not prohibitively expensive – about 50% more than the bus fare.

Pulau Sibu is one of the larger and more popular islands. Boats go to it from Mersing but, since it is further south, it can easily be reached by visitors from Singapore using ferries from Tanjong Sedili Besar at Teluk Mahkota (Jason's Bay).

WHERE TO STAY

Pulau Babi Besar
Radin Island Resort c/o 5 Gerai Majlis Daerah, Jalan Abu Bakar, 86800 Mersing; tel 07–794152/fax 07–791413

Besar Marina Resort c/o #10 Tourist Information Centre, Jalan Abu Bakar, 86800 Mersing; tel 07–793606

White Sand Beach Resort c/o 98 Jalan Harimau Tarum, Century Garden, 80250 Johor Bahru; tel 07–334669

Pulau Sibu
Sibu Island Cabanas Bsm Sdn Bhd c/o Suite 2–10, Pkeinj Building, Jalan Rebana, 80250 Johor Bahru; tel 07–317216
Sibu Island Resort Pulau Sibu; tel 07–818348

DO&H Kampung Huts c/o #9 Tourist Information Centre, Jalan Abu Bakar, Mersing; tel 07–793124

Sea Gypsy Village Resort c/o #9 Tourist Information Centre, Jalan Abu Bakar, Mersing; tel 07–793124

Pulau Rawa
The popular Rawa Safaris Island Resort can be booked through

Rawa Safaris Sdn Bhd Tourist Centre, 86800 Mersing Johor; tel 07–791204/5, fax 07–793848.

Pulau Babi Tengah
More accommodation is planned, but to date the main resort is

Pirate Bay Island Resort tel 07–241911 and 01–762042 (mobile)
Johor Bahru Office:
Suite 243, Johor Tower, 15 Jalan Gereja, 80100 Johor Bahru; tel 07–241911

Pulau Dayang
Dive Asia (see address below) has a resort on Pulau Dayang, on the beach opposite Pulau Aur and its main fishing village. They run weekly departures from both Mersing (4hr) and from their diving operation on Pulau Tioman (3hr). This is dormitory-style accommodation with three air-conditioned units, each for 12 people.

Pulau Pemanggil
Wira Chalets & Longhouse c/o Tioman Accommodation & Boat Services, 3 Jalan Abu Bakar, Mersing; tel 07–793048

WHERE TO EAT

Most of the places to eat on the islands are the restaurants attached to the accommodation – but this is not to say that you should feel yourself confined to eating where you happen to be staying. On Pulau Babi Besar try the open-air restaurant at the Radin Island Resort or the cheap-but-good Sundancer II restaurant. Pulau Sibu's DO&H Kampung Huts offers great curries alongside Western fare, while the Twin Beach Resort offers Chinese food. On the larger islands there can be excellent outdoor food stalls.

DIVE FACILITIES

White Sand Beach Resort c/o 98 Jalan Harimau Tarum, Century Garden, 80250 Johor Bahru; tel 07–334669

Sibu Island Cabanas Bsm Sdn Bhd c/o Suite 2–10, Pkeinj Building, Jalan Rebana, 80250 Johor Bahru; tel 07–317216

Dive Asia c/o Duncan Dominic, 169 Jalan Bukit, 86800 Mersing Johor; tel 07–794098 (office), 07–793014 (residence) fax 07–794099

FILM PROCESSING

Johor Bahru has several mini-labs for processing print film, E6 processing can be organized by:

Chau Wah Fotografi Sdn Bhd L–4, 72 & 73 Plaza Kotaraya, 80000 Johor Bahru; tel 07–246839

Johor Foto Enterprise G–24 Holiday Plaza, Jalan Dato Sulaiman, 80250 Johor Bahru; tel 07–310463

HOSPITALS

There is a small hospital in Mersing (tel 07–793333). The main hospital in Johor Bahru is:

Hospital Sultanah Aminah tel 07–231666

LOCAL HIGHLIGHTS

For local highlights on the mainland, refer to the directory covering Pahang Marine Parks which lists the main places of interest (page 80). Pulau Sibu offers canoeing and windsurfing (you can hire the relevant craft), and jungle treks are organized across the island; there is also some good walking along the beautiful beaches, although swimmers should beware of the currents. You can take a boat-trip (1hr) to Tanjung Leman, on the mainland about 30km (20 miles) south of Mersing; this tiny village is picturesque, but won't detain you long. Pulau Rawa's **Rawa Safaris Island Resort** offers canoeing, windsurfing and all sorts of other watersports. Again, the beaches are beautiful. Leatherback Turtles lay their eggs in July on Pulau Babi Tengah. If you get the opportunity, take a boat to Pulau Tinggi, which has a truly splendid beach. More to the point, however, the island is an extinct volcano; climbs up the mountain are pretty strenuous and take 4–5hr (round trip), but are worth it. Don't attempt the climb on your own, because it can be dangerous. A much safer option is to hire a local guide on the island. Other activities offered by Pulau Tinggi include **fishing**, **windsurfing** and **boating**. Pulau Babi Besar is geared to the conventional holidaymaker.

JOHOR BAHRU

Johor Bahru is a modern city and the gateway to Malaysia from the south. Accessed by the 1km (½ mile) causeway over the Johor Straits, the people of Singapore virtually use Johor Bahru as an extension of the island for shopping and eating out. Because of this, the causeway is extremely congested with traffic at weekends.

Desaru

The modern beach resort near Peninsular Malaysia's southeastern tip at Tanjung Penawar, now better known as Desaru, is a stretch of beach 20km (12 miles) long. Desaru is 90km (54 miles) east of Johor Bahru, but is in fact more easily reached from Singapore, where it has been heavily marketed: at weekends, particularly on Friday evenings and public holidays, Desaru is invaded by Singaporeans escaping city life. The beach is quite pretty in itself but offers nothing special to the international visitor.

However, when William Ong was running Pro Diving Services at the Desaru Golf Hotel he looked around for an interesting local sea-diving site to use as part of his Introductory Dive Courses. What he found was Feather Rock.

1 FEATHER ROCK

★★★★

Location: Just off the beach, 10min southeast by boat from the Desaru Golf Hotel.
Access: By boat.
Conditions: Generally calm; there can be some swell and undertow. Visibility is not great – about 5m (16ft).
Average depth: 5m (16ft)

Maximum depth: 9m (30ft)
The site covers 0.5ha (1 acre) and gets its name from the abundance of crinoids (feather stars) in evidence here. It offers an easy, shallow dive around rocks, with guided trails laid out underwater for novices.

There are many species of feather stars, soft corals, small gorgonian sea fans, sea squirts, fan worms and nudibranchs together with some sea grasses, and Christmas-tree Worms litter the boulder corals. The fish life is typical of rocks by a beach, with bottom-dwelling fish.

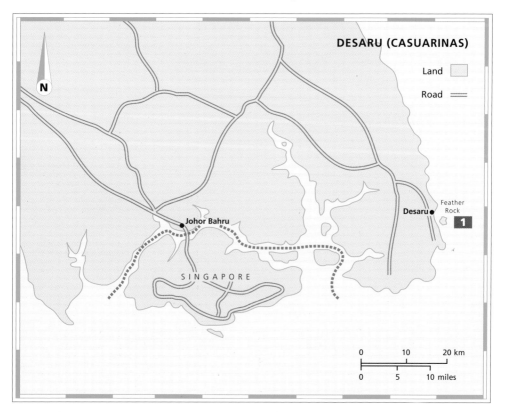

HOW TO GET THERE

From Johor Bahru, 90km (55 miles) to the west, the road connects to Desaru via Kota Tinggi; you can take a bus or a taxi from either.

Most people, however, come to Desaru from Singapore. There are regular ferries from Changi Point in Singapore; ask for Tanjung Pengileh, Kampung Pengerang or Belungkur, from any of which you can get a taxi to Desaru, while buses run frequently from Kampung Pengerang.

WHERE TO STAY

Desaru is a purpose-built up-market resort – the Desaru Garden Beach Resort (tel 07–821101) although cheaper accommodation is available.

Upper Price Range
Desaru Golf Hotel Tanjung Penawar, c/o PO Box 50, 81900 Kota Tinggi; tel 07–821101/fax 07–821480

Desaru View Hotel c/o PO Box 31, Bandar Penawar, 81900 Kota Tinggi; tel 07–821221/fax 07–821237
Sales Office:
#02–07/07A IBM Towers, 80 Anson Road, Singapore; tel 02–2232157 (from within Malaysia); 65–2232157 (international)/fax 02–2231673 (from within Malaysia); 65–2231673 (international)

Desaru Merlin Inn c/o PO Box 50, Tanjung Penawar, Kota Tinggi; tel 07–838101

Lower Price Range
Desaru Holiday Chalet c/o PO Box 20, Kota Tinggi; tel 07–821211/fax 07–821240

There is a campsite but it is poorly kept.

WHERE TO EAT

The hotels have their own, fairly expensive restaurants serving local, Japanese and Chinese food.

DIVE FACILITIES

Pro Dive Services SG–30 Wisma Abad Jalan Harimau Taman Century, 50250 Johor; tel 07–315026
Singapore Head Office:

Pro Diving Services 22 Bali Lane (entrance via North Bridge Road, opposite the Golden Landmark Hotel), Singapore 0718; tel 02–2912261 (from within Malaysia 65–2912261)/fax 02–2914136 (international), 65–29141369 (from within Malaysia) Full PADI courses.

FILM PROCESSING

The nearest film processing is in Singapore; for information refer to the directory covering Singapore (page 154) which lists addresses to mini-labs which handle E6 transparency processing.

HOSPITALS

The nearest hospitals are in Singapore:

Singapore General Hospital Outram Road; tel 65–2223322

Glen Eagles Hospital tel 65–4737222

Mount Elizabeth Hospital tel 65–7372666

In Johor Bahru the main hospital is:

Hospital Sultanah Aminah tel 07–231666

LOCAL HIGHLIGHTS

There's 20km (12 miles) of beach to walk along or just lie on, which is enough by way of leisure activity for many people. However, if the joys of sunbathing and the commercial activities offered by the **Desaru Garden Beach Resort** soon pall, your best idea is to take day trips to somewhere else.

Desaru's geographical location makes it easier to visit **Singapore** than the rest of Malaysia. However, you can take in **Johor Bahru** ('New Johor'); there is very little left of Johor Lama ('Old Johor'). Other interesting places in this area and, further north, in Pahang State are mentioned in the directory covering Pahang Marine Parks (see page 80).

Red Feather star (Himerometra robustipinna). The lower appendages, or cirri, on which the animal moves about can be seen clearly.

SARAWAK

L ying generally south of Labuan and Brunei, Sarawak has several large rivers depositing their sediment into the sea, so the coastline is mostly swamp. Moreover, the waters are very shallow: even 50km (30 miles) offshore depths reach no more than 15m (50ft). Visibility is, naturally, poor and most corals find it hard to survive. Although there are reports of developments in the pipeline, at the moment no one would think of going to Sarawak for the diving alone.

Captain Sim Yong Wah, a noted underwater writer and photographer, recommends the area around Pulau Talang–Talang Besar, Pulau Talang–Talang Kecil and Turtle Rock, 9km (5 miles) north–northwest of Sematan in the far northwest of Sarawak as having more coral and fish life than elsewhere in Sarawak, with some good small gorgonian sea fans, boulder corals and table corals.

KATORI MARU

Further out to sea, in 25m (80ft) of water, the wreck of the *Katori Maru* is probably the primary attraction for divers in these waters. A 10,000-ton Japanese troop-carrier, the *Katori Maru* was crippled by a Dutch submarine before finally being sunk by British aircraft bombing on 23 December 1941. The wreck lies 19km (10 nautical miles) north–northwest of Tanjung Sipang and is marked by a small buoy; the top of the vessel's bridge structure is at 12m (40ft). The ship is broken up and has little coral growth, but the fish life in and around the wreck is good.

PULAU SATANG BESAR

Several islands are turtle sanctuaries administered by the Turtles Management Board. Most of them are closed to visitors, but Pulau Satang Besar, 7km (4 miles) offshore and 18km (11 miles) from Damai Beach, not far from Kuching can be visited by day with permission from the Office of the Director of Kuching's Sarawak Museum.

Opposite: *View from a beach in the Santubong region, Sarawak, Malaysia.*
Above: *Gorgonian sea fans Subergorgia hicksoni are prolific in tropical waters.*

THE SPRATLYS
(Layang-Layang)

The Spratlys are some 600 islands, reefs and shoals stretching across the South China Sea from Borneo to Vietnam. Only about 30 are physically significant; the others are below sea-level for most of the time and are therefore marked on charts as 'awash' or 'existence doubtful'. The waterway is used by international shipping as a short-cut between the Pacific Ocean and the Indian Ocean via the Malacca Strait. With the lure of rich fishing grounds and the high probability of oil and gas reserves under the Spratlys, Malaysia, China, Vietnam, Taiwan, the Philippines and Brunei have all staked out claims. In 1988 the Chinese and Vietnamese navies clashed when Chinese troops occupied several reefs in the Spratlys, and since then Malaysia and the Philippines – as well as China and Vietnam – have reinforced those areas they regard as theirs.

THE SOUTH CHINA SEA
The Philippines regard the South China Sea as a buffer against possible attack, remembering that the Japanese launched their invasion of Southeast Asia by landing on Itu Aba, the largest island in the group. China considers the South China Sea strategically important; she used also to be particularly worried that the Soviet Union hoped to dominate the area through its proxy, Vietnam. In 1992 Beijing passed a law defining China's territorial waters as almost all of the South China Sea and part of the East Asia Sea, adjacent to Japan; the Chinese generated even more tension when they granted a US company a licence to explore for oil between the Spratlys and Vietnam. Meanwhile Taiwan claims territorial rights on the basis that she, and not the mainland Communist government, represents the rightful China; Vietnam is uneasy at the prospect of the Spratlys being under Chinese custody, as her own access to these seas could be threatened; and Brunei and Malaysia wish to protect their existing oilfields.

LAYANG-LAYANG
Quite naturally Malaysia claims the strip of the Spratlys nearest to her own landmass – i.e.,

Opposite: *A solitary sail-boat in the sunset on the South China Sea.*
Above: *A Green Turtle Chelonia mydas, rests on the sand.*

the area 306km (165 nautical miles) northwest of Kota Kinabalu in Borneo. Most of this region comprises reefs below sea-level, but there is a small – 6ha (15 acres) – barren low-lying island, Layang-Layang, or (in Bahasa Malaysian) Terumbu Layang-Layang; the full name translates as 'Swallows' Reef'. There are, oddly, no swallows on the reef! Instead, at the western tip of the island, there are nesting colonies of thousands of Brown Boobies (sometimes known as Asian Albatross), Noddy Terns, Sooty Terns and Great Crested Terns.

Pulau Layang-Layang lies on an atoll-like ring of 13 linked coral reefs in 1850m (6000ft) of water. Scientists are not sure whether the island is an extinct volcano, an uplifting like Pulau Sipadan (see page 130) or a sunken mountain. The atoll is 7.3km (4.5 miles) long and 2.2km (1.36 miles) wide, with a lagoon 60m (200ft) deep. There has been a Royal Malaysian Navy base at the eastern end of the island since 1982; more recently, M-Ocean has constructed a tourist resort. The lagoon's old entrance channel has been replaced through the blasting of a new one close to the resort and the naval base. The jetty is within the shelter of the lagoon. The weather is best from April to September.

The live-aboard boat MV *Coral Topaz* started diving and fishing cruises to Layang-Layang at the end of April 1991, and the area soon built up a reputation for wall-diving with lots of large pelagic species, good snorkelling and windsurfing in the lagoon and excellent bird-watching.

NEW ATOLL AIRSTRIP

The rudimentary airstrip originally built on Layang-Layang has recently been extended and upgraded to cater for Twin Otter flights. The construction work has temporarily spoilt some of the diving and legendary visibility close to the island and in the lagoon, but this situation should soon improve.

Opposite: *Barrel Sponge (Petrosia sp.) with Alabaster Sea Cucumbers (Opheodesoma sp.) and feather stars. These sea cucumbers are often found on sponges from which they may obtain certain nutrients.*

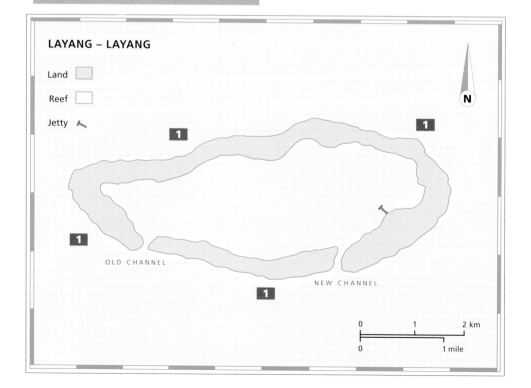

LAYANG – LAYANG

Land

Reef

Jetty

N

OLD CHANNEL

NEW CHANNEL

0   1   2 km

0   1 mile

1 TERUMBU LAYANG-LAYANG

★★★★★☆☆☆☆☆

Access and Conditions: The dives and their access depend very much on the weather and currents at the time. The weather can be very rough, and can turn bad very quickly. Divemasters and live-aboard cruise directors are still working out what is possible here and under what conditions safe diving can best be organized. One possibility is for divers to enter the water where two currents split and then drift one way or the other, according to conditions. Snorkelling in the lagoon is safe only away from the entrance channels, which can have rip currents as the lagoon fills and empties. There are some very strong currents and many deep dives: this area is for advanced divers only.

Average depth: 24m (80ft), but much of interest is below 40m (130ft)

Maximum depth: 900m–1850m (3000ft–6000ft)

This and the other reefs in the area are renowned for their wall-diving, with walls dropping to between 900m and 1850m (3000ft–6000ft). On the island itself, the northeast corner is renowned for its huge forest of large gorgonian sea fans. Before construction work started the entrance to the lagoon had prolific fish life. Unfortunately, these reefs have some very strong currents, and a lot of the interest lies deeper than most divers would wish to go. In general, the shallow areas here are not as interesting or as photogenic as at other Malaysian diving areas, such as those of Pulau Sipadan (see page 130).

As with any area where there are lots of pelagic species, much depends on luck: one day you might see everything possible and the next, on the same dive, you might see no pelagic species at all! However, dolphins frequently enter the lagoon, especially during rough weather, and turtles are seen on almost every dive.

In the upper 18m (60ft) are all the fish that frequent walls in fast currents, including jacks, barracuda, tuna and Rainbow Runners. In more sheltered areas angelfish, butterflyfish, clownfish, lionfish, scorpionfish, surgeonfish, stonefish, groupers and pufferfish are found. In shallow parts there are large table corals, and there is no shortage of soft corals and sponges under overhangs. On a dive, you may encounter Manta Rays, Whitetip Reef, Grey Reef and solitary Hammerhead Sharks.

On many wall dives there are two thermoclines. Usually the temperature is about 28°C (83°F) at the surface; then there is a thermocline from 18m to 24m (60–80ft), with a temperature of about 27°C (80°F); and finally, from 27m (90ft) down, the temperature is 24°C (75°F). It is in this deeper water that you find black corals, sponges and large barrel sponges. Below 40m (130ft) you may come across Silvertip Sharks, Eagle Rays and shoals of Hammerhead Sharks. There are many shoals and submerged reefs in the area that live-aboard dive boats are checking out.

Juvenile Whitetip Reef Shark (Triaenodon obesus) hiding in a cave for safety. Such juveniles are prey to larger sharks.

How to Get There

Kota Kinabalu is easily accessible by international flights from Kuala Lumpur, Hong Kong, Manila, Singapore, Bangkok, Brunei, Taipei and Seoul. It is also the take-off hub for flights to Tawau, Sandakan, Labuan and Kuching (Sarawak). The airport is 7km (4 miles) from the city centre.

There is an airport tax of five ringgits on local flights and 20 ringgits on international flights.

From Kota Kinabalu on either of two live-aboard boats, the MV *Coral Topaz* and the MV *Spirit of Borneo* (see below for details of both), the sea crossing to Layang-Layang takes about 17^1/$_2$hr. One problem for the resort is that the cruise out from Kota Kinabalu can be rough, and once you've arrived the weather can turn bad very quickly. However, the airstrip has recently been extended, and since May 1993 Malaysia Airlines have had scheduled flights using Twin Otter aircraft carrying 19 passengers to the island with a flight-time of 75min. Flight bookings are usually made in conjunction with the M-Ocean resort (address below) or the live-aboard you are joining.

It is no longer necessary to get special permission to go to Layang-Laying, but the Royal Malaysian Navy prefers, for safety reasons, to be informed. With so little accommodation available, it would be sensible to organize this in advance.

Where to Stay

The only accommodation on the island is the resort run by M-Ocean Diving. This resort has 15 deluxe rooms and two suites, all fully air-conditioned and with *en suite* facilities. It is situated on a 1.2km (^{3}/$_4$ mile) beach alongside the lagoon.

M-Ocean Diving 28–1 Jalan 8/70A Sri Hartamas, Jalan Duta, Kuala Lumpur, Malaysia; tel 03–2530048/fax 03–2530049

Dive Facilities

The M-Ocean resort offers the only facilities on Layang-Layang.

Live-aboard Boats

The MV *Coral Topaz* was the first live-aboard to run cruises out to Layang-Layang. It has recently been joined by the MV *Spirit of Borneo* (a subsidiary of M-Ocean Diving). Both live-aboards have scheduled trips to Layang-Layang from April to September, and the MV *Spirit of Borneo* also cruises to other nearby Malaysian reefs, including Dallas Reef, Investigator Shoal, Royal Charlotte Reef, Erica Reef, Louisa Reef, Mariveles Reef and the Ardasier Bank.

For full information concerning these boats, refer to the directory section covering Tunku Abdul Rahman Marine Park (page 106). The relevant addresses are:

MV Coral Topaz Coral Island Cruises Tours & Travel Sdn Bhd, G19, Ground Floor, Wisma Sabah, PO Box 14527, 88851 Kota Kinabalu, Sabah; tel 088–223490/fax 088–223404

MV Spirit of Borneo Tropical Dive Adventures Sdn Bhd, 28–1, Jalan 8/70A Sri Hartamas, Jalan Duta, 50480 Kuala Lumpur; tel 03–2530048/fax 03–2530049

Film Processing

There is no film processing at the resort. However, almost every street in the centre of Kota Kinabalu seems to have a selection of mini-labs who will process your print film. You can also find processing in Wisma Merdeka.

For reliable E6 transparency processing use the following:

Ban Loong Color Foto Centre AG52, Ground Floor, Wisma Merdeka, PO Box 12064, 88822 Kota Kinabalu, Sabah; tel 088–217950

Hospitals

Queen Elizabeth Hospital 88586 Kota Kinabalu; tel 088–218166/fax 088–211999

Health and Paramedic Service PO Box 11201, 88813 Kota Kinabalu; tel 088–50555/fax 088–221248

Local Highlights

The great thing about Layang-Layang is that the island is unspoilt! The corollary of this is, inevitably, that there is a significant dearth of things to do other than diving, fishing and bird-watching.

Pickhandle Barracuda (Sphyraena jello). Immature barracudas school in large shoals of 500-1000. Adults tend to swim singly and can become dangerous.

SABAH NORTHWEST COAST

The second largest state in Malaysia after Sarawak, Sabah's name came from the Arabic Zir-e Bad, meaning 'The Land Below the Wind', that refers to its position just below the typhoon belt. While Sarawak's chief characteristics are rainforests and rivers, Sabah is identified with mountains — in particular, the Crocker Range in the northwest region, which is dominated by Mount Kinabalu 4101m (13,455ft).

KOTA KINABALU

The focal point of Sabah's northwest coast is Kota Kinabalu, the state capital. Since the settlement was first established here as Jesselton by the British in 1883 (it was renamed in 1963) it has experienced a turbulent history, with pirates, rebellions and fires. It was completely destroyed by the Allies during World War II in order to stop the Japanese being able to use it as a base, but was later rebuilt mostly on reclaimed land in Gaya Bay.

Some time ago the northwest coast of Sabah was more generously endowed with beautiful coral reefs but, with a relatively high population density for the region, the reefs have suffered from siltation, destructive fishing methods and coral quarrying for construction.

MARINE PARKS

Tunku Abdul Rahman Marine Park is very close to Kota Kinabalu, so it gets crowded at weekends and during holiday periods. Tiga Park is more difficult to reach and is often quite empty of visitors, but it has only two real dive sites. Further south, off Labuan Federal Territory, the corals suffer from river run-off and siltation, but there is excellent wreck diving. Except for Labuan, this is not an area you would normally consider visiting specifically for its diving – especially as some of the best diving in the world is only a short flight away, at Pulau Sipadan on the east coast (see page 130). Since the water is relatively shallow, the visibility is soon spoilt by any windy weather. However, if you happen to be in the area anyway and the weather is fine, then bear in mind that the diving is very easy to get to and perfect for the training of novices.

Opposite: *The idyllic Sapi Island in the Tunku Abdul Rahman Marine Park.*
Above: *The Copperband Butterfly (Chelmon rostratus), common on silty inner reefs and wrecks.*

Tunku Abdul Rahman Marine Park

Lying 3–8km (2–5 miles) off Kota Kinabalu, the Tunku Abdul Rahman Marine Park consists of five islands: Pulau Gaya, Pulau Sapi, Pulau Manukan, Pulau Mamutik and Pulau Sulug. They are covered with lowland tropical rainforest; this is still undisturbed primary forest on Pulau Gaya within the park area, but on the other islands it is mostly secondary. These rainforest areas are home to a variety of interesting flora and fauna. Pulau Gaya, at 1483ha (3665 acres) by far the largest of the group – with a highest peak rising to 305m (1000ft) – is worth visiting just for the wildlife.

In 1974 most of Pulau Gaya and all of Pulau Sapi were declared the Tunku Abdul Rahman Marine Park, leaving only the small fishing village on the eastern promontory of Pulau Gaya out of the park (it remains so to this day). In 1979 the nearby Pulau Manukan, Pulau Mamutik and Pulau Sulug were added to the park.

ACCESS

All the islands can be reached by a 20min boat or ferry ride from the jetty by the Hyatt Kinabalu International Hotel, the Tanjung Aru Resort or the Kinabalu Yacht Club. This easy accessibility makes the islands very popular with local day-trippers at weekends. August is the high season for local holidays. There is an entrance fee of two ringgits per day per person to visit the islands on land.

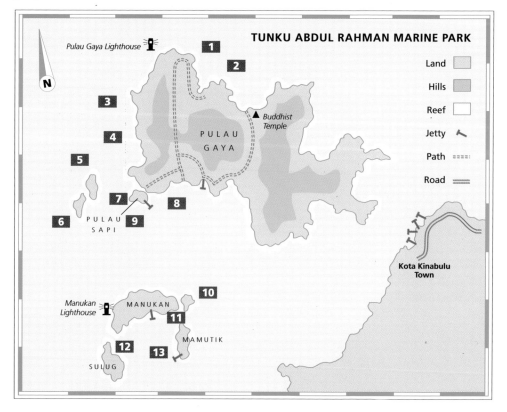

SHALLOW REEFS

The north and west shores of the islands have been ravaged by monsoon weather, so that there are rocky cliffs and banks of rubble, but the eastern and southern shores have golden beaches slowly shelving to reefs. These reefs are generally shallow, and most have been damaged by blast-fishing in the past, but where they are still intact they offer a profusion of brightly coloured stony corals, some of which are quite big.

THE CORAL

The corals are predominantly stony; in particular, there are large areas of colourful staghorn coral and large table corals (*Acropora*), there is lettuce coral, and (good news for snorkellers) very little fire coral. In among the larger corals are smaller areas of brain coral, mushroom corals, whip corals, bubble coral, blue and yellow sea squirts, sponges and large brown vase sponges. Also present are large blue sea stars, smaller green sea stars and cushion stars. Several colour varieties of feather stars are common in daylight, and there are lots of Christmas-tree Worms and fan worms.

FISH FAUNA

The fish fauna is more limited, but all the smaller reef fish can be seen, and there are quite large shoals of fusiliers; several varieties of anemones act as hosts to clownfish. Crabs and shells are still found, but very few lobsters. Whale Sharks can be seen here from January to April.

The Blue-spotted Lagoon Ray (Taeniura lymma), often camouflages its bright colours by covering itself in sand.

SURPRISE ROCK ISLAND

It is hard to equate modern Borneo with volcanic activity but all the signs are present: there are hot springs at Poring and active mud volcanoes in the Tiga and Turtle Islands parks, Pulau Sipadan is the result of volcanic uplift, and Mount Kinabalu, the youngest granite pluton in the world, is still rising by 5mm (0.2in) per year.

On 15 April 1988 local fishermen were startled when a new island, almost as big as a football pitch, was thrust up out of the sea 14km (9 miles) east of Pulau Banggi off the northern tip of Sabah, close to Philippines territorial waters. The nearby islanders named it Pulau Batu Hairan ('Surprise Rock Island'). Pulau Batu Hairan must have been quite a sight, with all its beautiful stony coral formations standing proud before they collapsed.

In fact, this area has been thrust up twice before during this century, first in 1914 and again in 1942. Unfortunately, in 1988 as before, the seabed was not thrust up far enough for the island to survive, and Pulau Batu Hairan was soon reclaimed by the waves.

BULIJONG BAY

The major beach area on Pulau Gaya is at Bulijong Bay, known locally as Police Beach because it used to be used by the police for target practice! This area has a 400m (440yd) beach with excellent swimming and some good snorkelling either side of the bay. It can get very busy, so most foreign visitors prefer the more secluded beaches on the smaller islands. There are forest trails and mangrove trails on board walks.

PULAU SAPI

Pulau Sapi, adjacent to the southwest tip of Pulau Gaya, is a small island – 10ha (25 acres) – with one of the best beaches in the park. It has most of the public facilities you would hope for, but no accommodation. You can camp if you have written permission from the Sabah Parks Office in Kota Kinabalu or from the park warden. There is a nature trail, and glass-bottomed boats are available for people who want to view the coral reef without getting wet. To the southeast there is good snorkelling.

PECULIAR BIRDS

Tunku Abdul Rahman Marine Park is home to a bizarre bird called the Megapode (*Megapodus freycinet*).

This bird incubates its eggs by burying them in mounds of sand and leaves; the leaves ferment like a compost heap and produce enough warmth to incubate the eggs until they are ready to hatch. A single mound may be used by several birds. The birds constantly tend the mound to control temperature. Now rarely found on Western Sabah's coast, the Megapode survives in small populations on all the islands in the Park except Pulau Mamutik; it is also found on the larger of Pulau Tiga Park's islands, further south.

Other birdlife on the Tunku Abdul Rahman Marine Park islands includes large species such as the White-bellied Sea Eagle, Green Heron and Pied Hornbill, as well as smaller and commoner species like sunbirds, flycatchers, Pink-necked Green Pigeon and sandpipers.

PULAU MANUKAN

Pulau Manukan covers 21ha (51 acres), and has the Park Headquarters. There are furnished chalets for rent, a swimming pool, football field, tennis and squash courts and a restaurant; the accommodation has to be booked through the Sabah Parks Office in Kota Kinabalu. Good snorkelling is to be had on the west, north and south coasts.

PULAU MAMUTIK

Pulau Mamutik is the smallest island – 6ha (15 acres) – and the nearest to the mainland. It has good beaches, but the one on the eastern side, facing Tanjung Aru, slopes down steeply. The island has a rest house, water and electricity, but you must bring your own food.

PULAU SULUG

Pulau Sulug, the island furthest away from Kota Kinabalu, covers 8ha (20 acres) and is relatively undeveloped, though there are some picnic shelters and toilets. At its eastern extremity is a long sand-spit and a beach; apart from this the island is rocky. It is popular with foreign tourists, who like the quiet, uncrowded atmosphere. There is good snorkelling at the island's southern end.

The wettest months in this region are during the southwest monsoon period, June to December, while the driest months are January to May. The best time for diving is April to August, with the calmest weather being in February to May.

The sites described below are all in warm shallow waters. They can be dived in bad weather, but the stirred-up sand renders visibility almost zero; otherwise, at all the sites the average visibility is about 10m (33ft). The depths given are for high tide.

1 PULAU GAYA: BULIJONG BAY

★★

Location: 500m (550yd) east of the northeast point of Bulijong Bay.
Access: By small boat to the east of the northeast end of the bay until the reef is visible.
Conditions: Some gentle currents, depending on the tide. Visibility is quickly ruined by windy weather.
Average depth: 10m (33ft)
Maximum depth: 21m (70ft)
A long gentle slope from 5m (16ft) to 21m (70ft) goes out to the north. There are table and staghorn corals, boulder corals, encrusting corals and sponges, blue sea stars, black sea urchins, nudibranchs, flat worms and small reef fish.

You can snorkel off the central section of the west side of Bulijong Bay.

2 PULAU GAYA: MERANGIS REEF

★★

Location: 400m (440yd) northeast of the eastern tip of Bulijong Bay.
Access: By small boat out to the east until the reef is visible.
Conditions: Calm in good weather; possibly some swell and surge as the tide changes.
Average depth: 9m (30ft)
Maximum depth: 26m (85ft)
A tongue slopes out in line with the promontory. The best diving is on the east side, but there is more marine life on the end, where a short wall drops to 26m (85ft). The site has table and staghorn corals, boulder and brain corals, encrusting corals and sponges, nudibranchs, sea stars, sea urchins and small reef fish.

You can snorkel off the north end of the promontory.

3 PULAU GAYA: AGILL REEF

★★

Location: At the centre of the west side of Pulau Gaya.
Access: By boat.
Conditions: Generally calm; possibly some swell and surge as the tide changes.
Average depth: 15m (50ft)
Maximum depth: 26m (85ft)
On a gentle slope from 8m (25ft) to 26m (85ft) are table, staghorn and boulder corals, with Christmas-tree Worms, brain corals, encrusting corals and sponges, sea anemones and small reef fish.

4 PULAU GAYA: CLEMENT REEF

★★★

Location: West–northwest of the gap between Pulau Sapi and Pulau Gaya.
Access: By boat.
Conditions: Generally calm; possibly some swell and surge as the tide turns.
Average depth: 15m (50ft)
Maximum depth: 26m (85ft)
A gentle slope from 8m (25ft) to 26m (85ft) has good large table, staghorn, lettuce, brain and boulder corals, encrusting corals and sponges, Christmas-tree Worms and fan worms, and vase and small barrel sponges. There are plenty of small reef fish, cuttlefish, catfish, sea urchins, sea stars, cushion stars and nudibranchs, lionfish, scorpionfish, stonefish and some groupers.

5 NORTH EDGELL PATCH

6 SOUTH EDGELL PATCH

★★

Location: West of Pulau Sapi.
Access: By small boat west from the island until the patch reefs are visible.
Conditions: Generally calm; possibly some swell and surge as the tide changes.
Average depth: 15m (50ft)
Maximum depth: 20m (65ft)
There is a gentle slope from 9m (30ft) to 20m (65ft). Both of these sites have been badly damaged by blast-fishing, leaving lots of coral rubble coated in encrusting coral, sponges and algae. There are small varieties of reef fish, black sea urchins, sea stars, cushion stars, sea cucumbers and nudibranchs. The two sites are open to the ocean, so there are occasional pelagic visitors, including Manta Rays.

ISLAND FORMATION

Geologically the islands of the Tunku Abdul Rahman Marine Park are part of the Crocker range, which stretches from the northern end of Sabah right down to the border with Sarawak. The islands were formed towards the end of the last ice age when rising sea levels isolated them from the mainland. The underlying sandstone of which they are formed can easily be seen around their coastlines, with outcrops sculpted by the weather into caves, honeycombs and deep crevasses.

7 PULAU SAPI: SOUTHWEST REEF
★★

Location: Off the southwest promontory of Pulau Sapi.
Access: By small boat to the west of the promontory.
Conditions: Generally calm; possibly some swell and surge as the tide turns.
Average depth: 6m (20ft) to 9m (30ft)
Maximum depth: 17m (56ft)
This site offers shallow diving in very easy conditions – ideal for novices.

8 PULAU SAPI: SAPI REEF
★★★★★★

Location: Off the southeast corner of Pulau Sapi.
Access: By boat.
Conditions: Generally calm; possibly some swell and surge as the tide turns.
Average depth: 9m (30ft)
Maximum depth: 17m (56ft)
Shallow diving in very easy conditions with table, staghorn, boulder, bubble and brain corals, encrusting corals and sponges, Christmas-tree Worms, fan worms, sea stars, cushion stars, sea cucumbers, sea squirts and sea urchins. There are lots of small reef fish, catfish, cuttlefish, lionfish, scorpionfish, stonefish, nudibranchs, flat worms and colourful feather stars. When the shallow water is surging it is quite difficult to achieve any good close-up photography of the smaller creatures.

There is quite good snorkelling off this corner of Pulau Sapi.

9 PULAU SAPI: RON REEF
★★★★★★

Location: South of Pulau Sapi.
Access: By boat.
Conditions: Generally calm; possibly some swell and surge as the tide changes.
Average depth: 9m (30ft)
Maximum depth: 17m (56ft)
Shallow diving in very easy conditions with boulders; the reef life and fish fauna are much the same as for the Sapi Reef (Site 8) including table, staghorn, boulder, bubble and brain corals, encrusting corals and sponges, Christmas-tree worms, fan worms, sea stars, cushion stars, sea cucumbers, sea squirts, sea urchins and many species of smaller reef fish.

The surging waters pose the same difficulties for close-up photography.

10 PULAU MANUKAN: MID REEF
★★★★

Location: Directly east of the east point of Pulau Manukan.
Access: By boat.
Conditions: Some light current, with swell and surge as the tide turns.
Average depth: 9m (30ft)
Maximum depth: 20m (65ft)
A gentle slope from 6m (20ft) to 20m (65ft) with few soft corals but lots of table, staghorn, lettuce, bubble, boulder and brain corals, encrusting corals and sponges, vase sponges and some small whip corals. There are Christmas-tree worms, nudibranchs and flat worms, sea squirts, sea stars, cushion stars, black sea urchins, sea cucumbers and lots of feather stars, as well as lionfish, scorpionfish, stonefish and shoals of small parrotfish, catfish, sweepers and fusiliers. Although anemones are frequent, few of them have attendant clownfish. Barracuda, groupers and turtles are common.

11 PULAU MANUKAN: MANUKAN REEF
★★★

Location: East-southeast of the southeast corner of Pulau Manukan.
Access: By boat from the southeast corner of Pulau Manukan towards Pulau Mamutik.
Conditions: Some currents and heavy boat traffic.
Average depth: 10m (33ft)
Maximum depth: 20m (65ft)
The site offers a gentle slope from 5m (16ft) to 20m (65ft). Small turtles and barracuda are often seen.

There tends to be heavy boat traffic here, so **this site is definitely not for snorkellers or for novices,** who might have trouble maintaining correct buoyancy and possibly float up when boats were passing. There is, however, good snorkelling off the north and south shores of Pulau Manukan.

12 PULAU SULUG: SULUG REEF
★★★★

Location: East of the beach and the north promontory of Pulau Sulug.
Access: By boat from north of Pulau Sulug.
Conditions: Some current and swell.
Average depth: 9m (30ft)
Maximum depth: 26m (85ft)
A tongue heading out east, with the best diving on the

south side and the most marine life at the eastern end. There are some very large table corals along with brain, boulder, staghorn and plate corals and encrusting corals and sponges. You will find lots of mushroom corals among the blast-fished rubble areas. There are also masses of blue sea stars, green sea stars, cushion stars, some big vase sponges, small barrel sponges, feather stars, Christmas-tree and fan worms, nudibranchs, lionfish, scorpionfish, stonefish, sea cucumbers and sea urchins. Jacks, barracuda, groupers and tuna may be seen occasionally.

There is good snorkelling to be found off the southeast tip of Pulau Sulug.

13 PULAU MAMUTIK: SOUTH REEF

Location: Southwest of Pulau Mamutik.
Access: By boat.
Conditions: Some current and swell.
Average depth: 9m (30ft)
Maximum depth: 18m (60ft)

This is an extremely small patch reef, which is not particularly good for diving or snorkelling.

SPINY-SKINNED CREATURES

Among the most conspicuous creatures on sandy sea beds are sea cucumbers, which can be up to 5m (16ft) long and are often very fat. Sea cucumbers are part of a widespread group, the echinoderms (meaning 'spiny skin'), all of which propel themselves on tiny tube feet activated by an unusual water-vascular system. Most echinoderms display fivefold symmetry, the features of their bodies being arranged in fives or multiples thereof. Some species of Sea urchins and many species of sea cucumbers are edible.

Other common echinoderms include:
- **Sea Stars**
  These usually have five or more arms radiating from a central body, each arm having its own organs for feeding, locomotion, respiration and reproduction.
- **Brittle stars**
  Often hidden away among corals, these trap zooplankton in their delicate spiny arms.
- **Sea urchins**
  These have no arms but an ellipsoidal or heart-shaped body and shell, sometimes flattened, with lots of spines. The Diadema urchin, with its long black spines, is among the commonest species.

The beautiful Sapi Island, Tunku Abdul Marine Park, has one of the best beaches in the park and offers excellent snorkelling.

HOW TO GET THERE

Kota Kinabalu is easily accessible by international flights from Kuala Lumpur, Hong Kong, Manila, Singapore, Bangkok, Brunei, Taipei and Seoul, and is the take-off hub for flights to Tawau, Sandakan, Labuan and Kuching (Sarawak). The airport is 7km (4 miles) from the city centre. Airport tax is M$5 on local flights and M$20 on international ones.

Boats go to the islands from near the Hotel Hyatt Kinabalu International in Kota Kinabalu. You can either go in a group and hire one much as you might a taxi or you can book on the daily (more frequent at weekends) ferry service run by Coral Island Cruises (address below) or the less regular service offered by Sea Quest (tel 088–230943). If you use one of the freelance operators, be prepared for some hard bargaining. Dive operators and operators at Shangri-La's Tanjung Aru Resort also run boats to the islands.

Helicopter Service

All have a payload limit of 425kg (935 pounds).
Kota Kinabalu
Sabah Air Pte Ltd Sabah Air Building, Locked Bag 113, Old Airport Road, 88999 Kota Kinabalu; tel 088–56733/fax 088–235195
Tawau
Sabah Air Pte Ltd Locked Bag 15, Tawau Airport, 91009 Tawau; tel 089–774005
Sandakan
Sabah Air Pte Ltd Sabah Air Hangar, Locked Bag 56, Sandakan Airport, 90009 Sandakan; tel 089–660527/fax 089–660545

WHERE TO STAY

All accommodation on the islands must be booked in advance through:

Sabah Parks Office Lot 3, Block K, PO Box 10626, Sinsuran Complex, Jalan Tun Fuad Stephens, 88806 Kota Kinabalu; tel 088–211585/fax 088–221001

Upper Price Range
Shangri-La's Tanjung Aru Resort (out of town), Jalan Pantai Aru
Postal Address:
Locked Bag 174, Kota Kinabalu; tel 088–58711/fax 088–217155

Hotel Shangri-La (Kota Kinabalu) 75 Bandaran Berjaya, PO Box 11718, 88819 Kota Kinabalu; tel 088–212800/fax 088–212078

Hotel Hyatt Kinabalu International Jalan Datuk Salleh Sulong, Kota Kinabalu; tel 088–221234/fax 088–225972

Medium Price Range
Borneo Rest House (out of town) Mile 3.5, Penampang Road, Tamam Fraser, PO Box 14799, 88855 Kota Kinabalu; tel 088–718855/fax 088–718955

Hotel Holiday Lots 1 & 2, Block F, Segama Complex, Kota Kinabalu; tel 088–213116/fax 088–215576
This hotel is popular with divers, so, if you want to meet other divers, it's the obvious place to go.

Hotel Capital 23 Jalan Haji Saman, PO Box 11223, 88813 Kota Kinabalu; tel 088–231999/fax 088–237222

Hotel Jesselton 66 Gaya Street, Kota Kinabalu; tel 088–223333/fax 088–240401

Sabah Inn 25 Jalan Pantai, PO Box 13455, 88839 Kota Kinabalu; tel 088–53177/fax 088–219660

Lower Price Range (but very clean)
Town Inn 31–33 Jalan Pantai, 88000 Kota Kinabalu; tel 088–225823/fax 088–217762

WHERE TO EAT

Kota Kinabalu has restaurants of all standards. The restaurants in Shangri-La's Tanjung Aru Resort, the Hyatt Kinabalu International Hotel and the Hotel Capital (addresses above) are highly recommended, as is:

Jaws Seafood Restaurant & Karaoke Lounge 4th Floor, Gaya Centre, Kota Kinabalu; tel 088–236009

If your proclivity is for Western fast food, there are also franchises of a couple of well known names ...

Burger King Block B, Segama Complex (opposite the Hyatt Hotel)

Kentucky Fried Chicken Ground Floor, Wisma Merdeka, Kota Kinabalu

DIVE FACILITIES

Dive-Shops
Borneo Divers and Sea Sports (Sabah) Sdn Bhd G-07, Ground Floor, Wisma Sabah, Kota Kinabalu; tel 088–222226

Kota Aquatics AG-04, Ground Floor, Wisma Merdeka, Kota Kinabalu; tel 088–218710

Diver Training
Borneo Divers and Sea Sports (Sabah) Sdn Bhd Rooms 401–409, 4th Floor, Wisma Sabah
Postal Address:
Locked Bag 194, 88999 Kota Kinabalu; tel

088–222226/fax 088–221550
Borneo Divers are Borneo's first and only PADI Five-Star IDC Dive Centre. They run courses up to Open-Water-Instructor level and have dive centres at Shangri-La's Tanjung Aru Resort, Labuan, Pulau Sipadan and Sangalakki. Refer to pages 140–141 for more about Borneo Divers and a list of the company's overseas agents.

The company has several female dive-masters – probably the only ones in Malaysia. Some beginners and children may feel more comfortable with them.

Andrew Chong PO Box 12130, 88823 Kota Kinabalu; tel 088–424280; 010 810335 (mobile)/fax 088–245752
Andrew Chong is a PADI OWSI/MFAI/IDC staff instructor who works part-time for Borneo Divers, Sipadan Dive Resort and the live-aboard boat MV *Coral Topaz* (see below). He is the local expert on Layang-Layang, having been involved in much of the early work there. Andrew has his own dive boat and is popular with local expatriates and their families.

Borneo Sea Adventures Sdn Bhd 1st Floor, 8A Karamunsing Warehouse, Kota Kinabalu
Postal Address:
PO Box 10134, 88801 Kota Kinabalu; tel 088–55390/fax 088–221106
PADI courses and diving trips off Sabah.

Diving Costs (all operators)
The standard rate is US$40 for one dive, US$70 for two dives on the same day.

LIVE-ABOARD BOATS

Kota Kinabalu is also the home port for the live-aboard dive boats MV *Coral Topaz* and MV *Spirit of Borneo*.

MV Coral Topaz
Coral Island Cruises Tours & Travel Sdn Bhd G19, Ground Floor, Wisma Sabah, PO Box 14527, 88851 Kota Kinabalu; tel 088–223490/fax 088–223404
Singapore Agent
Sharkeys Dive & Adventure Pte Ltd 1 Park Road, 3–53/54 Peoples Park Complex, Singapore 0105; tel 65–5383733/fax 65–5386919
The company also has a counter in the Hotel Hyatt Kinabalu International.

This boat has been running successfully for several years with trips to Layang-Layang when the weather permits and around Pulau Sipadan at other times.

The 46m (150ft) long, 7m (23ft) wide, 345-ton MV *Coral Topaz* was built in 1963 as a weather-research vessel. Equipped with twin stabilizers, she has a range of over 15,000km (10,000 miles) and a maximum speed of 10 knots (18.5kph).

Accommodation consists of five air-conditioned cabins plus a shared economy cabin with 17 bunks.

Andrew Chong (see address above) has been director of sea sports and divemaster on MV *Coral Topaz*, with particular reference to Layang-Layang.

MV *Spirit of Borneo*

Tropical Dive Adventures Sdn Bhd 28–1, Jalan 8/70A Sri Hartamas, Jalan Duta, 50480 Kuala Lumpur; tel 03–2530048/fax 03–2530049

This boat was advertised for two long years before finally coming into service; problems with its conversion in Australia caused most of its early departures to be cancelled.

It is now fully operational, and it is planned to make 10-day cruises out of Kota Kinabalu to the areas around Layang-Layang from April to September; then in October, when the monsoon arrives in this area, the MV *Spirit of Borneo* will move to the reefs off Indonesia and around Sipadan until February.

The MV *Spirit of Borneo* is an ex-research vessel. It is 37m (120ft) long, with air-conditioned accommodation for groups of 12–18 and a total capacity of 22.

Larger chase boats and E6 transparency processing are promised in the future.

MV *Spirit of Borneo* Overseas Agents

GERMANY

Club Montee Muncher Strasse 73, D-8228 Freilassing; tel 08654–1682/fax 08654–65600

SWITZERLAND

Dive Bubbles Dive Travel Dorfstrasse 15, 8630 Ruti; tel 055–317778/fax 055–313785

UK

Scuba Safaris Nastfield Cottage, The Green, Frampton-On-Severn, Gloucestershire GL2 7DY; tel 01452–740919/fax 01452–740943
Sure Dive Ltd 6 Pershore Grove, Ainsdale, Southport, Merseyside PR8 2SY; tel 01704–573714/fax 01704–570555

USA

See & Sea Travel Inc 50 Francisco Street, Suite 205, San Francisco, CA 94133; tel 415–4343400/fax 415–4343409

FILM PROCESSING

Kota Kinabalu has many mini-labs who will process your print film. They can be found in almost every street in the city centre and in Wisma Merdeka. For reliable E6 transparency processing use:
Ban Loong Color Foto Centre AG52, Ground Floor, Wisma Merdeka, PO Box 12064, 88822 Kota Kinabalu; tel 088–217950

HOSPITAL

Queen Elizabeth Hospital 88586 Kota Kinabalu; tel 088–218166/fax 088–211999

Health and Paramedic Service PO Box 11201, 88813 Kota Kinabalu; tel 088–50555/fax 088–221248

LOCAL HIGHLIGHTS

Kota Kinabalu – known as Jesselton under the British and until 1963 – is the centre for many interesting excursions. Within the small city itself are the **State Museum and Archives**, the **State Mosque**, the **Cathedral of the Sacred Heart**, the **Pek Nam Thong Buddhist Temple**, **Sembulan Bajau water village** and the **Sabah Foundation Building**. You could comfortably fit a visit to all of these, plus a drive up **Signal Hill** for a view over the city, into a half-day excursion if you so wished, although obviously you're likely to want to linger here and there. Your day could then be rounded off by spending a relaxing evening at the **Tanjung Aru Resort** looking out across the beach to the islands of Tunku Abdul Rahman Park and one of the justifiably famous sunsets.

If your visit to the area includes a Sunday, make a point of visiting the **Gaya Street Market**, which operates on that day. During the week you can suss out the **Filipino hawker stalls** and the busy **Central Market**.

Within easy reach of the city are **Mengkabong Bajau water village** (30min), probably the most-photographed water village in Malaysia, and, 45km (28 miles) away, **Poring Hot Springs**, where you can wallow in natural hot-sulphur baths and explore the primary-rainforest canopy from a walkway suspended 30m (100ft) up. There is also an orchid garden here.

If you're feeling more adventurous you could go white-water rafting on the Padas and Kiulu rivers, near **Papar** (20km; 12 miles away), or climb **Mount Kinabalu** (83km; 52 miles away), which at 4100m (13,455ft) is Southeast Asia's highest mountain. This two-day climb is highly organized: you must take a guide.

The area around the mountain is famous for its nine species of pitcher-plants and for its blooms of Rafflesia, the world's largest flower. **Mount Kinabalu National Park Centre** has collections of all the local flowers, including the orchids. Also, some 6km (3miles) from the Park Headquarters, you can visit the **Kundasang War Memorial** to the Allied prisoners-of-war who died on the death march in September 1944.

If you are particularly interested in *Rafflesia* flowers there is a good protected reserve at **Tambunan** in the **Crocker**

Mountains National Park, but be prepared for long walks on wet slippery paths with leeches (leech socks can be purchased at the reserve headquarters). It was raining heavily the day I was there, but nevertheless I found the trip worth it and saw three of these rare flowers.

There is a spectacular section of **railway** between Tenom and Beaufort, where the line follows the river Padas through the jungle. **Tenom** is the centre of the Murut tribes, but very little of their culture remains. At the northern tip of Sabah, near **Kudat**, some of the Rungus tribal people still live in communal longhouses, where the entire population of the village lives under one roof with separate rooms leading onto a long communal verandah. You can arrange to visit three of these in a long day's excursion from Kota Kinabalu, and it is also possible to stay overnight – but at a cost that is inordinately high by comparison with that of a day visit.

Most towns have traditional market days, *tamus*. Around the areas that I have mentioned these include:

- *Tuesday*: Kiulu
- *Saturday*: Beaufort
- *Sunday*: Kota Kinabalu (Gaya Street)
  Kota Belud
  Papar
  Tambunan
  Tenom

LOCAL TRAVEL AGENTS

Api Tours (Borneo) Sdn Bhd Lot G31/32, Ground Floor, Wisma Sabah, PO Box 12853, 88831 Kota Kinabalu; tel 088–221233/fax 088–221230

Borneo Expeditions Unit 306, 3rd Floor, Wisma Sabah, Jalan Tun Razak, 88831 Kota Kinabalu; tel 088–222721/fax 088–222720

Borneo Wildlife Adventures Sdn Bhd Lot 4, Block L, Ground Floor, Sinsuran Complex, 88000 Kota Kinabalu; tel 088–213668/fax 088–219089

Exotic Adventures (Borneo) Sdn Bhd Lot 6, Block J, 1st Floor, Segama Complex, PO Box 13805, 88844 Kota Kinabalu; tel 088–222499/fax 088–221749

For general information, visit
Tourist Office of the Government (TDC) 1 Jalan Segunting, Ground Floor, Wing Onn Life Building, 88000 Kota Kinabalu; tel 088–211732/fax 088–241764

Symbiosis is close association of two animal or plant species which may be of benefit to one or both participants. There are numerous examples of symbiosis among marine creatures, although it is not always obvious that both partners do in fact gain from the relationship.

SYMBIOSIS IN ACTION

Bigger fish are often shadowed by smaller ones who partly seek protection from predators but also use this as a means of approaching their own, even smaller, prey unnoticed; a common example is of jacks shadowing Humphead Wrasse and reef sharks. Also usually attendant on larger fishes – sharks, Humphead Wrasse, Manta Rays and turtles – are remoras (shark suckers), fishes of the family Echeneidae. Those on Manta Rays and Whale Sharks can attain 60cm (2ft) or more in length. The remoras pick up food scraps from their hosts' feeding, but it is uncertain what benefit the host gains in return – a thought that seems to have occurred to the sharks, too, for they are often seen trying to scrape the remoras off on the seabed or on coral. Perhaps the remoras remove some smaller parasites.

PILOTFISH

Pilotfish often travel just off the noses of the larger sharks, although frequently the shark can be seen snapping at them. As with remoras, the pilotfish may simply be seeking protection while at the same time picking up scraps from the larger fish's feeding.

CLEANER WRASSE

But not all partnerships are as one-sided. Cleaner Wrasse offer a valet service to larger fish at 'cleaning stations', eating parasites, fungal growths and dead scales and tissues. Their distinctive shape and striped body save them from being misidentified as prey, a factor exploited by some other species, which mimic the Cleaner Wrasse and can thus give the 'customer' a nasty surprise.

CLEANER SHRIMP

Some grazing fish act as cleaner fish to slow-moving marine animals like turtles, and the Transparent Cleaner Shrimp (Periclimenes) is often found living with other creatures including, among many others, moray eels, sea anemones, parrotfish, corals, sponges, the Spanish Dancer nudibranch and even the Crown-of-Thorns Starfish.

Pistol or Snapping Shrimps (Alpheidae) – sometimes called Bulldozer Shrimps – live in association with various species of goby. While the fish acts as a lookout, the poor-sighted shrimp excavates a burrow which both shrimp and goby then use as a hiding-place in daytime and a resting-place at night.

Various little creatures, including pipefish

Star Pufferfish (Arothron stellatus) with a Cleaner Wrasse (Labroides sp.).

CLOWNFISH SPECIES

Many species of clownfish are found in the waters off Malaysia and Singapore. Clownfish are members of the damselfish family. Of the 27 clownfish species, all but one belong to the genus Amphiprion, the odd one out being in the genus Premnas: Premnas clownfish look like the others but have a horizontal spine on the gill plate, just below the eye.

Each clownfish species favours a particular species of anemone as host.

and small crabs and cuttlefish as well as one anemone, Coeloplana, hide among the spines of long-spined sea urchins. Trumpetfish often hide in whip corals, and various crabs and shrimps and the Longnose Hawkfish conceal themselves amongst gorgonian sea fans of the same colour as themselves.

CLOWNFISH AND ANEMONES

But the best known marine partnership is that shared by clownfish (and some other dam-selfish) with sea anemones. The fish are more correctly called Anemonefish, but most divers and aquarists call them clownfish because of their gaudy colours and apparently eccentric behaviour as they charge, snap and grunt at other fish, at divers and even at their own reflection in a diver's mask. The origins of this behaviour are in fact largely territorial.

A SAFE HAVEN

The anemone gives the clownfish a haven to which it can retreat if threatened by predators and also provides it with a food source supple-mentary to its principal diet of floating zoo-plankton or algae growing nearby. The clown-fish's scavenging of food scraps, algae and parasites within the anemone helps keep the latter clean and healthy, and the movement of

the clownfish creates a respiratory current within the anemone. Clownfish have even been known to bring the anemone food, although it is not proven behaviour in the wild. Nevertheless, the clownfish would seem to get more out of the partnership than the anemone in that, while clownfish apparently cannot sur-vive for long without a host anemone, anemones can thrive without clownfish.

ANEMONE STING

Anemones, which in areas of high water movement can grow to be over 1m (40in) across, have other symbiotes, algae called zooxanthellae. They catch passing food with their sticky mucus and can kill live prey using the stinging nematocysts in their tentacles, but most of their nutrient comes from the symbiot-ic algae. Clownfish are not immune to the sting; however, the anemone's mucus contains chemicals that counter the sting, stopping each tentacle from stinging any of the others, or even itself, and the clownfish coat themselves in this. They also have a thick mucus layer which they generate themselves for protection.

Other small damselfish, notably the Domino Damselfish *Dascyllus trimaculatus*, can occupy anemones during their juvenile phase.

Richardsons Clownfish (Amphiprion rubrocinctus) with Radianthus anemone. The partnership is of benefit to both, though the clownfish has greater dependence.

Closed anemone, Radianthus ritteri, now known as Heteractis magnifica, with a Clownfish Amphiprion ocellaris, also known as Common Clownfish or Clown Anemonefish.

Pulau Tiga Park

Located 48km (30 miles) southwest of Kota Kinabalu, in Kimanis Bay, the Pulau Tiga National Park, gazetted in 1978, comprises Pulau Tiga and the two smaller islands Pulau Kalampunian Damit and Pulau Kalampunian Besar. Its total area is 15,864ha (39,200 acres).

PULAU TIGA

Pulau Tiga itself is a beautiful place heavily wooded with dipterocarp forest down to coconut palms at the beach edge. There are park rangers *in situ*, plus on the south of the island, a well laid-out campsite and picnic and barbecue areas along the fine white sandy beaches.The best time for diving is April to August, with the calmest weather being in February to May.

CORAL REEFS

The reefs off the two smaller islands and the north side of Pulau Tiga are heavily blast-fished, although there are two good dive sites to the south. All over, there are small table, lettuce, boulder and brain corals, antler-shaped corals and encrusting corals and sponges. Most of the stony corals are damaged and covered in silt, but in many places small soft corals thrive.

SNORKELLING

The park is noted for having more gorgonians and whip corals than normally found on Sabah's west coast. Visibility in this region is generally about 10m (33ft).You could snorkel out from the nearest point on the beach to both of the Picnic Beach dive sites described below but, if the tide reversed, it could be difficult to snorkel back against the current.

1 SOUTH OF THE NORTHWEST END OF PICNIC BEACH

★★★☆☆☆

Location: On Pulau Tiga, 80m (90yd) south of Picnic Beach's northwest corner.
Access: By boat or by snorkelling from the beach.
Conditions: Current, some swell and difficult surge.
Average depth: 9m (30ft)
Maximum depth: 17m (56ft)
Here you find a 30° slope from 4m (13ft) to 17m (56ft) with, despite all the coral debris from blast-fishing, a good fish fauna, especially in the deeper water. There are lettuce corals, brain corals, mushroom corals and boulder corals with Christmas-tree worms, although few table corals. Also present are some gorgonian sea fans – reaching 1m (40in) across – several whip corals, yellow sea squirts, blue tube sponges, blue sea stars and several anemones (lacking attendant clownfish). The fish life includes many small butterflyfish, catfish, small parrotfish, scorpionfish, lionfish, stonefish, surgeonfish and some groupers.

2 SOUTH OF THE SOUTHWEST END OF PICNIC BEACH

★★★

Location: On Pulau Tiga, 80m (90yd) south of Picnic Beach's southwest corner.
Access: By boat or by snorkelling from the beach.
Conditions: Current, some swell and difficult surge.
Average depth: 9m (30ft)
Maximum depth: 17m (56ft)
A gentle slope falls westward from 6m (20ft) to 17m (56ft). There is much coral rubble from blast-fishing but, even so, lots of small fish swim among good table and brain corals, whip corals, small soft corals and tiny gorgonian sea fans. There are congregations of black sea urchins, several cuttlefish, nudibranchs, sea cucumbers, shoals of small parrotfish and fusiliers, yellow sea squirts, blue tube sponges, big clams, Christmas-tree Worms, fan worms and anemones (most lacking attendant clownfish).

Previous page: *Sunset seen from Pulau Tiga Park, off the west coast of Sabah, Malaysia.*
Below: *Large Barrel Sponges (Petrosia sp.) can grow up to 2m (6¹/₂ft) and are extremely common in the Pacific.*

HOW TO GET THERE

Pulau Tiga is accessible directly by speedboat from Kota Kinabalu or by local boat from Kuala Penyu at the tip of the Klias peninsula.

The speedboats from Kota Kinabalu normally take about 2hr. However, if you are lucky you can get a passage on a fast boat with a 100HP engine; this makes the trip in about 1hr.

Kota Kinabalu is easily accessible by international flights from Kuala Lumpur, Hong Kong, Manila, Singapore, Bangkok, Brunei, Taipei and Seoul. It is also the take-off hub for flights to Tawau, Sandakan, Labuan and Kuching (Sarawak). The airport is 7km (4 miles) from the city centre.

There is an airport tax of five ringgits on local flights and 20 ringgits on international flights.

Kuala Penyu is 140km (87 miles) southwest of Kota Kinabalu, and can be reached on irregular local minibuses from either Beaufort or Papar, both of which have frequent services to Kuala Lumpur. From Kuala Penyu it takes about 45min on a small local boat to the park.

WHERE TO STAY

In theory, there is a resthouse with accommodation for six people next to the park headquarters; however, this seemed to be nothing more than an abandoned wreck when I visited in 1993, and I have no idea if there are any plans to open it.

Otherwise there is a campsite. Bookings are through

Sabah Parks Office Lot 3, Block K, PO Box 10626, Sinsuran Complex, Jalan Tun Fuad Stevens, 88806 Kota Kinabalu; tel 088–211585/fax 088–221001

Beaufort and Papar have a handful of medium-priced hotels and lodging houses.

For places to stay in Kota Kinabalu refer to the directory for the Tunku Abdul Rahman Marine Park (page 106).

DIVE FACILITIES

There are no dive facilities on the islands, so everything must be organized and transported from Kota Kinabalu; refer to the directory for the Tunku Abdul Rahman Marine Park (page 106) for details.

FILM PROCESSING

There is no film processing on the islands. For addresses in Kota Kinabalu refer to the directory for the Tunku Abdul Rahman Marine Park (page 106).

HOSPITAL

The most accessible hospital from the islands is in Kota Kinabalu:

Queen Elizabeth Hospital 88586 Kota Kinabalu; tel 088–218166/fax 088–211999

Health and Paramedic Service PO Box 11201, 88813 Kota Kinabalu; tel 088–50555/fax 088–221248

LOCAL HIGHLIGHTS

Named after a former British Governor of Borneo, Beaufort is a picturesque old town but offers very little by way of leisure-time activities once you've been round St Paul's Church. One idea is to take a return train-ride between here and Tenom, the railhead for the North Borneo Railway; the journey takes about 1–2hr, depending on the type of train you catch (the faster ones are more expensive), and the forest scenery is truly dramatic.

Papar is similarly tranquil (to euphemize), and seems to come alive only at the colourful Sunday *tamu* (market). The beach at Pantai Manis, nearby, is served by minibuses from Papar's centre.

For further ideas for things to do in the area, see the directory covering the Tunku Abdul Rahman Marine Park (page 106).

This jetty on Tiga Park Island is used by the park rangers rather than by tourists.

Labuan Federal Territory

Pulau Labuan is situated 115km (71 miles) south of Kota Kinabalu, 8km (5 miles) off the mainland of Sabah at the northern mouth of Brunei Bay; on the island the town of Labuan itself was formerly known as Victoria. The name Labuan comes from *labohan*, the Malay for 'anchorage'. The port has the largest and deepest harbour in the country – even the biggest tankers can anchor – and as a result the island has been a busy trading centre since historic times. In the 19th century Britain and other colonial powers used it as a trading and coaling station, exploiting locally mined coal.

The island has always been a military base, today being used by the federal government as a staging post for garrisons of the Malaysian Air Force, Army and Navy. It saw a great deal of action during World War II on the part of both the Allies and the Japanese. In 1984 Pulau Labuan was given to the federal government by the then chief minister, Datuk Harris. Datuk Harris formerly owned more than half of the island, which was incorporated into Sabah as part of the Federation of Malaysia in 1963.

LABUAN PORT

Labuan port has a thriving shipyard and handles the large reserves of oil and gas extracted from the nearby offshore oilfields. It was declared a duty-free port in 1956, and there is brisk trade with Filipinos smuggling duty-free goods into the southern Philippines port of Zamboanga (on Mindanao Island), where the smaller items are sold on the Barter Trade Market and larger items like cars quietly disappear.

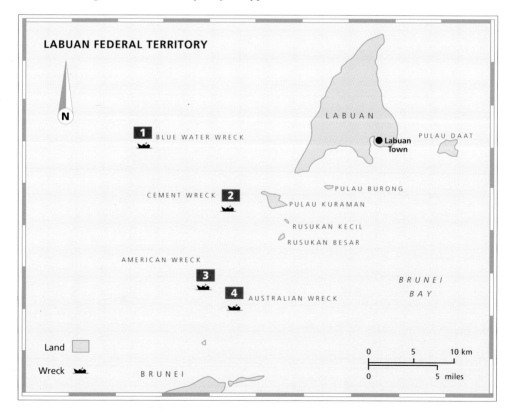

EXPANSION OF TOURISM

In 1990 Malaysia's federal government endorsed legislation establishing Labuan as an International Offshore Finance Centre, and the port is now undergoing expansion to cope with the anticipated investment and tourism boom. It has good links by both air and express ferry services with Kota Kinabalu, Brunei and Sarawak. A large new marina is being built – and this is where you will find Borneo Divers' new local office. From here the company oversees its sport-diving operation and dive-shop in addition to its commercial diving operation, which services the port as well as shipping and local oilfield industries.

WRECK DIVING

The reefs are not good for diving, being too near the outlets of sediment-laden rivers and having suffered from blast-fishing, but four good shipwrecks have been found. The wreck diving varies in difficulty from novice to serious, and is ideal for training courses on wreck diving. The fish fauna is good at all four sites, and the Cement Wreck has prolific colourful soft corals and feather stars. Visibility varies between 1.5 and 15m (5–50ft), with 8m (26ft) being a reasonable average. For some reason it is usually clearer on the Cement Wreck when it is bad on the others, even during the same day.

ACCESS TO THE WRECK SITES

All the shipwrecks are 40–50min by speedboat from the marina in Labuan. In good weather the dive operators use local landmarks to get near the wrecks, then finalize their position by echo sounder; when the surface visibility is really bad, Borneo Divers' divemasters carry a portable GPS (electronic Global Positioning System, using overhead satellites).

The journey out to the wreck sites can be rough in a small boat, with consequent damage to fragile cameras and flash guns unless they are well padded. The sites normally experience strong surface currents, and therefore it is essential to observe normal wreck-diving procedure and drop a shotline onto the wreck. Divers descend and ascend this shotline, which is tied off securely by the first diver down and released by the last diver to come up.

The wettest months in this region are during the southwest monsoon period, June to December, while the driest months are January to May. The best time for diving is April to August, with the calmest weather being in February to May.

Lionfish (Pterois volitans)
on the Cement Wreck
(Tung Hwang).

1 BLUE WATER WRECK

★★★★

Location: 30km (19 miles) due west of Pulau Labuan.
Access: By speedboat (50min) from the marina.
Conditions: Often choppy, with a strong surface current, though usually less current down on the wreck itself; there may be none at all in the lee of the hull. Suitable for all levels of diver, but only experienced divers should penetrate the hull.
Average depth: 28m (92ft)
Maximum depth: 35m (115ft)
This is the MV *Mabini Padre*, a Philippine stern trawler which sank while on tow after a fire on 13 November 1981. The 1654-tonne ship, measuring 80m (262ft) by 12m (40ft) by 6m (20ft), lies on her port side, with the starboard side at 24m (80ft) and the bottom at 35m (115ft). Although the coral life is poor, the wreck has quite a good fish fauna. There are small shoals of jacks, sweetlips, sweepers and cardinalfish, plus lone batfish, lionfish and scorpionfish. Large snappers and groupers shelter in the hull, and there are algae and sponges on the superstructure.

2 CEMENT WRECK

★★★★★

Location: 21km (11.5 miles) south–southwest of the Labuan Marina and west of Kuraman Island.
Access: By speedboat (40min) from the marina.
Conditions: Often choppy, with a strong surface current, though usually less current down on the wreck itself; there may be none at all in the lee of the hull. Suitable for all levels of diver, but only experienced divers should penetrate the hull. Visibility is often clearer on this wreck than on the others in the area.
Average depth: 20m (65ft)
Maximum depth: 31m (102ft)
This is the Japanese freighter *Tung Hwang*, whose last voyage was carrying cement from the Philippines destined for use on the Sultan of Brunei's palace; the builders rejected the cargo because of inferior quality. She was found sunk on 25 September 1980. The 2697-tonne ship, measuring 92m (300ft) by 15m (50ft) by 7.5m (25ft), sits absolutely upright on the bottom at 30m (100ft) with the anchor chain still out. Some of her masts

Opposite:*The superstructure of the Cement Wreck (Tung Hwang) is festooned with colourful soft corals and feather stars.*

have broken; those left rise to 8m (25ft). The roof of the wheelhouse is at 14m (45ft) and the main deck at 19m (65ft). In good visibility this wreck is extremely photogenic, and even in poor visibility she is well worth visiting for the colourful soft corals and feather stars that proliferate over all the superstructure.

This is one of the best wrecks for fish life, with shoals of sweetlips, barracuda, Rainbow Runners, fusiliers, batfish and the smaller sweepers and cardinalfish. Around the superstructure are large lionfish, hawkfish, filefish, Whitecheek Monocle Bream, angelfish, moray eels, Copperband Butterflyfish, scorpionfish, octopus, the occasional turtle and many smaller reef fish and nudibranchs. Large groupers and pufferfish hide in the hull, and Whitetip Reef Sharks are found by the stern. The superstructure around the funnel is a blaze of colour from soft corals, sponges and feather stars. There are also many sea urchins. Several fishing nets are snagged on the wreck.

3 AMERICAN WRECK

★★★★

Location: 24km (13 miles) southwest of Labuan Marina, southwest of the small Pulau Rusukan Besar on the Barat Banks; about 1.4km (3/4 mile) northwest of the Australian Wreck (Site 4).
Access: By speedboat (45min) from the marina.
Conditions: Often choppy, with a strong surface current, though usually less current down on the wreck itself; there may be none at all in the lee of the hull. Because of the way the ship has broken up, in poor conditions of visibility it can be difficult to keep your bearings while exploring the wreckage. Penetration of the hull is for experienced divers only.
Average depth: 20m (65ft)
Maximum depth: 30m (100ft)
The American Wreck has been identified as the US Navy's 808-tonne Admirable Class mine-hunter USS *Salute*. Measuring 56m (185ft) by 10m (33ft) by 5m (16ft), the ship was laid down on 11 November 1942 by the Winslow Marine Railway and Shipbuilding Co of Seattle; she was launched on 6 February 1943 (sponsored by Miss Patricia Lindgren) and commissioned on 4 December 1943. The ship was sunk by a Japanese mine on 17 June 1945, with the loss of over 100 men. The wreck is broken in half and folded back on itself, with the bow lying on top of the stern. The bottom is at 30m (100ft) on hard sand, and the shallowest part (the bow) is at 12m (40ft).

Although only experienced divers should contemplate penetrating the hull, there is plenty of marine life outside the wreck, and photographers will find no shortage of photogenic views. The fish fauna is good, with shoals of batfish, Spotted and Striped Sweetlips, cardinalfish,

ADVANCED WRECK DIVING

Penetrating large wrecks is advanced diving. You must be properly trained and equipped.

- Carry a sharp knife, a suitable monofilament line-cutter or scissors to cut fishing line and nets.
- Carry a good torch, plus a backup.
- Wear tough gloves.
- Choose to make your dive in slack water.
- If the wreck is not buoyed, drag a grapnel anchor onto it and buoy the line. The first pair of divers onto the wreck should tie the line off to it; the last pair of divers up should release it.
- On deep wrecks arrange a shotline as near vertical as you can to the part you wish to cover, so that descent and ascent are as quick as possible. Stage decompression can be carried out on the shotline, and for additional safety spare air cylinders, fitted with an octopus regulator, can be suspended on it at 10m (33ft) and 5m (16ft).
- Be extra vigilant at all times. Wrecks are always covered in fishing nets and lines. Visibility is often poor, and it is easy to make it poorer by stirring up sediment.
- When you move away from the shotline, take compass bearings and make a mental note of your movements. A tide-

change or stirred-up sediment can swiftly reduce visibility to near zero. If the visibility is really bad, fix a distance line to the base of the shotline.

If penetrating a wreck:

- Tie back or open entrance door or hatch so that it cannot close behind you.
- Tie off a lifeline and feed it out as you penetrate; alternatively, tie the lifeline to yourself and have your buddy (who remains outside) feed it out as you go through. If you become disorientated and sediment is stirred up, the lifeline will be your only guide to getting back out again.
- Don't forget to tie back any further doors or hatches you pass through.
- Beware parts of the wreck breaking up. Be especially careful with wooden wrecks, which often collapse.
- Leave yourself plenty of air to get out of the wreck and back to the shotline.
- If you have calculated slack water incorrectly there may be a strong current by the time you finish. A floating rope between the top of the shotline and the boat ladder is a useful precaution.

---

sweepers and fusiliers. There are also plenty of butterfly-fish, angelfish, scorpionfish, lionfish, octopus, grouper, moray eels, barracuda and small sharks, and large groupers, snappers and pufferfish hide in the hull. Not many corals are in evidence, but there are sponges, sea urchins, nudibranchs and algae.

4 AUSTRALIAN WRECK

★★★★

Location: 23km (14.5 miles) southwest of Labuan Marina, southwest of the small island of Rusukan Besar on the Barat Banks; about 1.4km (³/₄ mile) southeast of the American Wreck (Site 3).

Access: By speedboat (45min) from the marina.

Conditions: Often choppy, with a strong surface current, though usually less current down on the wreck itself; there may be none at all in the lee of the hull. Only experienced divers should penetrate the hull.

Average depth: 24m (80ft)

Maximum depth: 33m (110ft)

This is not the wreck of an Australian ship: the nickname derives from the fact that the ship was sunk in 1945 by the Australian Air Force. Measuring 85m (280ft) by 12m (40ft) by 6m (20ft), she was originally a Dutch passenger/cargo steamer, built in Rotterdam with Scottish engines in 1900; captured by the Japanese when they took Singapore in 1942, she was armed and then added to the Japanese fleet. She is thought to have been collecting booty from Brunei, Labuan, and Sarawak to take back to Japan when she was sunk. She now lies at a 50°

angle on her port side. The davits are at 18m (60ft) and the bottom is on sand at 33m (110ft); the starboard side is at 21m (70ft). The wooden decks have rotted away to leave just the skeleton.

There is an abundance of marine life: large shoals of jacks, snappers, sweetlips, fusiliers, cardinalfish and sweepers, with smaller shoals of batfish and barracuda. Large groupers, snappers and pufferfish hide in the hull. Large and small lionfish, scorpionfish, hawkfish, Whitecheek Monocle Bream, angelfish, butterflyfish, filefish, octopus and turtles can be seen around the superstructure, which is snagged with fishing nets and has many feather stars and soft corals. In good visibility there are many interesting angles for the photographer.

BARRACUDA

Although fearsome in appearance with protruding jaws and sharp teeth, barracudas found in this part of the world are not usually dangerous to divers. Barracudas are extremely effective predators. The body of the fish is streamlined for rapid movement, while the jaws are large with powerful fang-like teeth. They track down prey by sight and are attracted by the flash or glint in the sun of anything that could be taken for a sardine. Generally, barracudas do not threaten divers, however I have twice been attacked and bitten by a large, lone barracuda. The larger species seem to keep their distance which makes it difficult for underwater photographers to get a good close-up shot.

How to Get There

Labuan is easily accessible by air, sea or road, the final stage of your road journey being by ferry from Kota Kinabalu, Brunei or Sarawak. There are also direct flights to Labuan from Kuala Lumpur.

Kota Kinabalu is easily accessible by international flights from Kuala Lumpur, Hong Kong, Manila, Singapore, Bangkok, Brunei, Taipei and Seoul. It is also the take-off hub for flights to Tawau, Sandakan, Labuan and Kuching (Sarawak). The airport is 7km (4 miles) from the city centre.

By air-conditioned express ferry it is a 3hr trip from Kota Kinabalu. The ferry is in fact more convenient than flying, because in both Kota Kinabalu and Labuan the ferry terminal is right in the centre of town (in Kota Kinabalu it is in front of the Hotel Hyatt Kinabalu International); another point is that, returning this way, you don't have to worry about flying after diving. The one disadvantage is the fierce air-conditioning aboard the ferry: you might find a sweater useful.

Smaller boats ply between Labuan and the nearby Sabah mainland at Menumbok. They take about 1hr.

Where to Stay

Upper Price Range
Sheraton Manikar Resort Jalan Bata Manikar, Locked Bag 12, 87009 Labuan Federal Territory; tel 087–418700/ fax 087–418740

Medium Price Range
Mariner Hotel Jalan Tanjung Purun, PO Box 113, 87008 Labuan Federal Territory; tel 087–418822/fax 087–418811

Hotel Emas Labuan 27–28 Jalan Muhibbah, Labuan Federal Territory; tel 087–416288/fax 087–416255

Hotel Labuan Jalan Merdeka, PO Box 345 Labuan Federal Territory; tel 087–412311

Hotel Victoria Jalan Tun Mustapha, Labuan Federal Territory; tel 087–42411 Labuan Town used to be called Victoria.

Federal Inn PO Box 139, Jalan Dewan, Labuan Federal Territory; tel 087–417811/fax 087–417796

Lower Price Range
Kartika Saki Jalan Bunga Tanjung, Labuan Federal Territory; tel 087–414591

Hotel Pantai View Jalan Bunga Tanjung, Labuan Federal Territory; tel 087–411339

It is always worth doing a bit of haggling over the room-rates for cheaper accommodation in Labuan. One thing to beware of is that quite a few of the budget places are not so much hotels as houses of ill repute (the town is largely geared to entertain single oilmen on leave).

Where to Eat

There are top restaurants in the Sheraton and Emas hotels, and the Labuan Beach Restaurant, opposite the Hotel Tiara on Jalan Tanjung Batu, offers fairly expensive but very good food which you can eat on the terrace overlooking the beach. For cheaper meals the following is popular:

Seafood Sung Hwa 2nd Floor, Ujong Pasir, Jalan OKK Awang Besar, Labuan Federal Territory

There are also some excellent food-stalls, notably at the Medan Selera Labuan, down by the waterfront.

Dive Facilities

There are only two dive operators in Labuan, Borneo Divers and Ocean Sports. Both operators have dive-shops.

Borneo Divers Branch Office 359 Jalan Tanjung Purun, 87007 Labuan Federal Territory; tel 087–415867/fax 087–413454
Postal Address:
Locked Bag 15, 87009 Labuan Federal Territory
The Borneo Divers dive-shop is at the new marina, and all necessary equipment is available for rent.

Borneo Divers is Borneo's first and only professional full-service dive company, covering both sport and commercial diving. It is a PADI five-star Instructor Development Centre and, under Randy Davis at Labuan, a BSAC School. The wrecks off Labuan are ideal for Borneo Divers' PADI Wreck Diving Courses. Refer to page 140 for more about Borneo Divers and to page 141 for a list of the company's overseas agents.

Ocean Sports PO Box 179, 134 Jalan OKK Awang Besar, Labuan Federal Territory; tel 087–415389/fax 087–415697
The dive-shop is on these premises, and the training is under the PADI system.

Prices for diving with either operator, including transfers from accommodation, boat to and from the dive site, divemaster, tanks, weight belt and weights are US$40 for a single dive, US$70 for two dives on the same day.

Film Processing

The nearest E6 transparency processing is in Kota Kinabalu.

For the relevant addresses refer to the directory section covering Tunku Abdul Rahman Marine Park (page 107).

Hospital

Labuan Hospital
PO Box 6, 87008 Labuan; tel 087–413333/fax 087–413161

Local Highlights

Labuan is a federal territory governed directly from Kuala Lumpur. The island's duty-free status attracts people from Brunei and Malaysia on shopping sprees; however, when I was there in the autumn of 1993 I found little choice, and the prices were not especially low. Before October 1990 the duty exemptions did not include alcohol and cigarettes, but now the island has a real duty-free:

Labuan Duty Free
Bangunan Terminal, Jalan Merdeka; tel 087–411573.

Labuan is where the Japanese forces in North Borneo surrendered at the end of World War II, and there are appropriate memorials to both Allied and Japanese personnel who lost their lives here. It was also here that the Japanese officers responsible for the death march from Sandakan to Ranau were tried by an Australian war-crimes court.

Currently Labuan is mainly an oilman's port, and several bars cater for single oilmen on leave; best known of these are the **Relax Bar** and the larger **Jupiter Bar**. The locals favour karaoke bars which make for an enjoyable, if noisy, night out.

There is an old brick coal chimney at **Tanjung Kubong (Coal Point)**, and illegal cockfights, a great attraction for Filipinos, are held on Sunday afternoons.

The proximity of Labuan Federal Territory to Sabah, Sarawak and Brunei means that the tourist sites in these areas can be easily visited from there; refer to the regional directories covering Tunku Abdul Rahman Park, Turtle Islands Park and Pulau Sipadan (see pages 106, 126 and 138 respectively) for further details.

Kota Kinabalu travel agents (see page 97) can organize excursions in Sarawak. There you can travel up rivers to visit **tribal longhouses**, one of the world's largest caves and picturesque limestone pinnacles at **Mulu National Park**, and the **Orangutan sanctuary at Semongoh.** The Orangutans can be readily seen at a rehabilitation centre in the forest. They are mostly immature individuals. Mature, wild male Orangutans are immensely strong and there have been several reports of attacks on park rangers.

Night diving and snorkelling divide naturally into three periods. Dusk, when there is still plenty of light above water, is good for feather stars, brittle stars and basket stars, especially on fringing reefs. The normal time for night diving is between 19:00hrs and 21:00hrs. If you want to be sure of seeing parrotfish in their protective cocoons (see below) you should go much later – certainly after 22:00hrs, and possibly after midnight.

There is little to be gained by going deep: 3–5m (10–16ft) – a depth easy to snorkel to – is far enough down for you to see most things. From here you can easily watch basket stars, feather stars, urchins, crabs, lobsters, shellfish, sea hares, flat worms and the smaller nudibranchs and reef fish on top of the reef or along a shallow drop-off.

Choose an area where the wave and current action is minimal, and where there are easy marks for navigation; if you have not dived at night before, begin with a dusk dive. Either way, dive the area first during daylight to familiarize yourself with its topography. In terms of navigation, the easiest night dives are out and back along the face at a reef edge: go out at 6m (20ft), against the current (if any), and come back at 3m (10ft), with the current. Wear sufficient protective clothing: you are certain to bump into things. Before you enter the water, check all your diving and camera equipment is functioning correctly, and check it again once you are in the water.

LIGHTING

Lighting is obviously an important matter. In resorts or on boats where night diving and snorkelling are organized it is customary to have an underwater light or chemical lightstick to mark the entry/exit point. Elsewhere, if you are diving from a boat, fix chemical light-sticks to the boarding ladder and ascent/descent line; if you are diving from a beach align two lights on the shore in the direction of your exit.

TORCHES

For personal lighting as you explore you need a hand-torch. Helmet-mounted torches are merely a nuisance, because plankton and other small creatures attracted to the light swim around in front of your eyes, spoiling your vision by back-scattering light.

Torches can fail, of course, either from water leakage or because the batteries go flat, so it is worth carrying a spare. Remember that rechargeable torches go out with no warning as their nickel-cadmium batteries discharge;

use alkaline batteries in your back-up light. Small `Q light' torches make good, cheap back-up lights (or even as main lights), and photographers can also use them as focusing lights.

A wrist lanyard is another good idea: it will keep your torch conveniently nearby if you drop it, or if you need a spare hand for anything. Divers often keep a chemical light-stick attached to their cylinder or weight-belt so they can be easily found if their torches fail.

FLOODLIGHTS

Some resorts and boats set floodlights over the water so that clients above water can watch the antics of fish, octopuses and cuttlefish. However, these lights also attract hordes of small biting creatures to the surface. Swimming through these swarms can be uncomfortable, to say the least.

DANGERS

The dangers of night diving and snorkelling are not sharks, which are rarely seen at night, but more familiar creatures. While your vision is limited by the range and breadth of your torchlight it is easy to brush against organisms you would normally avoid, like fire coral, lionfish, stinging hydroids, spiny urchins,

scorpionfish and stonefish. In fact, scorpion-fish often get their camouflage wrong, so that they are easily seen bright red in the torch-light, but stonefish are even more difficult to see at night than they are during the day, often giving themselves away only by moving.

Opposite: *Darkband Fusilier (Pterocaesio tile), the most wide-ranging and often the most common of fusiliers, showing night-time coloration.*

Below: *Divers prepare for a night dive. Underwater exploration by torchlight can reveal a world hidden from sight during the day.*

SABAH: EAST/SOUTHEAST COAST

Eastern Sabah is less mountainous than the western part of the state and has traditionally been a land of cocoa and timber. However, in recent times world cocoa prices have fallen and eastern Sabah's timber is running out, so much of the land is now being made over to the cultivation of oil palms.

SANDAKAN

The region's biggest town is Sandakan, which used to be the state capital and was hugely prosperous because of the timber trade – at one time it was said to have more millionaires than anywhere else in the world. Due to its wealth and the large number of Chinese traders who settled here, it became known as Sabah's Hong Kong. All that changed at the end of World War II, when the town was flattened by Allied bombing. Soon afterwards the capital was transferred to Kota Kinabalu (then called Jesselton). But today Sandakan is thriving once again, exporting logs, palm oil and swiftlets' nests for use in making birds'-nest soup; it is also Malaysia's biggest fishing port and a major exporter of frozen prawns and other seafood.

To the visitor, Sandakan is the gateway to the Turtle Islands Park, the Kinabatangan River and the Sepilok Orangutan Sanctuary, one of only three in the world — the other two are in Sarawak and Sumatra, respectively. Another gateway is Tawau, previously known for logging and for cocoa estates: it is through Tawau that you reach the world-class diving at Pulau Sipadan and Pulau Sangalakki.

TRAVEL

Most visitors go by air between Kota Kinabalu, Sandakan and Tawau, since the road system in the region cannot be described as good. Moreover, although the area's many migrants and refugees from Indonesia and the southern Philippines are a source of cheap labour, their presence also presents problems, and the Malaysian government sets up road blocks to stop their free movement; bona fide visitors travelling overland can encounter difficulties at such places. Nevertheless, despite this, there is much to interest the dedicated traveller.

Opposite: *A beautiful tropical island off Semporna, on the east coast of Sabah, Malaysia.*
Above: *Hawksbill Turtle (Eretmochelys imbricata). This is the smallest of the marine turtle species.*

Turtle Islands Park

Turtle Islands Park lies close to the Philippines border, 40km (25 miles) north of Sandakan, and comprises three islands: Pulau Selingan, Pulau Gulisan and Pulau Bakkungan Kecil. The park was gazetted in 1977 to protect the Green and Hawksbill Turtles that lay eggs on the beaches here. Green Turtles (*Chelonia mydas*) make up 80% of the turtles in the park, with Pulau Selingan their preferred island for nesting. Hawksbill Turtles (*Eretmochelys imbricata*) prefer Pulau Gulisan. The turtles nest all year round, but the peak season for Green Turtles is August–October and that for Hawksbill Turtles February–April.

PULAU SELINGAN

On Pulau Selingan, the second largest island in the group – 8ha (20 acres) – lantanas grow under coconut palms. The main turtle beaches are on the east side of the island and on the southwest side near to the lighthouse beach; most of the northern shore is rocky. The beaches shelve off as sandy bottoms with some sea grasses; they are good for swimming but not for snorkelling.

TURTLE ISLANDS PARK CHRONOLOGY

- **1966 (1 August):** Malaysia's first turtle hatchery, financed by the Government, established on Pulau Selingan.
- **1971:** The Sabah government compulsorily buys the privately owned Pulau Selingan, Pulau Bakkungan Kecil and Pulau Gulisan for 89,000 ringgits.
- **1972:** The three islands are constituted as game and bird sanctuaries under the Forestry Department
- **1977:** The government converts the three islands, plus the surrounding coral reefs and the seas between the islands, into a 1740ha (4300-acre) Marine Park.

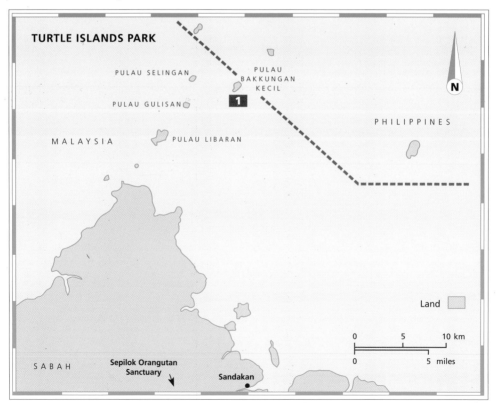

ACCOMMODATION

Pulau Selingan is the only island with accommodation: three multiple-room chalets (somewhat in need of repairs). For fresh water, rain is collected in tanks, and there is only intermittent electricity. There is also an information centre cum restaurant, which is in better condition, plus a ranger station and a turtle hatchery.

Pulau Bakkungan Kecil, the largest island – 8.5ha (21 acres) – is also the one closest to the Philippines border; it has a wide promontory to the southeast. Unlike the other two islands it boasts a small hill at its centre, with active mud volcanoes. The island has coconut palms over lalang grass. There are staff quarters for the hatchery.

Pulau Gulisan, the smallest island – only 1.6ha (4 acres) – is again covered in coconut palms and lalang grass.

Green Turtle (Chelonia mydas) returning to the sea at dawn after laying her eggs.

1 PULAU BAKKUNGAN KECIL: SOUTHERN END

★★★

Location: 100m (110yd) west from the southern end of Pulau Bakkungan Kecil.
Access: By boat (10min) from the accommodation on Pulau Selingan; you may be charged an extra 10 ringgits.
Conditions: Calm; average visibility about 20m (50ft).
Average depth: 1m (40in)
Maximum depth: 1.5m (5ft)

A stony coral garden that is as good as those at Pulau Sipadan (see page 130). There are good blue, green and yellow staghorn corals, large table corals, lots of blue sea stars, black sea cucumbers, salps, Chevron Butterflyfish, parrotfish, damselfish and shoals of fusiliers and catfish.

MAGANGS

En route to Pulau Selingan, in Sandakan Bay, you can see hundreds of *magangs*. These fish-traps, set in 12m (40ft) of water, consist of a bamboo framework supporting fine mesh nets. They are submerged at night, and kerosene lamps are lit on the framework above the water. The main catch is Whitebait.

Turtle Islands Park

HOW TO GET THERE

Kota Kinabalu to Sandakan is a 50min flight by Malaysian Airlines. At Sandakan you transfer to the main jetty, where you pick up a small speedboat for the 1hr 20min ride to Pulau Selingan. If you have not already arranged a boat you can fix one up through the local agents or barter at the jetty.

HELICOPTER SERVICE

Kota Kinabalu
Sabah Air Pte Ltd Sabah Air Building, Locked Bag 113, Old Airport Road, 88999 Kota Kinabalu; tel 088–56733/fax 088–235195

Tawau
Sabah Air Pte Ltd Locked Bag 15, Tawau Airport, 91009 Tawau; tel 089–774005

Sandakan
Sabah Air Pte Ltd, Sabah Air Hangar Locked Bag 56, Sandakan Airport, 90009 Sandakan; tel 089–660527/fax 089–660545 (payload limit 425kg; 935 pounds)

WHERE TO STAY

Accommodation on Pulau Selingan has to be organized on the mainland through

Park Warden Regional Office East Coast Parks Room 906, 9th Floor, Wisma Khoo Lebuh Tiga; tel 089–273453/fax 089–214570
Postal Address:
PO Box 768, Sandakan

You can do this direct or use one of the tour agents listed on page 127.

Sandakan
Upper Price Range
Ramada Renaissance Hotel Mile 1, Jalan Utara, 90007 Sandakan; tel 089–213299/fax 089–271271

Medium Price Range
Hotel Hsiang Garden Hsiang Garden Estate, Mile 1.5, Jalan Leila, Sandakan; tel 089–273122/fax 089–273127

Hotel Ramai Kilometre 1.5, Jalan Leila Sandakan; tel 089–273222/fax 089–271884

Hotel Nak Edinburgh Street, Sandakan; tel 089–272988/fax 089–272879

City View Hotel Lot 1, Block 23, 3rd Avenue, Sandakan; tel 089–271122/fax 089–273115

Hung Wing Hotel, Jalan Tiga, Sandakan; tel 089–218855/fax 089–18895

Uncle Tan's address on page 127

WHERE TO EAT

Sandakan is famous for inexpensive and delicious seafood; cuisines include Chinese, Indonesian/Malay and Indian Muslim, and you can also find Western, Japanese and Korean food. Try the **Ming Restaurant** in the Ramada Renaissance Hotel and the restaurant in the City View Hotel (addresses above), as well as:

XO Steak House Hsiang Garden Estate (opposite Hsiang Garden Hotel), Mile 1.5, Jalan Leila; tel 089–44033
Good selection of Western-style grilled and barbecued Australian Steak, plus seafood.

Seoul Garden Korean Restaurant Hsiang Garden Estate, Mile 1.5, Jalan Leila; tel 089–43891

DIVE FACILITIES

The nearest dive-shop is in Tawau and the nearest diving facilities are those of the Pulau Sipadan operators (see page 138).

FILM PROCESSING

There are several mini-labs for print film in Sandakan. E6 processing can be organized by **Sandakan Photo** on Jalan Dua.

HOSPITALS

Queen Elizabeth Hospital
88586 Kota Kinabalu; tel 088–218166/fax 088–211999

Health and Paramedic Service
PO Box 11201, 88813 Kota Kinabalu; tel 088–50555/fax 088–221248

LOCAL HIGHLIGHTS

It is well worth spending at least half a day looking around Sandakan town. The ornate Chinese temple of **Pui Gisin** is the largest in Sabah. The people of **Bajau water village**, the oldest village in Sandakan, are friendly and like being photographed. Other places worth going to include the house of **Agnes Newton Keith** (author of *The Land Below the Wind* [1939] and of various books describing life under the Japanese occupation), the **mosque** and the stone **Church of St Michael's of All Angels**. There is a **crocodile farm** at 8 Labuk Road, near the airport.

The **Sepilok Orangutan Rehabilitation Centre**, 25km (15 miles; 30min) outside Sandakan, is a must. Umbrellas/raincoats and mosquito repellent are useful. Feeding times are 10:00 and 14:30hrs daily except Fridays, when they are 09:30hrs and 14:30hrs. When I first visited the main feeding station it had too many visitors at feeding times, and the Orangutans and Long-tailed Macaques were snatching visitors' belong-

NEARBY ATTRACTIONS

There are many islands off the north and east coasts of Sabah. These have been heavily blast-fished, and some belong to other countries. Borneo Divers reconnoitred the diving on most of them and concluded that Sipadan and Sangalakki were better for their operations. However, the two live-aboard dive-boats MV Coral Topaz and MV Spirit of Borneo are currently looking at all these areas again to see what they can find.

ings; visitor numbers are now restricted, and the animals no longer give any problem.

Just outside Sandakan, at Mile 7 on Labuk Road, there is a **war memorial** to the hundreds of Australian prisoners of war who died under the Japanese in 1944 on the death marches to Ranau.

Across Sandakan Bay and some 20km (12miles) inland are the **Gomantong Caves**, famous for their bats and swiftlets' nests. The nests, made of saliva, are collected six-monthly for birds'-nest soup. The cave floors are 50cm (20in) or more deep in droppings, so wear sensible footwear.

Further afield is the **Kinabatangan River**, where you can see Proboscis Monkeys and Long-tailed Macaques (Crab-eating Monkeys). These come to the river only at dawn and at dusk, so to catch sight of them you must stay overnight in simple lodges around Sakau and cruise the river in small boats at the appropriate times. You will need fast film if you want to photograph the monkeys.

On the road to Lahad Datu, about 1km (0.6 mile) north of the Kinabatangan Bridge, is **Batuh Puteh Tulug** ('White Stone' or 'White Cliff'). Small caves high on this cliff contain very ancient wooden coffins; some

VISITORS AND TURTLES

On these islands the gravid turtles usually climb the beach between 20:00hrs and dawn, when the tide is high. Visitors are sensibly not allowed to walk around the beach at night, but the rangers carry portable radios and call up the visitors when they find the first turtle laying eggs. Only one turtle may be disturbed each night for photography, and then only once she has laid her eggs. Visitors are afterwards taken to the hatchery, where they can help collect and count the evening's hatchlings and release them into the sea.

of these have been removed to the **Sabah State Museum** in Kota Kinabalu, but those that remain are very interesting. Also in these caves you can get a close look at swiftlets' nests without having to make a dangerous climb.

TOUR AGENTS HANDLING TURTLE ISLANDS PARK

Kota Kinabalu
Api Tours (Borneo) Sdn Bhd Lot G31/32, Ground Floor, Wisma Sabah, PO Box 12853, 88831 Kota Kinabalu, Sabah, East Malaysia; tel 088–221233/fax 088–221230

Exotic Adventures (Borneo) Sdn Bhd 1st Floor,Lot 6, Block J, Segama Complex, PO Box 13805, 88844 Kota Kinabalu, Sabah; tel 088–222499/fax 088–221749

Sandakan
East Malaysia Travel Co. 53 Jalan Tiga, Sandakan; tel 089–212600

Intra Travel Service Sdn Bhd Ground Floor, Sandakan Rural District Council, Lot 2A & 2B, PO Box 1459

Alexander Ian Chong PO Box 521, 90007 Sandakan; tel 089–660241/fax 089–667688

SI Tours Lot 3B, 3rd Floor Yeng Ho Hong Building, Sandakan; tel 089–213502/fax 089–271513

Wildlife Expeditions Room 903, 9th Floor, Wisma Khoo Siak Chiew, Sandakan; tel 089–219616/fax 089–214570 (offices in the Ramada Renaissance Hotel)

Discovery Tours Room 1008, 10th Floor, Wisma Khoo Siak Chiew, Sandakan; tel 089–274106/fax 089–274107

Uncle Tan's Km 29 (Mile 17½) Labuk Road (5km; 3 miles) beyond the Sepilok junction); tel 089–216227/fax 089–271215 A specialist in cheaper accommodation and tours for the budget traveller.

This beach on Pulau Selingan, Turtle Islands Park, has overhanging branches which provide shelter for nesting turtles.

Semporna Marine Park

Semporna is a lively, bustling town, renowned for its delicious seafood. Fish markets on the waterfront sell crabs, lobsters, prawns and many varieties of fish.

SEMPORNA'S OFFSHORE ISLANDS
Semporna's offshore islands are gradually being discovered by the diving fraternity. However, even though the two groups of islands off Semporna, the Ligitan group and the Gaya group, have an underwater species diversity on a par with that of Australia's Great Barrier Reef – as good, in fact, as that around Pulau Sipadan. Pulau Sipadan remains the island of choice in the area.

DIVING OFF SEMPORNA

The resort on Pulau Mabul runs PADI courses up to Divemaster level and organizes three dives daily on Pulau Sipadan, 15km (9 miles; 15min) away by speedboat:

Sipadan-Mabul Resort
2nd Floor, Tong Hing Supermarket Building
55 Jalan Gaya (PO Box 14125)
88847 Kota Kinabalu
tel 088—230006
fax 088—242003

CONTINENTAL SHELF
The islands are all on the continental shelf, so the waters are shallow, with a maximum depth of 25m (82ft). The Ligitan group is on the edge of the shelf, south of which the seafloor falls away to 600m (2000ft) and more around Pulau Sipadan. It comprises three areas: Pulau Mabul, Pulau Kapalai and the Ligitan Reefs. This latter area bears the brunt of blast- and poison-fishing. Captain Sim recommends Pulau Kapalai for its nudibranch colonies and tells me that Pulau Mabul still has some good diving, as the presence of a police camp on the island protected it from the worst ravages of the blast-fishermen.

THE GAYA GROUP
The more important Gaya group consists of nine islets and reefs: Pulau Gaya, Pulau Mantabuan, Pulau Boheydulong, Pulau Maiga, Pulau Sibuon, Kapikan Reef, Church Reef, Pulau Sabangkat and Pulau Selakan. Located about 25km (16 miles) northeast of Semporna, the central islands of Pulau Boheydulong and Pulau Gaya comprise part of a now flooded volcanic caldera. These two islands are rugged, and there is a high peak – 455m (1493ft) – on Pulau Gaya. Both have been protected in the past: Pulau Boheydulong was declared a bird sanctuary in 1933, a status revoked in 1978, the year after the revocation of Pulau Gaya's Forest Reserve status. However, things are beginning to look up again: the first stage in gazetting Pulau Boheydulong as a Marine Park has recently been completed. Although in general these islands have been heavily exploited by an increasing population, luckily Pulau Boheydulong was until recently partially spared thanks to the presence there of a now defunct Japanese commercial pearl farm.

Borneo Divers and Pulau Sipadan Resort personnel have checked out most of the possible dive sites in the area, and WWF/Sabah Parks scientists completed detailed surveys in 1980 and 1987. Certainly there is some good diving and snorkelling here, but so far there is only one organized resort, on Pulau Mabul (see above).

Opposite: *An impressive view of Pulau Gaya, a crater island off Semporna in Sabah, Malaysia.*

Pulau Sipadan Marine Reserve

This is without doubt the destination that gained Malaysian diving its world-class reputation. Pulau Sipadan (the name means 'Border Island' in Malay) has the world's best beach diving, with a deep drop-off only a few swimming strokes from the accommodation run by two of its three dive operators.

Situated 35km (22 miles; 45min by speedboat) south of Semporna, off the southeast coast of Sabah, Pulau Sipadan lies just north of the equator in the Celebes (Sulawesi) Sea. It is 10km (6 miles) south of the continental shelf and is the peak of a volcanic base that rises steeply from depths of 600m (2000ft). Only 12ha (30 acres) in area and never more than a few metres above sea-level, the island is covered in tropical rainforest and ringed with a narrow, white sandy beach. You can walk right round this perimeter beach in 15–20min.

BIRD SANCTUARY
Though Pulau Sipadan was declared a bird sanctuary in 1933 and re-gazetted in 1963 after Independence, it was never managed in any way. Moreover, its ownership was regularly disputed between Malaysia and Indonesia – and, to a lesser extent, the Philippines – not to mention one Malaysian who still claims the island was given to his grandfather by the Sultan of Sulu.

DIVING DEVELOPMENTS
Sports divers began venturing into the area in the late 1970s, and a combined WWF/Sabah Parks team made a preliminary marine survey in 1980 (many of its members were in the

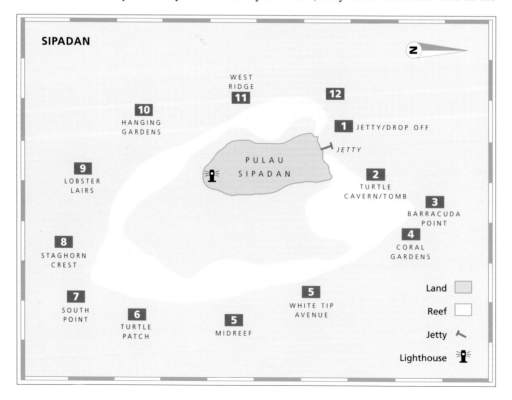

team that completed a second survey in 1992). Poor anchorage, regular pirate activity and blast-fishing (as late as 1985) kept visitors down, and the few who did venture here used self-contained boats or camped on the beach. By 1988, however, Borneo Divers gained permission to build more permanent accommodation (opened 1989), and Mike Wong came on the first of many visits which culminated in his evocative book *Sipadan – Borneo's Underwater Paradise* (1991). In 1989 Jacques Cousteau and his team arrived with the research vessel *Calypso*; the great Frenchman was moved to say: 'I have seen other places like Sipadan, 45 years ago, but now no more. Now we have found an untouched piece of art.'

OUTSTANDING MARINE LIFE

Underwater, Pulau Sipadan has just about everything the Indo-Pacific has to offer. The waters teem with fish, many inquisitive enough to approach divers: expect to be regularly buzzed by shoals of fusiliers, barracuda, batfish, sweetlips, jacks, goatfish and a huge shoal of Bumphead Parrotfish. At least six species of clownfish inhabit the colourful sea anemones. Timid Whitetip Reef Sharks are common, but the other sharks less so – although Hammerhead, Grey Reef and Variegated (Leopard) Sharks are seen occasionally, as are Manta Rays and Eagle Rays, with Blue-spotted Rays being common. If you dive down a shotline in open water off the reef you may encounter tuna.

A CORAL PARADISE

Pulau Sipadan's coral, fish and turtle life is prolific: more than 200 species of fish have been recorded and over 70 genera of corals, so that the area matches Australia's Great Barrier Reef in terms of species diversity.

The shallow-water areas are largely covered with corals in excellent condition, with broad expanses of staghorn and table corals, plate and lettuce corals, boulder and brain corals, encrusting corals, bubble corals and solitary mushroom corals. Interspersed among the stony corals are large leathery *Sarcophyton* and *Sinularia* corals, constantly pulsating *Xenia* corals and colourful *Dendronephthya* soft-tree corals. Here, too, are sponges, including vase and barrel sponges, plus sea squirts, oysters and Giant Clams. Although fire coral is uncommon, there are plenty of stinging hydroids.

The drop-off walls are less luxuriant, but have gardens of colourful *Tubastrea* and *Dendrophyllia* species under overhangs, together with sponges, gorgonian sea fans and *Dendronephthya* soft-tree corals. Deeper down on the walls are huge gorgonian sea fans, black corals, large barrel sponges covered in Alabaster Sea Cucumbers, and very big *Dendronephthya* soft corals.

TURTLES

But what makes Pulau Sipadan really stand out are the turtles. Massive 140kg (300-pound) Green Turtles and smaller Hawksbill Turtles are everywhere. Often you can see 20–30 on a single dive; usually they ignore you entirely so that they can concentrate on the serious business of eating, sleeping and scratching parasites off their backs on the coral. The main time for nesting is in August. Official egg collectors legally operate here, but nests near the resorts are often sponsored by tourists to allow the eggs to hatch out. Currently the island is in the care of the Ministry of Tourism and Environmental Development under the Department of Wildlife, which has stationed a team of park rangers on the island to oversee its affairs. The turtles should never be disturbed before they start laying or they will give up and return to the sea, so walking around the island at night without a ranger is forbidden.

On land, aside from rare fowl and migratory birds, there are Monitor Lizards as well as huge Robber Crabs (*Birgus latro*); now rare elsewhere, these are often called Coconut Crabs because of their habit of climbing coconut palms to feed on the fruit. Fruit bats active at night can be extremely noisy.

Pulau Sipadan can be dived all year round, but the weather is calmest and driest from May to October. August is the local holiday high season. Visibility is unpredictable – it can be murky one day and crystal-clear the next – but in general you can expect it to be about 30m (100ft).

EXCELLENT DIVING

The diving on offer usually consists of three daily boat dives plus unlimited shore dives; if you dive to the limit you should take a day off to de-gas after four or five days. To eliminate anchor damage, the boat dives, from small fibreglass boats holding up to eight divers always accompanied by a resort divemaster, are all drift-dives, even if there is no current. The dive sites are never more than 10min from the resort, so you board the boats from the beach fully kitted up.

On most sites there is excellent diving, whether in deep water on the wall or shallow water on the reef crest. The obvious scheme is to start with the deepest point, gradually rising to shallow water beside or over the reef top, where you can de-gas pleasantly while observing the beauty at this depth. At all sites except Turtle Cavern you can snorkel happily along the edge of the drop-off and see just as much reef life as the divers, although of course you would miss the gorgonian sea fans, black corals and deeper-dwelling sharks and pelagic visitors.

Shore dives and night dives are from the beach in front of the chalets, where a swim of 5–10m (16–33ft), depending on the height of the tide, brings you to the drop-off.

On morning dives you are regularly shaken by blast-fishing explosions off nearby islands. There is a legend that a huge scarlet octopus used to frighten fishermen off the island, but unfortunately this monster did not deter all of them, as there are some shallow-water areas where blast-fishing has occured.

However it is not effective in deep water so most of Pulau Sipadan has been spared.

Opposite: *Gorgonian Sea fan (Melithaea squamata).*

Below: *Pulau Sipadan is a diver's paradise of coral and teeming marine life.*

1 THE JETTY, JETTY BEACH AND DROP-OFF BELOW

★★★★★★☆☆☆☆

Location: In front of Borneo Divers and Pulau Sipadan Resort.
Access: Enter the water and swim out 5–10m (16–33ft), depending on the height of the tide.
Conditions: Generally calm; occasionally a slight current.
Average depth: Whatever you like
Maximum depth: 600m (2000ft)

This has to be the world's best beach dive and one of the world's top night dives. The drop-off goes down deeper than divers can dive and of course snorkellers will be limited in their depth, but there is a tremendous amount of interest just in the top 10m (33ft) or so. Under the jetty and to the east of it you find coral with shoals of goatfish and catfish, sea urchins, sea stars and crabs. West of the jetty there is sand frequented by small shoals of fish plus gobies with Bulldozer Shrimps and the occasional large barracuda. (At night I have photographed the rare Zebra Lionfish on this sand.)

Once you go over the drop-off you encounter a huge shoal of jacks and smaller shoals of Spotted Sweetlips and juvenile batfish. Descending the drop-off from 10m to 20m (33–65ft) you come to overhangs and caverns which during the day contain colourful angelfish, butterfly fish, Map and Porcupine Pufferfish, lionfish, scorpionfish and leaf fish, Spotted and Vlaming's Unicornfish, Moorish Idols, Orange-striped and Clown Triggerfish, Giant Moray Eels, various nudibranchs and flat worms, blue and yellow sea squirts, and assorted sponges and anemones (including a rare small white anemone) with clownfish. At night these caves contain parrotfish sleeping in their cocoons, Bumphead Parrotfish, turtles and pufferfish, large *Linckia* sea stars, flashlight fish, scorpionfish, crabs, shrimps and Snowflake Moray Eels. On many night dives here I have been able to study huge sleeping Bumphead Parrotfish and a colossal male Green Turtle at less than arm's-length. Whitetip Reef Sharks patrol the face at dawn and dusk.

2 TURTLE CAVERN

★★★★★

Location: East of the jetty.
Access: Swim out from the jetty beach over the drop-off, turn right (east) and continue along the wall until you reach the cavern entrance on a sandy patch at 18m (60ft).
Conditions: This is an advanced dive on which it is possible to get dangerously lost; the resort operators sensibly insist you are accompanied by one of their divemasters. You require a reliable and powerful underwater light and

a backup. It is easy to stir up silt and spoil the visibility. There may be some current along the wall. Snorkelling is not possible.
Average depth: 15–20m (50–65ft), but the main entrance is at the deepest point
Maximum depth: 21m (70ft)

The famous Turtle Cavern has been romanticized as the place where turtles go to die. The truth is more straightforward. The drowned turtles here probably entered at dusk and got lost in the interconnecting caverns because, when darkness fell, there was no light to guide them out. One of the bodies on view was put here by a film crew.

The caverns were formed as a result of weathering during the last Ice Age when sea levels were 100m (330ft) or so lower than at present. The main entrance is a large cavern on sand at 18m (60ft) with a resident Star Pufferfish and various little shoals of smaller fish. This cavern descends to 21m (70ft). At the back of it you swim up through a tunnel into a smaller cavern which now contains a marlin skeleton (put here by a resort divemaster). The various interconnecting caverns rise to less than 4m (13ft) from the surface and at the furthest point are 70m (230ft) inland from the main entrance. The dark caverns are also home to shoals of flashlight fish and specialized shrimps and crabs.

3 BARRACUDA POINT

★★★★★★☆☆☆☆

Location: The northernmost point, on the east side of the reef.
Access: By boat (a few min) east from jetty beach.
Conditions: This dive can be a bit rough, with variable and possibly strong currents that sometimes reverse. Novices should stay with the divemaster.
Average depth: 14m (45ft)
Maximum depth: 600m (2000ft)

This dive got its name from the very large shoal (500–1000) of barracuda often seen on the point. (This shoal is often seen also at the South Point [Site 7] and sometimes disappears for a couple of weeks.) It is interesting to enter the eye of the shoal and experience this immense number of fish circling around you – although some divers freak out when they find so many eyes watching them!

The site varies with depth. In the shallower waters it has coral heads on coral rubble and sand, sloping gently out and down. At the point itself there are Garden Eels; the many Whitetip Reef Sharks that lie on the sand during the day are very timid and difficult to approach closely.

There are few angelfish and butterflyfish here but plenty of just about everything else, including blue and yellow seas quirts, nudibranchs, flat worms, sting rays, moray eels, cuttlefish, many varieties of pufferfish, scorpionfish, stonefish, surgeonfish, flounders and crocodilefish. The area has many large Green Turtles, either sleeping under coral heads while surgeonfish feed on the algae on their shells or scratching themselves on the coral to try to remove barnacles. Trumpetfish hide in whip corals, colourful feather stars spread out in the current on any support they can find, and various pelagic species cruise around.

4 CORAL GARDENS

★★★★★★☆☆☆☆

Location: The northeast face of the reef, southeast of Barracuda Point.
Access: By boat (5min) east and then south around the island from the jetty beach.
Conditions: Normally a gentle current; occasionally stronger.
Average depth: 10m (33ft) along the reef crest
Maximum depth: 600m (2000ft)
You can descend the drop-off, but the beauty of this dive is to be found on the coral crest. Vast fields of stony corals are interspersed with smaller areas of soft corals, large boulder corals and large leathery corals and sponges. The staghorn corals are particularly prolific and colourful. This is a paradise for photographers, with just about every type of colourful Pacific reef fish you could think of, from tiny Anthias, Fire Gobies, Chromis, sergeant majors and damselfish through most of the smaller angelfish and butterflyfish to the larger Emperor, Yellowmask and Six-band angelfish. There are shoals of jacks, Rainbow Runners, fusiliers, goatfish and snappers. On one dive here I encountered a shoal of nearly 100 Bumphead Parrotfish. Batfish hover at cleaning stations, and Powder-blue Surgeonfish, Sleek, Spotted and Vlaming's Unicornfish, Picasso, Orange-striped, Titan and Clown Triggerfish, Moorish Idols and bannerfish all flit among the corals. Groupers, Coral Trout, hawkfish, soldierfish, Golden Rabbitfish, squirrelfish and bigeyes pause on or under corals. Parrotfish and Giant Wrasse cruise around, and a remarkable variety of anemones play host

to clownfish. Colourful feather stars are everywhere.

As well as the more common Green Turtles, Hawksbill Turtles can be found on the edge of the drop-off, often feeding on sponges.

5 WHITETIP AVENUE AND MID REEF

★★★★★☆☆☆☆☆

Location: The central part of the east face of the reef.
Access: By boat (10min) east and then south around the island from the jetty beach.
Conditions: Current usually gentle; can get stronger. Suitable for inexperienced divers *except* deep over the drop-off.
Average depth: 16m (52ft) for the reef crest
Maximum depth: 600m (2000ft)
There are two dives here, either on the reef crest or over the drop-off in deeper water. The reef crest is covered in stony and soft corals with most of the colourful Pacific reef fish you associate with them as well as oysters, Giant Clams and many turtles.

In deeper water over the drop-off, especially between 30m (100ft) and 50m (165ft), there are big black corals, huge gorgonian sea fans (often hiding Longnose Hawkfish and adorned with feather stars) and many large barrel sponges covered in Alabaster Sea Cucumbers. In strong currents *Dendronephthya* soft-tree corals swell up to impressive dimensions. Further down, Whitetip Reef Sharks and Grey Reef Sharks cruise the wall. In strong currents, I have started a dive at Mid Reef or Turtle Patch (Site 6) and finished at the jetty beach, having in the interim used up the 36-exposure films in both my cameras!

6 TURTLE PATCH

★★★★★☆☆☆☆☆

Location: The southern end of the east face of the reef.
Access: By boat (10min) east and then south around the island from the jetty beach.
Conditions: Usually calm with a light current, but the current can get stronger.
Average depth: 14m (45ft)
Maximum depth: 600m (2000ft)
This dive is very similar to Mid Reef and Whitetip Avenue (Site 5) but with even more turtles. I once spent 20min here photographing a Hawksbill Turtle close-up while it ripped apart a sponge deep in a crevice between corals; it was too intent on feeding to pay any attention to me! This is another area where I have encountered the huge shoal of Bumphead Parrotfish mentioned at Site 4. Immature Whitetip Reef Sharks can be found hiding in small coral crevices. There are lots of very large table corals.

7 SOUTH POINT

8 STAGHORN CREST

9 LOBSTER LAIRS

★★★★★☆☆☆☆☆

Location: The southern end of the reef: the South Point is the southernmost point of the east face; Staghorn Crest is immediately west of South Point; Lobster Lairs is at the southern end of the west face.

Access: By boat (10min) either way around the island from the jetty beach.

Conditions: Like Barracuda Point (Site 3) these dives can be a bit rough, with variable and often strong currents which may reverse during the dive. Novices should stay with the divemaster.

Average depth: 20m (65ft)

Maximum depth: 600m (2000ft)

In many ways these dives are rather similar to Barracuda Point (Site 3), with coral heads on coral rubble and sand. The currents are often too strong for the less sturdy corals and their associated fish, but just about everything else is to be found here.

Bracing yourself for photography can be difficult, but there is plenty worth photographing. The huge Barracuda shoal (see Site 3) is often seen on the South Point, as are other pelagic species including Manta Rays and Eagle Rays. A dozen or more Whitetip Reef Sharks and the occasional Leopard (Variegated) Shark rest on the sand at the point. There are lots of shoaling fish, especially fusiliers, snappers and Rainbow Runners, plus unicornfish, batfish, surgeonfish, jacks, scorpionfish, stonefish, crocodilefish, flounders, moray eels, pufferfish, feather stars and the inevitable turtles – large lone Green Turtles sleeping or scratching themselves and Hawksbill Turtles feeding. There are some big blast-fishing craters around the South Point and Staghorn Crest, and lots of broken coral at Lobster Lairs. Also at Lobster Lairs are

several narrow crevices in the coral where lobsters hide. The reef slopes gently out and down, but there is not much of interest below 30m (100ft).

10 HANGING GARDENS

11 WEST RIDGE

12 NORTH POINT

★★★★★☆☆☆☆☆

Location: The west face of the reef: Hanging Gardens is west–southwest of the navigation light tower; West Ridge is west of the island itself; North Point is the northernmost point of the west face.

Access: By boat (5min) west and then south around the island from the jetty beach.

Conditions: Usually some current, often enough to push you all the way back to the jetty beach. Snorkelling is possible but not under the overhangs in deep water.

Average depth: 18m (60ft)

Maximum depth: 600m (2000ft)

You swim above a shallow coral-covered reef crest, then over the drop-off and down the wall, which has lots of overhangs containing *Tubastrea* and *Dendrophyllia* corals, large gorgonian sea fans (hiding Longnose Hawkfish), black corals, sponges and barrel sponges – hence the name 'Hanging Gardens'. There are also plenty of nudibranchs, flat worms and feather stars.

The reef crest covering consists of hard and soft corals with all varieties of Pacific reef fish including lionfish, scorpionfish, stonefish, pufferfish, batfish, rabbitfish, barracuda and moray eels. There are also shoals of jacks, sweetlips, snappers, fusiliers, Rainbow Runners and goatfish, plus many species of sea anemones and clownfish.

The Coral Trout (Cephalopholis Miniata), one of the most common members of the grouper family.

Above: *The tiny Long-nosed Hawkfish (Oxycirrhites typus) less than 5cm (2in). It is seen here camouflaged on a gorgonian sea fan.*

Below: *During the day the Goggle Eye or Big Eye (Priacanthus hamrur) can be found hanging under reefs or in caves. It feeds at night.*

Pulau Sipadan

How to Get There

Kota Kinabalu is easily accessible by international flights from Kuala Lumpur, Hong Kong, Manila, Singapore, Bangkok, Brunei, Taipei and Seoul. There is an airport tax of five ringgits on local flights and 20 ringgits on international flights. From Kota Kinabalu you take a short flight by Malaysian Airlines Boeing 737 to Tawau.

From Tawau you transfer by road to the jetty by the Dragon Inn in Semporna. This can take 1–2hr depending on the vehicle and the driver. From Semporna it is 45min by speedboat to Pulau Sipadan. This crossing can be bumpy, so make sure that fragile equipment – such as cameras and flash guns – is suitably packed.

Wealthy clients can now take a helicopter direct from Tawau Airport to the resorts on Pulau Sipadan.

Helicopter Services

For details of the services available, refer to the directory section covering Turtle Islands Park (page 126).

Where to Stay

Most divers will arrive as part of a package trip and would normally stay overnight in Kota Kinabalu before taking an early-morning flight to Tawau, then travelling on to Semporna and Pulau Sipadan.

If you wish to stay in Semporna there is the Dragon Inn, near the departure jetty for Pulau Sipadan. Constructed of wood and built on stilts above the water, it is similar to the houses in the nearby Bajau water villages. It has its own restaurant but you would be wise to avoid the lobsters, which are kept in cages below the hotel in water which contains much of the village's effluent.

Dragon Inn Hotel Jalan Tastan, PO Box 6 91307 Semporna; tel 089–781088

The cheaper hotels in Tawau are best avoided. The most commonly used is:

Hotel Emas Jalan Utara
Postal Address:
PO Box 33, New North Road, 91007 Tawau; tel 089–762000/fax 089–763569

Others include (both in the upper price range):

Hotel Marco Polo
Jalan Clinic, PO Box 1003, 91007 Tawau; tel 089–777988/fax 089–763739

Hotel Merdeka Jalan Masjid, 91007 Tawau; tel 089–776655/fax 089–761743

For details of the accommodation offered by the dive operators, see below.

Where to Eat

These hotels have their own westernized restaurants.

If you are looking for fast food, turn right out of the main entrance of hotel Emas and right again; on the next corner there is a Kentucky Fried Chicken-type restaurant. If, on the other hand, you are looking for a top-quality Western-style restaurant I can recommend

XO Steakhouse Ground Floor, TB 330B, Block 42, Fajar Complex, Tawau; tel 089–764186
Steak imported from Australia, plus seafood.

Dive Facilities

There are now three dive operators on the island and one or two live-aboard boats lie offshore when the monsoon weather stops them from operating around Layang-Layang. Another operator is setting up on Pulau Mabul, an island 15km (9 miles; 15min by speedboat) away.

The resort operators on Pulau Sipadan itself are required by law to use water-desalination plants for fresh water and to ensure that sewage and rubbish do not find their way into the sea.

Borneo Divers (address below), the original and the largest Pulau Sipadan operator, has the prime position along the beach either side of the jetty, with easy access across the beach to the drop-off. The company is very strong in the US, European and Australian markets, and prefers to deal through agents in the country of sale. These agents handle flights from the country of origin to Kota Kinabalu, where Borneo Divers takes over, handling accommodation, transfers and any side tours within Malaysia or Indonesia (Sangalakki). Refer to pages 140–141 for more about Borneo Divers and a list of the company's overseas agents.

Borneo Divers have several female divemasters, which some novices, ladies and families may feel more comfortable with.

The smaller **Pulau Sipadan Resort** also caters for deep-sea fishing and local non-diving tourists, and has more of a local atmosphere. It is situated along the beach west of and adjacent to Borneo Divers, also having easy access across the beach to the drop-off.

Pulau Sipadan Resort deals in direct bookings as well as agency bookings. It is popular with local and expatriate divers from Brunei, Malaysia and Singapore. Contact Veronica Lee by fax, post or telephone (see details below) and she will handle all accommodation and transfers from Kota Kinabalu.

The newest operator, Sipadan Dive Centre, is situated further away from the jetty and the drop-off, east and south of Borneo Divers. It is oriented to the Japanese and Hong Kong markets.

All three operators offer similar accommodation and have diving standards suited to the requirements of their main clientele. Accommodation is in traditional `A`-frame wooden chalets, each with two single beds, a ceiling fan and UK-type 240-volt three-square-pin electric wall sockets for charging (110-volt also available). Showers and toilets are communal, with separate male and female quarters. Prices include three meals a day plus snacks and hot drinks; alcoholic and carbonated beverages extra. English-speaking staff do the cooking, cleaning, most of your fetching and carrying and man the dive boats.

Dive-shops
The dive operators have small shops on the island selling T-shirts, batteries, print film, toiletries and other sundry items. Basic diving and snorkelling equipment is available for hire. Borneo Divers also have a dive-shop at their Tawau office:

Borneo Divers, TB 46 Jalan Dunlop, Tawau; tel 089–761259/fax 089–761691

Diver Training
Borneo Divers and Sea Sports (Sabah) Sdn Bhd Rooms 401–409, 4th Floor, Wisma Sabah, 88000 Kota Kinabalu; tel 088–222226/fax 088–221550
Postal Address:
Locked Bag 194, 88999 Kota Kinabalu; tel 088–222226/fax 088–221550
To protect the reef, Borneo Divers run only advanced and speciality courses at Pulau Sipadan.

Approximate diving costs ex Kota Kinabalu:
4 days/3 nights US$770

Price includes air fare and transfers from and to your hotel in Kota Kinabalu. Non-divers deduct 10% from the above prices.

Pulau Sipadan Resort & Tours Sdn Bhd 484 Block P, Bandar Sabindo, PO Box 61120, 91021 Tawau, Sabah; tel 089–765200/fax 089–763575
Singapore Agent
Sharkeys Dive & Adventure Ltd
1 Park Road, 3–53/54 Peoples Park Complex, Singapore 0105; tel 65–5383733/fax 65–5386919
Pulau Sipadan Resort has PADI and NAUI instructors.

Peninsular Malaysia Agent
Sea Divers Sdn Bhd 18, Jalan Utara (off Jalan Imbi), 55100 Kuala Lumpur; tel 03–9855201/fax 03–9855202

Approximate diving costs ex Tawau Airport:
4 days/3 nights US$550. Prices include transfers from and to Tawau airport.

Sipadan Dive Centre Sdn Bhd A 1026, 10th Floor, Wisma Merdeka, Jalan Tun Razak, 88000 Kota Kinabalu, Sabah; tel 088–240584/fax 088–240415 PADI instructors.

LIVE-ABOARD BOATS

Kota Kinabalu is the home port for the live-aboard dive boats MV *Coral Topaz* and MV *Spirit of Borneo*. For details see the directory covering the Tunku Abdul Rahman Marine Park (page 106).

FILM PROCESSING

There are no processing facilities on the island. The nearest are at Sandakan and Kota Kinabalu; refer to the directories covering Turtle Islands Park (page 126) and Tunku Abdul Rahman Marine Park (page 106) respectively.

HOSPITALS

Tawau General Hospital PO Box 67, 91007 Tawau; tel 089–763533

Semporna District Hospital PO Box 80 91307, Semporna; tel 089–781522

LOCAL HIGHLIGHTS

Nearby are the islands of the proposed Semporna Marine Park (see page 128), but these are of little interest by comparison with Pulau Sipadan itself.

Semporna has a busy market and Bajau water villages. The Semporna Ocean Tourism Centre is worth a visit if only to admire its location on stilts atop a causeway; its aquarium is best left unmentioned. From Semporna you can take day-trips to the beaches (good for swimming and snorkelling) of Pulau Gaya, Pulau Mabul (where there is some diving – see page 128) and Pulau Sibuon.

The people in the 'Icebox' **Bajau water village** in Tawau are very friendly. Tawau made its money from logging, rubber-tapping and cocoa, but now much of the land has been turned over to oil palms. You can organize a day visit to the **cocoa estates and factory** through Hotel Emas (see address above).

If you are energetic, try a few days' trekking along the jungle trails of the **Danum Valley Field Centre**. Accommodation is limited (I had to camp), so organize this – and transport – in advance. The area has been maintained as primary rainforest for research purposes, and there are plenty of local birds and animals in evidence. One option is to organize a night drive, often the most successful way to see the animals, as they freeze in the vehicle's headlights. If you have a head for heights you can climb a vertical ladder 40m (130ft) up a tree to a platform and view the rainforest canopy. Bookings are through Innoprise Corporation Sdn Bhd, Sadong Jaya, Kota Kinabalu (tel 088–243245), which also has a regional office in Lahad Datu (tel 089–81092).

If you have the time to go by road from Semporna to Sandakan, then as well as Danum Valley you can visit **Batuh Peteh Tulug Burial Caves** and the **Gomantong**

KINABANTANGAN RIVER AND GOMANTONG CAVES

Nature enthusiasts will enjoy a trip on the **Kinabantangan River**. Here in Lower Kinabantangan, you can see the strange-looking proboscis monkeys with their big protruding noses. The species is known as *Orang Belanda* or 'Dutchman', named after early Dutch missionaries whose European noses seemed large to the local people. These monkeys can be seen crashing from tree to tree by the water. Orangutans and elephants also inhabit this area but are rarely to be seen. Between the road to the village of Sukau and the Kinabantangan River lie the **Gomantong Caves**, home to millions of bats and swiftlets whose nests are much prized by the Chinese for birds' nest soup.

Caves, and take a look at the Proboscis Monkeys on the **Kinabatangan River**.

Don't miss the **Sepilok Orangutan Rehabilitation Centre**.

A tranquil scene at Borneo Divers' resort on Pulau Sipadan which can be dived all year round.

Randy Davis and Ron Holland, two expatriate divers who worked professionally in Sabah, Labuan and Sarawak, as well as diving for pleasure, found themselves regularly being asked to train others. In 1983 they got together with Clement Lee and Samson Shak to set up Borneo Divers. The company opened for business in 1984 and was incorporated under Malaysian Law on 10 August. It operated from a small dive-shop beside the Tanjung Aru Resort, outside Kota Kinabalu.

RAPID EXPANSION

After initial hiccups the business rapidly expanded in the fields of both commercial and recreational diving. Borneo Divers started taking trips to Pulau Sipadan in 1985, sleeping in tents; the company built its first dive-lodge there in 1989. In 1991 Clement Lee became Malaysia's first PADI course director, the highest level of teaching within PADI.

In 1992 the company transferred its jointly owned commercial section, Borneo Subsea Services (Malaysia) Sdn Bhd, to the Asia Supply Base at Labuan, also opening another recreational centre and dive-shop there. In 1993 it opened P.T. Sangalakki Dive Resort.

A THRIVING DIVE COMPANY

Today Borneo Divers is the biggest professional full-service dive company in Southeast Asia, with over 130 employees. The original four directors remain in office and still dive regularly, a fact that may have no small influence on the company's commercial success. In a recent management reorganization Clement Lee became Managing Director and Jenny Majalap the Dive Tours Manager, with Randy Davis looking after Borneo Subsea Services.

The main headquarters in Kota Kinabalu covers most of the fourth floor of Wisma Sabah, and there are branches in East Malaysia at Shangri-La's Tanjung Aru Resort, Labuan, Tawau and Sipadan Dive Lodge, and in Kalimantan (Indonesian Borneo) at Tarakan and P.T. Sangalakki Dive Resort. The company has dive-shops at its Kota Kinabalu, Labuan and Tawau offices and at its Yaohan

outlet in Kota Kinabalu. It runs PADI courses up to Open Water Instructor level and, under Randy Davis at Labuan, functions as a BSAC school; to date over 4000 divers have been trained by Borneo Divers.

The company's commercial operation, based at Labuan, is ideally situated for rapid transport to the offshore oilfields industry as well as for local underwater inspection and surveys, with capabilities for air diving to 50m (165ft), mixed-gas facilities and Remote Operated Vehicles (ROVs). It has its own recompression chamber for offshore work.

ENVIRONMENTALLY FRIENDLY

Borneo Divers has always been at the forefront of conservation, both on land and underwater. Clients are not allowed to spear fish or collect marine animals, dead or alive. The company has sponsored numerous underwater and beach clean-ups as well as Crown-of-Thorns Starfish harvests from threatened areas in Tunku Abdul Rahman Park. It actively promotes PADI's project AWARE – Aquatic World Awareness Responsibility Education – which is a 10-year programme to educate new divers and re-educate existing divers about taking care of, and cleaning up, the marine environment. It has co-sponsored several WWF–University of Malaysia environmental studies on Pulau Sipadan, where it was the first to instal a water-desalination plant and use biodegradable soaps and other items. It is now implementing the same policies at P.T. Sangalakki Dive Resort.

AGENTS

Borneo Divers have agents all over the world. The contact details opposite are only a selection. If you need further details contact the main office at the following address:

Borneo Divers, Rooms 401-409, 4th Floor, Wisma Sabah, 88000 Kota Kinabalu, Sabah, Malaysia, tel 088-22226/fax 088-221550.

AGENTS

AUSTRALIA
Dive Adventures
Level 9, 32 York Street
Sydney
NSW 2000
tel 02–9070322
fax 02–2994644

FRANCE
Blue Lagoon
26 rue de Maubeuge
75009 Paris
tel 01–42829540
fax 01–40230143

GERMANY
Bernard TTS Gmbh
Tauchreisen Dive Tour
D-65929 Frankfurt
tel 069–333153
fax 069–303094

Nautico Sportriesen Gmbh
Wondsbaken Chaussee
315–317
22089 Hamburg
tel 040–201377
fax 040–201057

HOLLAND
Sport Reizen Services
Diving Adventures
Nijverheindsweg 14
NL-4731
CZ Oudenbosch
tel 165213463
fax 165218493

ITALY
Aquadiving Tours Bl Blue
'n Green
Via Mameli 72C/203
61100 Pesaro
tel 0721–400562
fax 0721–400581

JAPAN
Cruise International Co Ltd
Room 603 Arkcity
Ikebukuro 2–45–1
Ikebukuro Toshima–Ku
Tokyo 171
tel 03–59520915
fax 03–59520917

PENINSULAR MALAYSIA
Underwater photographer
and videographer Daniel
D'Orville acts as Borneo
Divers' agent here:

Daniel D'Orville
62,SS 22/25 Damansara Jaya
47400 Petaling Jaya
Selangor
tel 03–7173066
fax 03–7184303

SWEDEN
Flying Diving Travels
Carl Bondes Vag 58
162 41 Vallingby
Stockholm
tel 8–890186
fax 8–890187

SWITZERLAND
Intens Travel Agency
Dorfplatz 6
6330 Cham
tel 042–363366
fax 042–369039

UNITED KINGDOM
Scuba Safaris
Nastfield Cottage
The Green
Frampton–On–Severn
Gloucestershire
GL2 7DY
tel 01452–740919
fax 01452–740943

USA
Eastquest Inc
1 Beekman Street #607
New York
NY 10038
tel 212–4062224
fax 212–4068793

Island Dreams Travel
8585 Katy Freeway
Suite 118, Houston
tel 800–3466116
fax 713–9739300

Sea Safaris
3700 Highland Ave, Suite
102, Manhattan Beach
CA 90266
tel 213–5462464
fax 310–5451672

Pulau Sipadan must have the best and easiest shore diving in the world. The drop-off is only a few metres from your accommodation.

SANGALAKKI (DIVING'S NEW FRONTIER)

Sangalakki is in fact in Indonesia, but I have included it here because it is most easily accessible from Malaysian Borneo.

Once the company had completed its dive resort on Pulau Sipadan (see page 130), Borneo Divers began reconnoitring for good diving among the islands and reefs south of that island. Local fishermen told the company of an island, Pulau Kakaban, which had a lake containing millions of jellyfish. Pulau Kakaban was found indeed to offer good diving, but its surrounding mangrove swamps made it unsuitable for resort development. However, the nearby island of Pulau Sangalakki also had good diving and was similar to Pulau Sipadan, 190km (120 miles) to the north, so it was decided to develop Pulau Sangalakki Resort.

A TROPICAL PARADISE

About 12ha (30 acres) in area, the island is covered in dense tropical forest surrounded by white, sandy beaches that are perfect for turtles laying eggs. You can walk right round it in 20min. The tidal range is 2.5m (8ft) and the reefs extend some 600–1000m (660–1100yd) out, continuing as gentle slopes. A small boat channel has been cut through the outer reef. All the dive sites around Pulau Sangalakki are 10–15min from the resort by fast speedboat. Most of the diving is drift-diving. You can snorkel from the boat, particularly among the Manta Rays, which are very approachable. When the tide is in you can board the dive boat at the beach, but by the time you return the boat will ground some 150m (500ft) out, leaving you to walk the rest of the way. Similarly, you will have to walk out to the boat for the next dive, but by the time you return the tide will allow the boat right up to the main beach again. This walking is no particular hardship, as there are plenty of willing Borneo Divers staff to carry your equipment.

PULAU KAKABAN

Some 25min away by boat is Pulau Kakaban, where there are walls to 240m (800ft) with lots of pelagic species. In Kakaban's freshwater lake, reminiscent of the lake on Palau in

Opposite: *Sangalakki dive boats moored off the beach.*
Above: *Colourful Nudibranch or sea slug (Chromodoris bullocki) on a sea squirt (Polycarpa aurata).*

Micronesia, are three species of non-stinging jellyfish. What species these actually are is as yet unknown, although Dr Tomas Tomascik, a Canadian marine biologist working for the Indonesian Government, arrived to investigate this matter just as I was leaving. Borneo Divers has improved the track to the lake and supplies porters to carry your equipment, so you can dive as well as snorkel here.

Both islands are good for observing birds and butterflies, and at Sangalakki the circumstances are excellent for catching sight of turtles and turtle hatchlings. All the buildings are larger than those at Sipadan, but they are built well back from the beach and situated behind bushes so that their lights do not disturb turtles nesting at night. This, together with the fact that Borneo Divers has bought up the egg-collecting concession, means that on many nights 20–50 turtles come ashore to lay eggs, and turtle hatchlings are often seen. I soon learnt to carry a torch when I went to the restaurant at night in case I tripped over turtles on the way back to my chalet!

CURRENTS

The currents vary from medium to strong; their strength and direction depend on the tide at the time of your dive. Where they are strong, novices should stay beside the divemaster. Average visibility is almost everywhere about 30m (100ft).

A VARIETY OF MARINE LIFE

On almost every dive you can see Manta Rays, Eagle Rays, stingrays, cuttlefish, batfish, barracuda and Barramundi Cod, Coral Trout, groupers, many species of pufferfish, Spotted and Striped Sweetlips, hawkfish, Threadfin Bream, lionfish, scorpionfish, stonefish, dam-

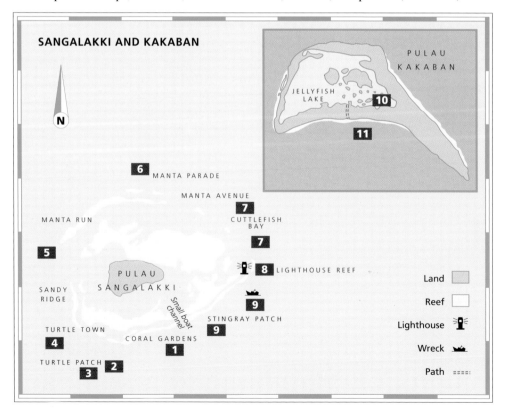

selfish, Anthias, Chromis, wrasse and moray eels. Small sharks are around, usually Grey Reef, Whitetip Reef, Blacktip Reef and Leopard (Variegated). Also in evidence are shoals of fusiliers, snappers, catfish and jacks.

On the sand there are large barrel sponges covered with Alabaster Sea Cucumbers, as well as (truly giant) Giant Clams, some as much as 1m (40in) across, plus flat worms, fan worms, sea pens, sea stars, cushion stars, sea cucumbers, sea anemones (with and without clownfish), sponges and nudibranchs.

SANDY RIDGE

At Sandy Ridge there is a patch of Garden Eels. All around are isolated gorgonian sea fans, some very large and at remarkably shallow depths; these and many corals rising in the current are adorned with multicoloured feather stars. As well as large fields of stony corals, predominantly lettuce coral interspersed with boulder and brain coral, there are smaller fields of soft corals and many tube sponges.

The reef-fish fauna is as varied as at Sipadan but less concentrated; it includes Clown, Orange-striped and Titan Triggerfish, squirrelfish, surgeonfish and many species of angelfish and butterflyfish. There are remarkably few parrotfish, and those present are small.

At the time of my visit (September 1993) the Sangalakki resort was still under construction and the divemasters had yet to cover all the diving possibilities. Since then they may well have found more dive sites than those described here, as well as different ways to dive some of these. More recently, the resort has been closed on a temporary basis. You will therefore need to make enquiries as to the current situation when planning a trip; Borneo Divers should have up-to-date information.

The Yellow-saddle Goatfish (Parupeneus cyclostomus) uses the long whisker-like barbels on its chin to search for food in the sands. Goatfish usually forage in small groups.

1 CORAL GARDENS

★★★★★

Location: Just west outside the small boat channel.
Access: By boat, turning out of the small boat channel.
Conditions: Usually calm with a light current.
Average depth: 15m (50ft)
Maximum depth: 27m (90ft)
Mixed stony and soft corals shelve out gradually to 27m (90ft), after which there is flat sand. All the common Pacific reef fish, turtles, cuttlefish, nudibranchs, flat worms, sea stars, cushion stars, sea cucumbers, frogfish, lizardfish, goatfish and feather stars are in evidence.

2 DRIFTING FROM CORAL GARDENS TO TURTLE TOWN TO SANDY RIDGE

★★★★★

Location: The southwest area of the reef.
Access: By boat, turning west out of the small boat channel.
Conditions: Usually calm with a medium to strong current. Novices should stay with the divemaster.
Average depth: 24m (80ft)
Maximum depth: 28m (92ft)
The bottom here comprises an undulating expanse of stony corals, mostly vast fields of lettuce coral with some small soft corals, big whip corals and big gorgonian sea fans covered in feather stars. There are plenty of large shoals of fish, juvenile angelfish and butterflyfish, and all the expected Pacific reef fish, including Moorish Idols. Also in evidence are turtles, stingrays, groupers, small parrotfish, Barramundi Cod, sea stars, sea anemones, clownfish, cuttlefish and nudibranchs.

Outside this area is a field of large soft corals known as Sherwood Forest.

3 TURTLE PATCH

★★★★★

Location: At the southwest corner of the reef, between Turtle Town and Coral Gardens (see Site 2).
Access: By boat, west from the boat channel.
Conditions: Usually calm with a gentle current.
Average depth: 12m (40ft)
Maximum depth: 13m (43ft)
A level area of stony lettuce corals, with some large boulder corals forming overhangs that shelter many turtles. Some huge gorgonian sea fans are present at a depth of only 12m (40ft); you can see also lots of cuttlefish, Bandit and Porcupine Pufferfish and sea anemones with clown-

fish. In addition there are many leathery soft corals tinged with blue, all the expected reef fish, shoals of jacks and fusiliers, and, spread out on all the high points, feather stars.

4 TURTLE TOWN

★★★★★

Location: The southwest corner of the reef.
Access: By boat, west from the small boat channel.
Conditions: Usually calm with a light to medium current.
Average depth: 15m (50ft)
Maximum depth: 15m (50ft)
Here there are gullies and small ridges on stony coral in all directions. As the dive's name implies, there are lots of turtles. All the expected Pacific reef fish are here, too, along with sea stars and feather stars.

5 DRIFTING FROM MANTA RUN TO SANDY RIDGE

★★★★★

Location: The northwest to west area of the reef.
Access: By boat, either way around the island from the small boat channel.
Conditions: Generally calm but almost always some current, which can be strong. Novices should stay with the divemaster.
Average depth: 15m (50ft)
Maximum depth: 28m (92ft)
An undulating sandy bottom is dotted with coral heads, gorgonian sea fans and large barrel sponges. You can expect to see at least 20 Manta Rays in any one dive, and often these are curious enough to give you a close inspection. There are some patches of lettuce coral, individual *Dendronephthya* soft corals and sea anemones, sea cucumbers (many species) and sea stars, including cushion stars. There are also lots of small pufferfish, all the expected reef fish and many sea anemones (without attendant clownfish). There is a large patch of garden eels on Sandy Ridge by an old anchor.

6 MANTA PARADE

★★★★★

Location: The northernmost area of the reef.
Access: By boat from the small boat channel north around the east side of the reef.
Conditions: Generally calm but almost always some current, which can be strong. Novices should stay with the divemaster.

Average depth: 15m (50ft)
Maximum depth: 15m (50ft)
A flat sandy bottom is scattered with small coral heads, large barrel sponges covered in Alabaster Sea Cucumbers, and gorgonian sea fans, up to 1.5m (5ft) across, that act as a feeding platform for feather stars. There are many soft corals, sea anemones (with clownfish), flat worms, fan worms, nudibranchs, sea stars, cushion stars, sea cucumbers and all the expected reef fish, including frogfish, crocodilefish, lionfish, scorpionfish and stonefish.

As the dive's name indicates, Manta Rays parade up and down this area; if you stay calm and quiet they will approach you. Snorkelling among them is particularly good fun.

7 DRIFTING FROM MANTA AVENUE TO CUTTLEFISH BAY TO LIGHTHOUSE REEF

★★★★★

Location: The northeast area of the reef to the lighthouse reef.
Access: By boat around the east side of the island from the small boat channel.
Conditions: Usually calm with a medium or strong current. Novices should stay with the divemaster.
Average depth: 12m (40ft)
Maximum depth: 16m (52ft)
Here you find a slope rising gently from 16m (52ft) to 5m

Gorgonian sea whip (Lophogorgia sp.) on a reef wall angled to the current.

(16ft) with a mixture of everything: stony and soft corals, gorgonian sea fans, sea whips, sea pens, sea stars, cushion stars, sea anemones, nudibranchs, flat worms, sea cucumbers, all the expected reef fish and shoals of catfish, jacks and fusiliers. Colourful feather stars feed on the plankton in the current.

Just as at Manta Parade (Site 6), Manta Rays promenade up and down Manta Avenue and approach divers who stay calm and quiet. Snorkellers can likewise get close to them.

8 LIGHTHOUSE REEF

★★★★

Location: The lighthouse.
Access: By boat, east from the small boat channel.
Conditions: Usually calm; the current is gentle enough that you can easily swim against it.
Average depth: 14m (45ft)
Maximum depth: 14m (45ft)
The only dive on this reef that is not a drift-dive: the boat can be moored to the lighthouse and you can make a circular tour, taking in the wrecks (one recent) of two small wooden boats; the older wreck has some quite large *Dendronephthya* soft corals and a good fish fauna, including sweetlips and groupers.

Otherwise a flat sandy bottom is interspersed with small coral heads. There are lots of different sea anemones with various attendant clownfish, several sea anemones without attendant clownfish, frogfish, scorpionfish, lionfish, sea cucumbers, sea stars, sea urchins, all the expected reef fish and some huge Giant Clams – over 1m (40in) across.

9 DRIFTING FROM LIGHTHOUSE REEF TO STING RAY PATCH TO CORAL GARDENS

★★★★★

Location: The lighthouse.
Access: By boat, east from the small boat channel.
Conditions: Normally calm with a medium current.
Average depth: 25m (82ft)
Maximum depth: 27m (90ft)
Here you are offered an undulating bottom of coral gardens, with most varieties of stony, gorgonian and soft corals interspersed with sandy patches. On every high point colourful feather stars open themselves out in the current which is a beautiful sight.

Also in evidence are Eagle Rays, Hawksbill Turtles, Green Turtles, lots of cuttlefish, moray eels, Barramundi Cod, lionfish, stonefish, several scorpionfish, nudibranchs, sea anemones, Black-spotted Butterflyfish, Emperor Angelfish and all the common reef fish.

10 KAKABAN ISLAND: JELLYFISH LAKE

★★★★★☆☆☆☆☆

Location: Covers most of Kakaban Island.
Access: The path from the shore, reached by boat from Pulau Sangalakki (25min), starts at almost the centre of the southern bay of Kakaban Island; despite improvements, it can be slippery when wet – wear sandals, trainers or bootees. Borneo Divers staff carry your equipment to the lake for you.
Conditions: This trip is undertaken only when the weather is calm enough for a comfortable crossing between the two islands. The visibility in the lake is generally only about 15m (50ft).
Average depth: Your own choice
Maximum depth: Not known
Swimming through millions of jellyfish – even non-stinging ones! – is not everyone's idea of fun. So far only the shallow edges of the lake have been dived. Some people find it too spooky, or worry about snakes and other threats. In the end it's up to you – but certainly this is a unique experience. Many of the jellyfish sink to the bottom where, in the grassy areas, white anemones devour some of them. Many of the roots of the mangroves that surround the lake are encrusted with sponges.

11 KAKABAN ISLAND DROP-OFF

★★★★★☆☆☆☆☆

Location: Along the south coast of Pulau Kakaban.
Access: By boat (25min) from Pulau Sangalakki.
Conditions: Usually calm with some current. Like all deep walls, this has great visibility.
Average depth: Your own choice
Maximum depth: 240m (800ft)
This is a deep wall offering all the variety you would expect. You could be lucky and see any of the pelagic species, and certainly you can expect to encounter shoals of smaller fish. Sharks, groupers, tuna, jacks, barracuda and Manta Rays are common.

JELLYFISH

These unusual-looking creatures range from microscopic to enormous in size. One species - Lion's Mane Jellyfish - when mature, has tentacles that reach a length of ten metres. Jellyfish are coral relatives and are perhaps best known for their sting which can be extremely painful. They propel themselves by pulsations of a bell-like body but are unable to withstand tides or currents which often deposit them on the shore.

How to Get There

Although Sangalakki is in Indonesia it is easiest to get there via Malaysia. To visit Indonesia by this route you must have an Indonesian visa. Borneo Divers (see address below) can obtain visas for you same-day in Kota Kinabalu if you have not already obtained one before you get there.

Kota Kinabalu is easily accessible by international flights from Kuala Lumpur, Hong Kong, Manila, Singapore, Bangkok, Brunei, Taipei and Seoul. From Kota Kinabalu you take a short flight by Malaysian Airlines Boeing 737 to Tawau as if you were going to Pulau Sipadan (see page 130). From Tawau you transfer to a 19-seat Malaysian Airlines Twin Otter or a similar small aircraft run by Bouraq (Indonesian) Airlines. The flight to Tarakan in Indonesia takes about 40min. There is a baggage limit of 10kg (22 pounds), with excess-baggage charges of US$1 per kilogram (2.2 pounds) on the flight from Tawau to Tarakan, though I was charged US$2 per kilogram on the return from Tarakan to Tawau! Even aside from the cost factor, it is wise to keep your baggage to a minimum on this sector: if the plane is full there is no guarantee that your excess baggage will fly with it! My hand baggage was not weighed.

Although it was not yet in operation when I visited in late 1993, Borneo Divers now have a catamaran service running from Tarakan to Sangalakki (3-hr). At present departures to Sangalakki via Tarakan from Kota Kinabalu and Tawau are on Mondays and Saturdays. Returns are on Fridays and Sundays, with an overnight stop in Tarakan. Borneo Divers' staff assist you at all transfers. Some divers prefer to combine a week at Sipadan with a week at Sangalakki.

Where to Stay

Medium Price Range
Hotel Tarakan Plaza Jalan Jos Sudarso, Tarakan, Indonesia; tel 0551–21870/fax 0551–21029

Lower Price Range
Hotel Bahetra Jalan Sulawesi, Tarakan, Indonesia; tel 0551–21821

Dive Facilities

P.T. Sangalakki Dive Resort is wholly operated by Borneo Divers, who with their Indonesian partners have an exclusive arrangement with the local Indonesian government. They have two 8.5m by 2m (28ft by 6¹/₂ft) custom-built dive boats, powered by twin 65HP outboard engines. Each boat can carry 10 divers. Three boat dives a day are offered, except when visiting Kakaban. Accommodation is in twin-share beach chalets built with natural materials in local Indonesian style. Each chalet has 240-volt electricity including a fan and continental-type two-round-pin sockets for charging, etc.; a 110-volt two-flat-pin socket supply is also available. Mosquito nets and insect repellent come in useful after rain. Eight huts have so far been built, with a maximum of 20 envisaged. Toilets and showers are in a large central block with separate male and female quarters. There is a large dining hall cum bar/lounge at the eastern end by the dive hut. English-speaking staff do the cooking, cleaning, most of your fetching and carrying and man the dive boats. Bearing in mind the 10kg (22-pound) baggage limit on the Tawau–Tarakan flight, Borneo Divers have complete sets of diving equipment for hire at the resort.

Borneo Divers & Sea Sports (Sabah) Sdn Bhd Room 401–409, 4th Floor, Wisma Sabah, 88000 Kota Kinabalu; tel 60–88–222226/fax 60–88–221550
Postal Address:
Locked Bag 194, 88999 Kota Kinabalu
Tawau Office and Dive Shop:
TB46, First Floor, Jalan Dunlop, Tawau; tel 089–761259/fax 089–761691
Borneo Divers, Borneo's first and only PADI Five-Star IDC Dive Centre, run courses up to Open-Water Instructor level and have dive centres at Shangri-La's Tanjung Aru Resort, Labuan, Sipadan island and Sangalakki. They have several female divemasters.

Approximate diving costs ex-Tawau:
5 days/4 nights US$1390

Prices include airport–hotel–airport transfers in Kota Kinabalu, Tawau or Tarakan on arrival and departure days; a return Tawau–Tarakan air ticket; Tarakan–Sangalakki–Tarakan transfers by boat; and all food and drink except alcoholic and carbonated beverages while at the dive resort. They do not include accommodation and meals in Kota Kinabalu, Tawau or Tarakan, if required.

Film Processing

There are no processing facilities on the island. The nearest are at Sandakan and Kota Kinabalu; refer to the directories covering Turtle Islands Park (page 126) and Tunku Abdul Rahman Marine Park (page 107) respectively.

Hospitals

Tawau General Hospital PO Box 67, 91007 Tawau; tel 089–763533

Semporna District Hospital PO Box 80 91307, Semporna; tel 089–781522

Local Highlights

This area of Kalimantan is covered in wild rainforest and mangrove swamps. None of it is organized for foreign visitors.

Tarakan is a small frontier town on Tarakan Island; it expanded as an oil town, but has largely subsided again, and now has little more to offer than a small souk and some little restaurants. However, *en route* to Tarakan through Malaysia you have access to all the highlights accessible from Kota Kinabalu, Tawau and Sandakan: refer to the directories covering Turtle Islands Park (page 126) and Tunku Abdul Rahman Marine Park (page 107) respectively.

Beach hut accommodation hidden away in the shrubbery.

SINGAPORE

Many of the workaholics and expatriates who drive the dynamic economy of Singapore are also avid divers. These local enthusiasts are lucky enough to be at the hub of much of Southeast Asia's diving. Borneo, the southern islands of Peninsular Malaysia and the nearer dive sites of Indonesia can be easily reached for a weekend; and for longer breaks there is simple access to Indonesia's more distant dive sites as well as those in Thailand, the Philippines and Palau.

LIMITED VISIBILITY

However, the diving off Singapore itself is not good. The waters are shallow and there are heavy shipping movements and continuous construction projects which often involve land-fill reclamation of coastal waters. In short, the diving off the southern islands is best described (in the words of William Ong) as 'limited-visibility diving': a visibility of 1.5m (5ft) is considered a fine thing! The marine life is in fact pretty good – it is just difficult to see it. Surprises do occur; for example, a shoal of pink dolphins was observed between Pulau Tekong and Pulau Pengerang in April 1993, and dugongs sometimes show themselves in November by the fire jetty where the water fireboats are kept.

DANGEROUS CURRENTS

Many areas have strong and treacherous currents, and others are off-limits either for indus-trial reasons or because they are live-firing practice ranges. Nevertheless, a few areas are utilized for training novices or to allow more experienced divers to keep fit at weekends. Water temperatures average 27°C (81°F), and on a lucky day visibility can reach 5m (16ft), the best visibility occurring during the cooler months of October to April.

At weekends bumboats (converted lighters) depart from the Jardine Steps by the World Trade Centre around 08:00 taking picnickers, sunbathers, divers and snorkellers to Pulau Hantu, the Sisters Islands, St John's Island and Pulau Kusu.

Opposite: *The skyline of Singapore at night.*
Above: *Soft tree corals are a delightful sight in all Indo-Pacific waters.*

1 PULAU HANTU (GHOST ISLAND)

★★★★

Location: West–southwest of Pulau Bukom.
Access: By boat (about 45min) west–southwest from the Jardine Steps, around Sentosa Island and Pulau Bukom.
Conditions: Dive here only in calm conditions. Average visibility is about 1.2m (4ft).
Average depth: 12m (40ft)
Maximum depth: 15m (50ft)
This is Singapore's most popular location for diver training: a small island with patch reefs on the west side, which are sheltered from the main currents (though there are strong currents on the north side).

The fringing reef is made up of stony corals and rocks. A channel 12m (40ft) deep runs between the main island and the patch reefs, giving a choice of two slopes to a sandy bottom. There is some boulder coral, staghorn coral, lettuce coral, bubble coral, mushroom corals, encrusting corals and sponges, sea anemones (with clownfish), lionfish, scorpionfish, batfish, razorfish and feather stars. Down on the sand are sea stars, white and black sea urchins, sea cucumbers, nudibranchs, stingrays and gobies with alpheid shrimps. Turtles, sea snakes and sea horses are occasionally seen, and *Sargassum* may be found in the coldest season (October to February).

PULAU AUR

For better diving that is still relatively near home, Singapore Dive Operators now offer trips lasting 3—5 days to Pulau Aur (see page 84), off the east coast of Peninsular Malaysia, and to the Anambas archipelago, further east into Indonesian waters, where there are also convenient wrecks for wreck-diving courses.

Non-diving excursions go by fast ferry to the Indonesian island of Pulau Batam, which is about two-thirds the size of Singapore. With Singaporean help, Pulau Batam is fast becoming a 'second Singapore'.

---

2 PULAU SALU

★★★★

Location: West–southwest of the Jardine Steps, north of Pulau Sudong (Site 7).
Access: By boat (about 50min) west–southwest from the Jardine Steps.
Conditions: Dive here only in calm conditions. Novices should be wary: there can be strong currents. Average visibility is about 1.2m (4ft).
Average depth: 12m (40ft)
Maximum depth: 21m (70ft)
Pulau Salu is in a restricted area, but is dived for the

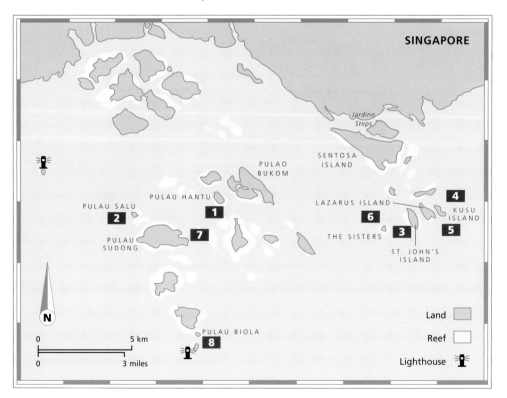

greater variety of marine life it offers than you can generally find elsewhere among Singapore's dive sites. There are good corals on the west side, and the western tip generally has the least current. Nurse Sharks have been seen on the reef.

3 ST JOHN'S ISLAND (PULAU SAKIJANG BENDERA; BARKING DEER ISLAND)
4 PULAU KUSU (TURTLE ISLAND)

★★★★

Location: Southeast of Sentosa Island.
Access: By boat (about 45min) from the Jardine Steps around and southeast of Sentosa Island.
Conditions: Dive at these sites only in calm conditions. There can be strong currents, so novices should not go out unescorted.
Average depth: 20m (65ft)
Maximum depth: 30m (100ft)
These are primarily tourist islands, and thus boast changing rooms and swimming lagoons. St John's is the larger of the two. Both islands have waters down to 30m (100ft), but the visibility is usually bad (1m; 40ft). St John's has stony corals and the occasional pelagic fish or sea snake, while the reef on the northeast side of Pulau Kusu has some gorgonian sea fans, table corals and, occasionally, turtles.

5 PULAU LAZARUS

★★

Location: Between St John's Island and Pulau Kusu (Sites 3 and 4).
Access: By boat (about 45min) from the Jardine Steps around and southeast of Sentosa Island.
Conditions: Dive here only in calm conditions. The very strong currents that sometimes prevail make the site unsuitable for novices.Poor visibility: about 1m (40in).
Average depth: 15m (50ft)
Maximum depth: 18m (60ft)
This site, with its very strong currents, has little to recommend it except, on the southern tip, a wreck in 18m (60ft) of water.

6 SISTERS ISLANDS (PULAU SUBER LAUT)

★★★★

Location: South of Sentosa Island.
Access: By boat (about 45min) south from the Jardine Steps and around Sentosa Island.

Conditions: Dive here only in calm conditions. There can be some very strong currents, and only experienced divers should descend to the wreck. Average visibility is quite good for Singapore – at 1.5m (5ft)!
Average depth: 10m (33ft)
Maximum depth: 21m (70ft)
These two islands, west of St John's Island (Site 3), are close together and resemble each other in shape. There is a shallow reef at 6m (20ft) and the broken-up wreck of a steel barge in 21m (70ft) of water. Penetrating the wreck can be dangerous – divers have died in it. It is wise to inspect the wreck only from the outside.

7 PULAU SUDONG: EAST SIDE

★★

Location: West–southwest of the Jardine Steps, south of Pulau Hantu.
Access: By boat (about 45min) from the Jardine Steps and around Pulau Bukom.
Conditions: Dive here only in calm conditions. Novices should beware: there are very strong currents. Average visibility is poor: about 1m (40in).
Average depth: 9m (30ft)
Maximum depth: 20m (65ft)
The east side of Pulau Sudong is outside the restricted area but in the shipping lane. Currents are always strong. There is similar marine life to that at nearby Pulau Hantu (Site 1). About 150m (500ft) offshore to the north a beacon marks the wreck of a large steel barge on sand at 20m (65ft), with the deck at 9m (30ft). The wreck is mostly intact and has become a fine artificial reef, with excellent stony and soft corals. Fish fauna includes filefish – rare on the fringing reefs.

8 PULAU BIOLA (VIOLIN ISLAND) AND RAFFLES LIGHTHOUSE

★★

Location: Southwest of Sentosa Island.
Access: By boat (about 1hr) from the Jardine Steps and around Sentosa Island.
Conditions: Can be very rough, with big waves and heavy swells. Average visibility is poor: about 1m (40in).
Average depth: 34m (110ft)
Maximum depth: 34m (110ft)
The area between Pulau Pawai, Pulau Senang, Pulau Biola and Raffles Lighthouse is restricted for live-firing practice, and it has strong currents. Yet the area attracts experienced divers because it has better marine life than you can find elsewhere off Singapore. Local boatmen sink their old boats here, but these are mostly made of wood and so are unsafe to enter.

Singapore

HOW TO GET THERE

Singapore is easily accessible by road or rail from Malaysia and Thailand, by ferry from Malaysia and Indonesia and by international flights from all over the world.

WHERE TO STAY

There is accommodation of every standard, from the immortalized Raffles Hotel to camping sites.

Upper Price Range
Raffles Hotel 1 Beach Road; tel 3378041

Hilton International 581 Orchard Road; tel 7372233

Carlton Hotel 76 Bras Basah Road; tel 3388333

Shangri–La 22 Orange Grove Road; tel 7373644

Medium Price Range
Hotel Bencoolen 47 Bencoolen Street; tel 3360822/fax 3364384

Hotel Peninsula 3 Coleman Street; tel 3372200

Strand Hotel 25 Bencoolen Street; tel 338166

YMCA International House 1 Orchard Road; tel 3373444

Lower Price Range
South East Asia Hotel 190 Waterloo Street; tel 3382394

Kian Hua Hotel 81 Bencoolen Street; tel 3383492

Shan Wah Hotel 36 Bencoolen Street; tel 3362428

WHERE TO EAT

There are restaurants of all standards and cuisines – far too many to contemplate listing them here. Your best idea is to get hold of a tourist directory on arrival; alternatively, invest in a comprehensive guidebook. International fast-food outlets have taken off in a big way, including Burger King, McDonald's, Pizza Hut and Delifrance.

DIVE FACILITIES

Singapore Club Aquanaut (non-profit dive club), #05/33–34, 190 Clemenceau Avenue, Singapore Shopping Centre, Singapore 0923; tel 3343454/fax 3340855
This is the premier local dive club.

Pro Diving Services (William & Ruby Ong) 32, Bali Lane (entrance via North Bridge Road, opposite the Landmark Hotel), Singapore 0718; tel 2912261/fax 2914136
PADI Five-Star facility offering excursions to Malaysia and Indonesia.

Sharkeys Dive & Adventure Pte Ltd (Peter Reiser & Michael Lim)
1 Park Road, #03-53/54 Peoples Park Complex, Singapore 0105; tel 5383733/fax 5386919
SSI courses of all standards; branches in Malaysia (Pulau Tioman) and Thailand (Phuket); excursions to Indonesia, Malaysia and Thailand.

Sentosa Water Sports World Trade Centre #1–6, 1 Maritime Square; tel 2745612/fax 2741087

Mako Sub-Aquatics #05–01/03, 71 Ayer Rajah Crescent; tel 7741440

Aqua Divers, Block 75 #01–503, Commonwealth Drive, Singapore 0314; tel 4712875/fax 4799583

Scuba Craft 5001 Beach Road, Golden Mile Complex #02–17, Singapore 0719; tel 2994072/fax 2998089

Great Blue Dive Shop Holland Road Shopping Centre, 211 Holland Avenue #03–05, Singapore 1027; tel 4670767/fax 4696752
NAUI courses and excursions.

Diving Travel
Dive Spots (Asia Aquatic) #07–37 Cuppage Centre, 55 Cuppage Road, Singapore 0922; tel 7388158/fax 7388153
Diving excursions.

Travelhouse Pte Ltd #11–07 Shenton House, 3 Shenton Way, Singapore 0106; tel 2278020/fax 2277025

LIVE-ABOARD BOATS

Trips on the MV *Sea Rover* can be booked through

Kwok Wai Tours c/o Octo-Tech Industrial Pte Ltd, 1004 Toa Payoh Industrial Park #03–1489, Singapore 1231; tel 2733333

FILM PROCESSING

There are many mini-labs for processing print film. E6 transparency processing is handled by the following laboratories:

Albert Colour Labs #01–07 Tanglin Shopping Centre, Singapore 1023; tel 2351845
and
#B1–15 Orchard Towers, Singapore 0923; tel 2352815
and
#B1–10 Orchard Hotel Shopping Arcade; tel 7344689

Pacific Colour Enterprise – Raffles City
PO Box 0597, Singapore 9117; tel 5340882
and
PO Box 0105, 133 Newbridge Road #02–60; tel 5340882

Raffles Commercial Colour Labs Block 1008 – Toa Payoh North #04–09/15; tel 2565458
and
Takashimaya Department Store, 3rd Floor, Orchard Road, Ngee Ann City, Singapore 0923

Rainbow Colour Service Pte Ltd 59 Rowell Road, Singapore 0820; tel 2930971/fax 2924601

Robert Lam Colour Shop 103 Beach Road, Singapore 0718; tel 3346146/fax 3346147

Singapore Colour Centre 565 Macpherson Road #03–06, Singapore 1336; tel 2829122

UNDERWATER PHOTOGRAPHIC EQUIPMENT

Andrew Yeo #02–15 The Adelphi, 1 Coleman Street, Singapore 0617; tel 3376334/fax 3391869
Aquaflash, Sea & Sea, Anthis Nexus and Subal.

HOSPITALS

Singapore General Hospital Outram Road; tel 2223322

Glen Eagles Hospital tel 4737222

Mount Elizabeth Hospital tel 7372666

ADAPTING TO NEW ENVIRONMENTS

Western divers are unlikely to have difficulty adapting to Singapore — unless they've been travelling elsewhere in Asia and are unprepared for Singapore's squeaky-clean environment!

LOCAL HIGHLIGHTS

Singapore is a cosmopolitan city. Aside from the skyscrapers of the bustling modern city there are Chinese, Arab and Indian areas. Public transport is so good that it is just as easy to get around on your own as to opt for guided tours. There are one- and three-day explorer tickets on the buses and the special 'Singapore Trolley' buses, whose routes are specifically designed for city sightseeing.

A wide range of **cruises** operate on the Singapore River, around the harbour and to the nearby Singaporean, Malaysian and Indonesian islands.

The main shopping district is in the vicinity of **Orchard Road**; while here you can visit the famous **Raffles Hotel**. Other places to visit include **Chinatown, Little India** and **Arab Street, St Andrew's Cathedral**, the **Thian Hock Keng Temple**, the **Kong Meng San Phor Kark See Temple**, the **Sri Mariamman Temple**, the **Temple of 1000 Lights**, the **Siong Lim Temple**, the **Sultan Mosque**, the **Al-Abrar Mosque** and the **Hajjah Fatimah Mosque**. Then, as if that were not enough, there are the **National Museum and Art Gallery**, the many gardens, the **Jurong Bird Park and Crocodile Park**, the zoo and the mythologically based **Merlion** Statue by Clifford Pier, which is synonymous with Singapore the same way

that Big Ben is of London or the Little Mermaid of Copenhagen. **Sentosa Island**, a UK military base until 1970, is now one large theme park. You can cross to Sentosa by one of the regular ferries that go from the World Trade Centre, but a better deal is to buy an all-in ticket at the cable-car station by the World Trade Centre: this gives you not only the cable-car ride to the summit of **Faber Mountain**, Singapore's highest point, but also buses and the monorail on Sentosa Island and entrance to several of the attractions there. Those attractions include the **Surrender Chambers, Fort Siloso**, the **Maritime Museum, Underwater World,** the **Coralarium, Fun World** and **Sun World,** with its swimming lagoons and artificial beach of imported sand.

Guided tours to nearby areas in Malaysia and Indonesia can be organized through your hotel or directly with a tour operator.

RMG Tours Pte Ltd 25 Hoot Kiam Road, Singapore 1024; tel 7387776/fax 2355256

Franco Asian Travel tel 2938282

Tour East 163 Tanglin Road; tel 2355703

Water Tours 70 Collyer Quay, #01–31 Clifford Quay, Singapore 0104; tel

SINGAPOREAN CLEANLINESS

Singapore is renowned as a 'clean, green' city, but this reputation has not been achieved without a number of draconian laws aimed to control personal behaviour. These laws apply equally to tourists.

- Littering is punishable by a hefty S$1000 fine.
- Smoking in public places (including restaurants) is punishable by a S$500 fine.
- Eating and drinking are prohibited on the whole of the MRT system.
- The authorities have decided that chewing-gum is too difficult to clean up, and have accordingly banned it from the country entirely.

5339811/fax 5357743

Singapore River Cruises & Leisure Pte Ltd 62 Cecil Street, #01–00 TPI Building, Singapore; tel 2279678/fax 2277287

Bantayan (Eye-patch) Butterflyfish (Chaetodon adiergastos) tend to stay with the same partner until one of them dies.

The Marine Environment

SOUTHEAST ASIAN REEFS AND REEF LIFE

Most of the reefs around Southeast Asia are – at least in geological terms – quite young. Towards the end of the last ice age, sea levels were as much as 100m (330ft) lower than they are today, and much of the area between the large islands of Borneo, Sumatra and Java was dry land. Since then the sea has reasserted itself, so that now this area is flooded with warm, shallow water dotted with islands and reefs.

THE NATURE OF CORALS AND REEFS

Tropical reefs are built mainly from corals, primitive animals closely related to sea anemones. Most of the coral types that contribute to reef construction are colonial; that is, numerous individuals – polyps – come together to create what is essentially a single compound organism. The polyps produce calcareous skeletons; when thousands of millions of them are present in a single colony they form large, stony (in fact, limestone) structures which build up as reefs. What happens is that, when corals die, some of the skeleton remains intact, thus adding to the reef. Cracks and holes then fill with sand and the calcareous remains of other reef plants and animals, and gradually the whole becomes consolidated, with new corals growing on the surface of the mass. Thus only the outermost layer of the growing reef is actually alive.

There are about 450 species of reef-building coral in the seas around Southeast Asia. Corals grow slowly, adding about 1–10cm (0.4–4in) growth in a year. Once over a certain age they start being able to reproduce, releasing tiny forms that float freely among the plankton for a few weeks until settling to continue the growth of the reef. The forms corals create as they grow vary enormously according to the species and to the place on the reef where it is growing. Colonies range in size from a few centimetres in diameter to giants several metres across and many hundreds of years old. Some are branched or bushy, others tree-like, others in the form of plates, tables or delicate leafy fronds, and yet others are encrusting, lobed, rounded or massive.

Microscopic plants called zooxanthellae are of great importance to the growth and health of many corals. These are packed in their millions into the living tissues of most reef-building corals (and of various other reef animals, such as Giant Clams). Although reef corals capture planktonic organisms from the water, a significant amount of their food comes directly from the zooxanthellae. It is for this reason that the most prolific coral growths are in the shallow, well lit waters where the zooxanthellae thrive. The presence of coral communities does not, necessarily lead to the development of thick deposits of reef limestone; for example, the Krakatoa

Islands off the southern tip of Sumatra consist mainly of slabs of volcanic rock with a patchy veneer of corals.

Types of Reef

In most regions with plentiful coral communities, the calcareous skeletons have built up to form a variety of different types of reef:
- fringing reefs
- patch reefs, banks and shoals
- barrier reefs
- atolls

Fringing Reefs

Fringing reefs occur in shallow water near to land. Typically they extend to depths of 15m–45m (50–150ft), depending on factors such as the profile and depth of the seabed and the clarity of the water. Islands that stand in deep water, like Pulau Sipadan, have precipitous fringing reefs that descend hundreds of metres, but these are exceptions rather than the rule. Many mainland coastlines in Southeast Asia are too close to river estuaries for reefs to develop, and instead support stands of mangroves – another marine ecosystem of enormous importance in the region. But the offshore islands, away from the influence of freshwater run-off, are often surrounded by reefs. In Malaysia and Thailand a large proportion of reefs are of this type.

Patch Reefs, Banks and Shoals

In theory, reefs can develop anywhere that the underlying rock has at some time been close enough to the surface for corals to become established and grow. Sea levels may have risen considerably since then, or other geological changes may have occurred to lower the depth of the bed beneath the surface; either way, there are many places where reefs exist as isolated mounds or hillocks on the seabed. Such patch reefs are widespread throughout the Southeast Asian region in relatively shallow waters surrounding the islands and on the continental shelves. They vary in size from tens to thousands of metres in diameter, usually with their tops coming to within a few metres of the surface – indeed, some emerge above the surface and are topped by sand cays. Patch reefs further

---

Opposite: *Redcoat Squirrelfish Adioryx (Holocentrus) ruber with mixed corals and feather stars. Squirrelfish (Holocentridae) are primarily nocturnal, feeding mainly on crustaceans at night and hovering singly or in groups, near to or amongst corals and rocks during the day.*

offshore, lying in waters hundreds of metres deep and with even their tops 20m (66ft) or more below the surface, are usually referred to as banks or shoals. Some of the most extensive lie in the South China Sea.

Barrier Reefs
Barrier reefs occur along the edges of island or continental shelves, and are substantial structures. The major difference, apart from size, between them and fringing reefs is that they are separated from the shore by a wide, deep lagoon.

The outer edge of the barrier drops away steeply to the ocean floor beyond. Initially these reefs formed in shallow waters; then, as sea levels increased, they built progressively upwards so that their living topmost parts were still near the surface of the water.

There are a few barrier reefs in the Philippines and Indonesia, but the best-developed are found around Papua New Guinea – for example, the 180km (110-mile) barrier running along the outside of the Louisiade Archipelago off the southern tip of the mainland.

Atolls
These are formations of ancient origin – millions of years old – and take the form of ring-shaped reefs enclosing a shallow lagoon and dropping away to deep water on their outsides. Atolls begun life as fringing reefs around volcanic islands and kept growing as the underlying base gradually subsided beneath the water level.

Most of the world's atolls are in the Indian and Pacific oceans, but there are a number to explore in Southeast Asian waters, particularly around Papua New Guinea and the eastern provinces of Indonesia. Taka Bone Rate Atoll, reputedly the third largest atoll in the world, is off the southern coastline of Sulawesi.

REEF LIFE
The reef ecologies of Southeast Asia – and those off northern Australia – harbour a greater range of species than anywhere else in the Indo-Pacific: they are packed with all manner of bizarre and beautiful plants and exotic animals.

It is likely the region became established as a centre of evolutionary diversification millions of years ago; it has remained so, despite changes in sea levels and in the fortunes of individual reefs, right up until the present day.

On most reefs your attention is likely to be held initially by the fish life: in a single dive's casual observation you might see well over 50 different species, while a more concentrated effort would reveal hundreds. Even that is only part of the story.

The reefs and associated marine habitats of most Southeast Asian countries support well over 1000 species, but many are hidden from view within the complex framework of the reef – gobies, for example, usually in fact the most numerous of all the fish species on a reef, are seldom noticed.

Reef Zones and Habitats
Reefs can be divided into a number of zones reflecting differences in such features as depth, profile, distance from the shore, amount of wave action, and type of seabed. Associated with each zone are characteristic types of marine life.

The Back Reef and Lagoon
The back reef and lagoon fill the area between the shore and the seaward reef. Here the seabed is usually a mixture of sand, coral rubble, limestone slabs and living coral colonies. The water depth varies from a few metres to 50m (165ft) or more, and the size of the lagoon can be anywhere from a few hundred to thousands of square metres. The largest and deepest lagoons are those associated with barrier reefs and atolls, and may be dotted with islands and smaller reefs.

Sites within lagoons are obviously more sheltered than those on the seaward reef, and are also more affected by sedimentation. Here you will find many attractive seaweeds; most of the corals are delicate, branching types. Large sand-dwelling anemones are often found, and in places soft corals and 'false corals' are likely to form mats over the seabed. Especially where there is a current you may encounter extensive beds of seagrasses, the only flowering plants to occur in the sea. Among the many species of animals that make these pastures their home are the longest Sea Cucumbers you will find anywhere around the reef.

Although some typical reef fishes are absent from this environment, there is no shortage of interesting species. On the one hand there are roving predators – snappers, wrasse, triggerfish, emperors and others – on the lookout for worms, crustaceans, gastropods, sea urchins and small fish. Then there are the bottom-dwelling fish that burrow into the sand until completely hidden, emerging only when they need to feed.

Most entertaining to watch – if you spot them – are the small gobies that live in association with Pistol Shrimps. In this partnership the shrimp is the digger and the goby, stationed at the entrance to the burrow, is the sentry. The small fish remains ever on the alert, ready to retreat hurriedly into the burrow at the first sign of disturbance. The shrimp has very poor eyesight; it keeps its antennae in close touch with the goby so that it can pick up the danger signal and, likewise, retire swiftly to the safety of the burrow.

The Reef Flat
Reef flats are formed as their associated reefs push steadily seaward, leaving behind limestone areas that are eroded and planed almost flat by the action of the sea. The reef flat is essentially an intertidal area, but at high tide it can provide interesting snorkelling.

The inner part of the reef flat is the area most sheltered from the waves, and here you may find beautiful pools full of corals and small fish. Among the common sights are 'micro-atolls' of the coral genus Porites; their distinctive doughnut (toroidal) shape, with a ring of coral surrounding a small, sandy-bottomed pool, occurs as a result of low water level and hot sun inhibiting the upward growth of the coral. In deeper water, as on the reef rim, the same coral forms huge rounded colonies.

Towards the outer edge of the reef flat, where wave action is much more significant, surfaces are often encrusted with calcareous red algae, and elsewhere you will usually find a fine mat of filamentous algae that serves as grazing pasture for fish, sea urchins, gastropods, molluscs and other animals. Some fish are permanent inhabitants of the reef-flat area, retreating to pools if necessary at low tide; but others, like parrotfish and surgeonfish, spend much of their time in deeper water, and then crowding over onto the reef flat with the rising tide.

The Seaward Reef Front

Most divers ignore the shoreward zones of the reef and head straight for sites on the reef front, on the basis that here they are most likely to see spectacular features and impressive displays of marine life. Brightly lit, clean, plankton-rich water provides ideal growing conditions for corals, and the colonies they form help create habitats of considerable complexity. There is infinite variety, from shallow gardens of delicate branching corals to walls festooned with soft corals and sea fans.

The top 20m (66ft) or so of the seaward reef is especially full of life. Here small, brilliantly coloured damselfish and anthias swarm around the coral, darting into open water to feed on plankton. Butterflyfish show their dazzling arrays of spots, stripes and intricate patterns as they probe into crevices or pick at coral polyps – many have elongated snouts especially adapted for this delicate task. By contrast, you can see parrotfish biting and scraping at the coral, over time leaving characteristic white scars.

Open-water species like fusiliers, snappers and sharks cover quite large areas when feeding, and wrasse often forage far and wide over the reef. But many species are more localized and can be highly territorial, on occasion even being prepared to take on a trespassing diver. Clownfishes (Amphiprion spp) and Premnas biaculeatus are among the boldest, dashing out from the safety of anemone tentacles to give chase.

Fish-watching can give you endless pleasure, but there is much else to see. Any bare spaces created on the reef are soon colonized, and in some places the surface is covered with large organisms that may be tens or even hundreds of years old. These sedentary reef-dwellers primarily rely on, aside from the omnipresent algae, waterborne food. Corals and their close relatives – anemones, sea fans and black corals – capture planktonic organisms using their tiny stinging cells. Sea squirts and sponges strain the plankton as seawater passes through special canals in their body-walls. Other organisms have rather different techniques: the Christmas-tree Worm, for exam-

ple, filters out food with the aid of its beautiful feathery 'crown' of tentacles.

Apart from the fish and the sedentary organisms there is a huge array of other lifeforms for you to observe on the reef. Tiny crabs live among the coral branches and larger ones wedge themselves into appropriate nooks and crannies, often emerging to feed at night. Spiny lobsters hide in caverns, coming out to hunt under cover of darkness. Gastropod molluscs are another type of marine creature seldom seen during the day, but they are in fact present in very large numbers, especially on the shallower parts of the reef; many of them are small, but on occasion you might come across one of the larger species, like the Giant Triton (Charonia tritonis).

Some of the most easily spotted of the mobile invertebrates are the echinoderms, well represented on Southeast Asian reefs. Most primitive of these are the feather stars, sporting long delicate arms in all colours from bright yellow to green, red and black. The best-known of their relatives, the sea urchins, is the black, spiny variety that lives in shallow reef areas and is a potential hazard to anyone walking onto the reef.

Many of the small, brightly coloured starfish that wander over the reef face feed on the surface film of detritus and micro-organisms. Others are carnivorous, browsing on sponges and sea mats, and a few feed on living coral polyps. The damage they cause depends on their size, their appetite and, collectively, their population density. Potentially the most damaging of all is the large predator Acanthaster planci, the Crown-of-Thorns Starfish; fortunately populations of this creature have so far reached plague proportions on relatively few of the Southeast Asian reefs, and so extensive damage caused by it is not yet commonplace.

Whether brilliantly attractive or frankly plain, whether swiftly darting or sessile, all the life forms you find on the reef are part of the reef's finely balanced ecosystem. You are not: you are an intruder, albeit a friendly one. It is your obligation to cause as little disturbance and destruction among these creatures as possible.

MARINE CONSERVATION

Reefs in the Southeast Asian region are among the most biologically diverse in the world; they are also valuable to the local people as fishing grounds and as sources of other important natural products including shells. Unfortunately, in the past few decades they have come under increasing pressure from human activities, and as a result they are, in places, showing signs of wear and tear.

Corals are slow-growing: if damaged or removed they may require years to recover or be replaced. In the natural course of events, storm-driven waves from time to time create havoc on coral reefs, especially in the typhoon belt. But some human activities are similarly destructive, especially blast fishing and the indiscriminate collection of corals to sell as marine curios.

Overfishing is a further deadly hazard to reef environments, and has already led to perilously declining populations of target species in some areas. Another way overfishing can cause grave damage is through altering the balance of local ecosystems; for example, decreasing the populations of herbivorous fish can lead to an explosive increase in the algae on which those species feed, so the corals of the reef may be overgrown and suffer.

Some areas are being damaged by pollution, especially where reefs occur close to large centres of human population. Corals and other reef creatures are sensitive to dirty, sediment-laden water, and are at risk of being smothered when silt settles on the bottom. Sewage, nutrients from agricultural fertilizers and other organic materials washed into the sea encourage the growth of algae, sometimes to the extent that – again – corals become overgrown.

One final point affects us divers directly. Although, like other visitors to the reef, we wish simply to enjoy ourselves, and although most of us are conscious of conservation issues and take steps to reduce any deleterious effects of our presence, tourism and development in general have created many problems for the reefs. Harbours, jetties and sea walls are on occasion built so close to reefs – sometimes even on top of them! – that the environment is drastically altered and populations of reef organisms plummet. Visiting boats often damage the corals through inadvertent grounding or careless or insouciant anchoring. And divers themselves, once they get in the water, may, unintentionally cause damage as they move about on the reef.

Growing awareness of environmental issues has given rise to 'ecotourism'. The main underlying principle is often summarized as 'take nothing but photographs, leave nothing but footprints', but even footprints – indeed, any form of touching – can be a problem in fragile environments, particularly among corals. A better way to think of ecotourism is in terms of managing tourism and the tourists themselves in such a way as to make the industry ecologically sustainable. The necessary capital investment is minimal, and thereafter much-needed employment becomes available for the local population. In the long term the profits would exceed those from logging or overfishing.

Although divers, as well as many dive operators and resorts, have been at the forefront in protecting reefs and marine ecosystems, we all need somewhere to eat and sleep. If a small resort is built without a waste-treatment system, the nearby reefs may not be irreparably damaged; but if those same reefs start to attract increasing numbers of divers and spawn further resorts, strict controls become necessary.

In such discussions of ecotourism we are looking at the larger scale. It is too easy to forget that 'tourists' and 'divers' are not amorphous groups but collections of individuals, with individual responsibilities and capable of making individual decisions. Keeping reefs ecologically sustainable depends as much on each of us as it does on the dive and resort operators. Here are just some of the ways in which you, as a diver, can help preserve the reefs that have given you so much:

- Try not to touch living marine organisms with either your body or your diving equipment. Be particularly careful to control your fins, since their size and the force of kicking can damage large areas of coral. Don't use deep fin-strokes next to the reef, since the surge of water can disturb delicate organisms.

- Learn the skills of good buoyancy control – too much damage is caused by divers descending too rapidly or crashing into corals while trying to adjust their buoyancy. Make sure you are properly weighted and learn to achieve neutral buoyancy. If you haven't dived for a while, practise your skills somewhere you won't cause any damage.

- Avoid kicking up sand. Clouds of sand settling on the reef can smother corals. Snorkellers should be careful not to kick up sand when treading water in shallow reef areas.

- Never stand on corals, however robust they may seem. Living polyps are easily damaged by the slightest touch. Never pose for pictures or stand inside giant basket or barrel sponges.

- If you are out of control and about to collide with the reef, steady yourself with your fingertips on a part of the reef that is already dead or covered in algae. If you need to adjust your diving equipment or mask, try to do so in a sandy area well away from the reef.

- Don't collect or buy shells, corals, starfish or any other marine souvenirs.

- On any excursion, whether with an operator or privately organized, make sure you take your garbage back for proper disposal on land.

- Take great care in underwater caverns and caves. Avoid lots of people crowding into the cave, and don't stay too long: your air bubbles collect in pockets on the roof of the cave, and delicate creatures living there can 'drown in air'.

- If booking a live-aboard dive trip, ask about the company's environmental policy – particularly on the discharge of sewage and anchoring. Avoid boats that cause unnecessary anchor damage, have bad oil leaks, or discharge untreated sewage near reefs.

- Don't participate in spearfishing for sport – it is anyway now banned in many countries. If you are living on a boat and relying on spearfishing for food, make sure you are familiar with all local fish and game regulations and obtain any necessary licensing.

- Don't feed fish. It may seem harmless but it can upset their normal feeding patterns and provoke aggressive behaviour – and be unhealthy for them if you give them food that is not part of their normal diet.

- Don't move marine organisms around to photograph or play with them. In particular, don't hitch rides on turtles: it causes them considerable stress.

CONSERVATION IN MALAYSIA

The main causes of reef destruction in Malaysia are removal of coral for building, damage caused by blast fishing or trawlers getting too close to reefs, river run-off, and effluent and sewage discharge into the sea.

Blast fishing, illegal since 1985, has been curbed to some extent, but still continues in a few areas. How much damage has been caused by sedimentation is not really known, but in Peninsular Malaysia it has been noticeable around Pangkor and the Sembilan Islands and in the Pulau Perhentian and Pulau Redang groups. In Sabah, sedimentation damage has occurred in the Tunku Abdul Rahman Marine Park and around Kota Kinabalu.

Malaysian reefs and adjacent waters are important for both subsistence and commercial fishing, and in some areas reef fish comprise as much as 30% of the total fish catch. As with other countries, there has been a marked decline in fisheries in certain areas (e.g., the Strait of Malacca), and populations of marine turtles have declined throughout.

Providing long-term protection for coral reefs is a complex task, since it is not only a question of protecting the reef itself but also of ensuring that nearby land-based activities do not adversely affect the corals and marine life. Marine parks are often only really effective if part of a coastal-management programme that also encompasses terrestrial habitats. Thus the integration of protected areas requires considerable resources as well as commitment on the part of national governments.

Another important component of coral-reef conservation is the use of Environmental Impact Assessment (EIA) studies, which help pinpoint potential problem areas in the development of coastal regions. Finally, community involvement and public education are vital if the need for sustainable management is to be understood and carried through at local level.

The Malaysian government has recognized the need for integrated planning and management of both land and sea to control and minimize adverse effects on the marine environment. About 25 Marine Protected Areas (MPAs) are either planned or already in existence. In terms of public education and, just as important, the provision of improved economic opportunities (so that no one need damage reefs to sustain their livelihood), several government agencies and NGOs are active in the community. Despite the government's commitment to marine conservation, there are major challenges to be faced. EIAs are mandatory in Malaysian law for only some development projects, and there are many shortcomings in the procedures which will need rectification if they are to become truly effective. Planning at the regional level often fails to incorporate environmental criteria, and it can take up to four years to implement management plans even when agreed upon. Securing consensus between the different levels of government is another problem, since political approval for conservation measures also has to be gained at local and state level. Finally, trained marine personnel are in short supply.

The growth of sport diving in Malaysia provides a powerful economic incentive to improve the effectiveness of marine-conservation measures and, ultimately, a sustainable future for the country's marine heritage.

CONSERVATION IN SINGAPORE

The recent history of Singapore is one of continuous construction, particularly on the southern coast and the southern islands. Inland construction projects deposit silt into the rivers and hence the sea, while coastal construction projects are mostly on land reclaimed using landfill. Many thousands of tonnes of sand have been used to make the artificial beaches of Sentosa Island. The level of siltation is exacerbated by regular construction on the nearby Indonesian islands, busy shipping movements and industrial pollution.

Fortunately Singapore has some very vociferous and active conservation societies, both marine and terrestrial. The Republic of Singapore Yacht Club, the Singapore Underwater Federation and the Singapore Institute of Biology, supported by the Singapore Sea Sports Liaison Committee, spent four years making extensive surveys of Singapore's coral reefs, using hundreds of volunteer divers. They presented a comprehensive report to the government in 1991. The Marine Conservation Group of the Malayan Nature Society (Singapore Branch) recently organized the transplantation of corals from threatened reefs to an area of Sentosa Island where no reef existed. This 'coral-reef rescue project' was sponsored by the Care-for-Nature Trust Fund and the Hong Kong Bank. The key organizer was marine biologist Helen Newman, with the help of volunteer divers from local dive clubs, dive shops and universities.

Opinions vary about this type of project. Some say that often the wrong types of corals for the site might be transplanted and would soon die, so it would have been better to install an artificial reef. However, the transplanted corals have been constantly monitored and scientific knowledge gained. The ensuing publicity has done much to develop public awareness, and another similar project is now under way – to transplant to Sentosa Island the corals of Pulau Air Chawan, off Jurong.

COMMON FISH

Angelfish (family Pomacanthidae)
These beautiful fish, with their minute, brushlike teeth, browse on sponges, algae and corals. Their vibrant colouring varies according to the species, like those of the butterflyfish and were once thought part of the same family. However, they are distin-guishable by a short spike extend-ing from the gill cover. Angelfish are territorial in habit and tend to occupy the same caves or ledges for a period of time.

Emperor Angelfish, 30cm (12in)
Pomancanthus Imperator

Barracuda (family Sphyraenidae)
With their elongated, streamlined, silvery body and sinis-ter-looking jaws, barracudas tend to appear rather fear-some. However, even though they rarely threaten divers, caution on approach is advisable. Barracudas are effec-tive reef predators . They tend to school in large numbers when young but by the time they mature to a length of two metres or longer, they prefer to hunt singly or in pairs.

Pickhandle Barracuda, 2m (6½ft)
Sphyraena Jello (& Remora)

Bigeyes (family Priacanthidae)
As their name suggests, these small, nocturnal fish have extremely large eyes. Bigeyes are effective predators which hide in pro-tective holes in the coral by day and venture out at night to feed on other small fish, crabs, larvae and the larger plank-tonic animals (the organic life which is found floating at various depths.

Big Eye, 30cm (12in)
Priacanthus Hamrur

Blenny (family Blennidae)
Blennies are often incredibly hard to spot, since they are usually well camouflaged and blend into the rubble- or algae-covered reef bottom where they live. The carnivo-rous blennies are ferocious hunters, whipping out so quickly from their hiding places to snatch small prey that the entire split-sec-ond action can go completely unno-ticed unless you know exactly what you're looking for and where to look.

Blenny, 15cm (6in)
Blennidae

Butterflyfish (family Chaetodontidae)
Among the most colourful of reef inhabitants, butterfly-fish have flat, thin bodies, usually with a stripe through the eye and sometimes with a dark blotch near the tail: this serves as camouflage and confuses predators, who lunge for the wrong end of the fish. Butterflyfish can also, unusually, swim backwards to escape danger. Many species live as mated pairs and have territories while others school in large numbers.

Racoon Butterflyfish, 21cm (8in)
Chaetodon Lunula

Damselfish and Clownfish (family Pomacentridae)
These pugnacious little fish often farm their own patch of algae. Found almost everywhere on the reef, they also sometimes form large aggregations to feed on plankton. Clownfishes (*Amphiprion spp*) and *Premnas Biaculeatus*, which live among the stinging tenta-cles of the sea anemone, are also members of this family. Of the 27 clownfish species known from the Indo-Pacific, 15 are found on the reefs of Southeast Asia.

Clownfish, 5cm (2in)
Amphiprion Rubrocinctus

Cardinalfish (family Apogonidae)
These tiny fish live in a wide range of depths down the reef. Their colours vary widely, but most have large eyes which help their night vision as they come out of hiding to feed on the plankton that rises up through the water as night falls. Cardinalfish also have large mouths and, in some species,

Largetooth Cardinal Fish, 12cm (5in)
Cheilodipterus Macrodon

the male incubates the eggs inside its mouth. During this period, the male juggles the egg mass from time to time and refrains from feeding. This process is known as mouth brooding and is a reproductive strategy that is used by certain species of marine fish.

Goatfish (family Mullidae)

Easily recognized by their chin whiskers, a pair of long barbels which they use to hunt for food, goatfish are often seen moving along sandflats, stirring up small clouds of sand as they feel beneath the surface for prey. They sometimes forage in small groups or large schools. Goatfish are benthic, or 'bottom dwellers', which is the name for fish that either feed or lie camouflaged on the ocean floor.

Yellowsaddle Goatfish, 25-30cm (10-12in)
Parupeneus Cyclostomus

Goby (family Gobiidae)

The Goby is another 'bottom dweller' which can remain undetected on the sea bed for long periods of time. They have large, protruding eyes which are raised above the level of the head and powerful jaws which enable them to snatch prey and dart back to safety. Gobies are among the most successful reef families, with literally hundreds of species. Their colouring varies from brightly coloured to quite drab.

Hector's Goby, 15cm (6in)
Amblygobius Hectori

Grouper (family Serranidae)

Groupers range from just a few centimetres long to the massive Giant Grouper, 3.5m (12ft) long. They vary enormously in colour; grey with darker spots is the most common. Movement is slow except when attacking prey with remarkable speed. All groupers are carnivorous, feeding on invertebrates and other fish. Like wrasse and parrotfish, some start out as females and become males later while others are hermaphroditic.

Lunartail Grouper, 35cm (14in)
Variola Louti

Jack and Trevally (family Carangidae)

Jacks and trevallies are fast predators which range in size from small to very large. they can be silver, black, green or yellow. They are usually found in the open water but are occasional visitors to the reef since they follow the current as they feed. Cruising the outer slopes, they dash in with lightning speed to snatch unwary reef fish. They can be seen singly, schooling or in small groups.

Yellowspotted Jack Fish, 30cm (12in)
Carangoides Fulvoguttatus

Moray Eel (family Muraenidae)

This ancient species of fish have gained their undeserved reputation for ferocity largely because, as they breathe, they open and close the mouth to reveal their numerous sharp teeth. They do not have fins or scales. Moray Eels anchor the rear portion of their bodies in a selected coral crevice and stay hidden during the day. They emerge at night to feed on shrimp, octopuses and mussels and are immediately attracted by the smell of dead or injured fish.

Giant Moray Eel, 2m (6½ft)
Gymnothorax Javanicus

Moorish Idol (family Zanclidae)

This graceful and flamboyant fish reaches a maximum size of 20cm. It is easily distinguished by its long dorsal fin, thick protuding lips and pointed snout. It probes for food (mostly algae and invertebrates) in nooks and crannies. Moorish Idols are usually seen individually, but may sometimes form large aggregations prior to spawning. Moorish Idols are related to surgeonfish even though their body shape is quite different.

Moorish Idol, 18cm (7in)
Zanclus Cornutus

Parrotfish (family Scaridae)

So-called because of their sharp, parrot-like beaks and bright colours, the parrotfishes are among the most important herbivores on the reef. Many change colour and sex as they grow, the terminal-phase males developing striking coloration by comparison with the drabness of the initial-phase males and females. Many build transparent cocoons of mucus to sleep in at night, the mucus acting as a scent barrier against predators. The beak of the Parrotfish enable them to crunch the surface of coral rock to feed on algal stubble and boring algae within.

Swarthy Parrotfish, 40cm (16cm)
Scarus Niger

Pipefish and Seahorse (family Syngathidae)
Pipefish and seahorses, are poor swimmers. They tend to lurk in seagrass beds or amongst coral away from currents. Seahorses use their tails to wrap themselves around corals and seagrasses to stop themselves being swept away. Their vulnerability has forced them to become masters of disguise, sometimes mimicking a blade of grass or a gorgonian coral.

Pipefish, 14cm (5½in)
Corythoichthys

Pufferfish (family Tetraodontidae)
These small to medium-size, highly poisonous, omnivores feed on algae, worms, molluscs and crustaceans. Pufferfish are found all the way down the reef to depths of around 30m (100ft). They are slow moving but when threatened, they inflate themselves into big, round balls by sucking water into the abdomen, so that it becomes almost an impossible task for predators to try and swallow them.

Map Pufferfish, 50cm (20in)
Arothron Mappa

Snapper (family Lutjanidae)
Snappers are important carnivores on the reef, feeding mostly at night. Many are inshore-dwellers, although the Yellowtail Snapper is a midwater fish and the commercially exploited Red Snapper dwells at all depths. Snappers are becoming much rarer on the reefs because they are

Checkered Snapper, 22cm (9in)
Lutjanus Decussatus

long-lived and slow-growing which means that once the populations are drastically reduced they unfortunately take a long time to replenish.

Soldierfish and Squirrelfish (family Holocentridae)
Both species are nocturnal fish and are often confused with each other. Soldierfish have a rounder, bulkier body and are more evenly coloured than squirrelfish. The red or reddish-orange coloration and large eyes are also common among other nocturnal fishes like bigeyes. Dozing under rocks or corals by day, they emerge by night to feed. They have serrated, spiny scales and sharp defensive fins.

Blotch Eye Soldierfish, 12cm (5in)
Myripristis Murdjan

Triggerfish (family Balistidae)
Triggerfish are medium to large fish with flattened bodies and often striking markings (e.g., the Picasso Triggerfish [*Rhinecanthus aculeatus*]), these have powerful teeth and feed on crustaceans and echinoderms on the mid-reef. Large species cruise coral looking for food. When a triggerfish is threatened it squeezes itself into a crevice and erects its first dorsal spine, locking it into place with a second, smaller spine: this stays wedged until the 'trigger' is released.

Orange Striped Triggerfish, 18cm (7in)
Balistapus Undulatus

Wrasse and Hogfish (family Labridae)
Wrasse vary enormously in size, from the tiny Cleaner Wrasse (*Labroides spp*) to the giant Napoleon Wrasse (*Cheilinus undulatus*), which can reach nearly 2m (6½ft) in length. Wrasse are usually brightly coloured and go through various colour and sex changes as they mature. Their distinctive buck teeth are well adapted to pulling molluscs from rocks or picking off crustaceans. Most live in shallow reef areas, although some will frequent greater depths.

Giant Humphead Wrasse, 1m (40in)
Cheilinus Undulatus

UNDERWATER PHOTOGRAPHY

Photography has become one of the most popular underwater pastimes. Being able to capture on film some of the amazing creatures we see underwater is highly rewarding, but can also prove incredibly frustrating, as the real difficulties of underwater photography – backscatter, fish that refuse to stay still, flooded camera housings and so on – become apparent. You need a lot of perseverance – and some luck – to get really good results, but if you're prepared to persist you'll find you've developed a passion that will last for a lifetime of diving.

Shallow-Water Cameras

There are several cameras on the market that are suitable for snorkelling. Kodak and Fuji both offer cheap, single-use cameras that are waterproof down to about 2m (6^1/$_2$ft) and work well enough in clear, sunlit waters. If you object to disposables, Minolta and Canon make slightly more expensive cameras that can be used down to depths of about 5m (16ft).

Submersible Cameras and Housings

You have essentially two main options for serious underwater photography. The first is to lash out on a purpose-built waterproof camera; the second is to buy a waterproof housing for your normal SLR land camera. Each system has its pros and cons.

The submersible camera used by most professionals is the Nikonos, a 35mm non-reflex camera with TTL (through-the-lens) automatic exposure system and dedicated flashguns. (A popular alternative is the Sea & Sea Motor Marine II.) The specially designed Nikonos lenses give sharper results underwater than any housed lenses, but the lack of reflex focusing makes it difficult to compose pictures, and you can easily cut off part of a subject. Lenses range from 15mm to 80mm in focal length, but must be changed in air. Underwater, the 35mm lens is of much use only with extension tubes or close-up outfits, though it can be used in air. The 28mm lens should be considered the standard.

Other companies supply accessories for the Nikonos: lenses, lens converters, extension tubes and housings to accommodate fish-eye and superwide land-camera lenses. Lens converters are convenient: they can be changed underwater. The Motor Marine II makes good use of these, with converters for wide-angle and macro. The Nikonos close-up kit can also be changed underwater.

Nikonos have recently introduced the RS-AF, a fully waterproof reflex camera with autofocus and dedicated lenses and flashgun, but it is extremely heavy and expensive. It is a poor buy by comparison with land cameras like Nikon's 801, F90 and F4 in housings; these are more versatile, weigh less, and can be used also on land.

Land cameras can be used underwater in specialist metal or plexiglass housings. Housings without controls, as used for fully automatic cameras, require fast films to obtain reasonable shutter speeds and lens apertures in the low ambient light underwater. Housings are available for all top-grade reflex cameras, but there are advantages and disadvantages to each system:

- Metal housings are strong, reliable, work well at depth and last a long time if properly maintained; they are heavier to carry, but are buoyant in water. Their higher cost is justified if your camera is expensive and deserves the extra protection.

- Plexiglass housings are fragile and need careful handling both in and out of the water; they are available for a wide range of cameras. They are lightweight, which is convenient on land, but in water are often too buoyant, so that you have to attach extra weights to them. Some models compress at depth, so the control rods miss the camera controls ... but, if you adjust the rods to work at depths they do not function properly near the surface! However, as most underwater photographs are taken near the surface, in practice this drawback is not usually serious.

E6 PUSH/PULL PROCESSING

If you have been on holiday or on a longer trip, there is always a possibility that, unknown to you, your cameras, flashguns or meters may not have been performing correctly. The exposures may be wrong: while colour negative films allow an exposure latitude of four f-stops (black-and-white films even more), colour transparency films are sensitive to within a quarter of an f-stop. Your problems do not stop there: the processor can suffer from power cuts or machinery failures.

In light of these considerations, professional photographers never have all their exposed film processed at the same time. Instead, they have it done in small batches.

This way you can review the results of the film processed so far. If all is not right, the processing of an E6 film can be adjusted by a professional laboratory so that, in effect, the exposure is made faster by up to two f-stops or slower by up to one f-stop. Some changes in colour and contrast result, but they are not significant.

Kodachrome films can likewise be adjusted in the processing, although not to the same extent. This can be done by various laboratories in the USA or, in the UK, by the Kodak Professional Laboratory at Wimbledon.

If you suspect a particular film, have a clip test done. This involves the initial few frames being cut off and processed first so that you can have a look at the results.

'O' Rings

Underwater cameras, housings, flashguns and cables have 'O' ring seals. These and their mating surfaces or grooves must be kept scrupulously clean. 'O' rings should be lightly greased with silicone grease to prevent flooding; too much grease will attract grit and hairs. Silicone spray should not be used, as the cooling can crack the 'O' ring.

Removable 'O' rings should be stored off the unit to stop them becoming flat, and the unit itself should be sealed in a plastic bag to keep out moisture. User-removable 'O' rings on Nikonos cameras and flash-synchronization cables are best replaced every 12 months; nonremovable 'O' rings should be serviced every 12–18 months. The 'O' rings on housings usually last the life of the housing.

Lighting

Sunlight can give spectacular effects underwater, especially in silhouette shots. When the sun is at a low angle, or in choppy seas, much of the light fails to penetrate surface. To get the best of it, photograph two hours either side of the sun's highest point. Generally you should have the sun behind you and on your subject.

Water acts as a cyan (blue–green) filter, cutting back red, so photographs taken with colour film have a blue–green cast. Different filters can correct this in either cold or tropical waters, but they reduce the already limited amount of light available. The answer is flash, which will put back the colour and increase apparent sharpness.

Modern flashguns have TTL automatic-exposure systems. Underwater, large flashguns give good wide-angle performance up to 1.5m (5ft). Smaller flashguns have a narrower angle and work up to only 1m (40in); diffusers widen the angle of cover, but you lose at least one f-stop in output. Some land flashguns can be housed for underwater use.

Flashguns used on or near the camera make suspended particles in the water light up like white stars in a black sky (backscatter); the closer these are to the camera, the larger they appear. The solution is to keep the flash as far as possible above and to one side of the camera. Two narrow-angle flashguns, one each side of the camera, often produce a better result than a single wide-angle flashgun. In a multiple-flash set-up the prime flashgun will meter by TTL (if available); any other flashgun connected will give its pre-programmed output, so should be set low to achieve modelling light.

When photographing divers, remember the eyes within the mask must be lit. Flashguns with a colour temperature of 4500°K give more accurate skin tones and colour.

Fish scales reflect light in different ways depending on the angle of the fish to the camera. Silver fish reflect more light than coloured fish, and black fish almost none at all, so to make sure you get a good result you should bracket exposures. If using an automatic camera, do this by altering the film-speed setting. At distances under 1m

(40in) most automatic flashguns tend to overexpose, so allow for this. The easiest way to balance flash with available light is to use TTL flash with a camera set on aperture-priority metering. Take a reading of the mid-water background that agrees with your chosen flash-synchronization speed, and set the aperture one number higher to give a deeper blue. Set your flash to TTL and it will correctly light your subject.

Once you have learnt the correct exposures for different situations you can begin experimenting aesthetically with manual exposure.

Film

For b/w photography, fast 400 ISO film is best. For beginners wishing to use colour, negative print film is best as it has plenty of exposure latitude. (Reversal film is better for reproduction, but requires very accurate exposure.) Kodachrome films are ideal for close work but can give mid-water shots a blue–green water background; although this is in fact accurate, people are conditioned to a 'blue' sea. Ektachrome and Fujichrome produce blue water backgrounds; 50–100 ISO films present the best compromise between exposure and grain, and pale yellow filters can be used to cut down the blue.

Subjects

What you photograph depends on your personal interests. Macro photography, with extension tubes and fixed frames, is easiest to get right: the lens-to-subject and flash-to-subject distances are fixed, and the effects of silting in the water are minimized. Expose a test film at a variety of exposures with a fixed set-up; the best result tells you the exposure to use in future for this particular setting and film. Some fish are strongly territorial. Surgeonfish, triggerfish and sharks may make mock attacks; you can get strong pictures if you are brave enough to stand your ground. Manta rays are curious and will keep coming back if you react quietly and do not chase them. Angelfish and Butterflyfish swim off when you first enter their territory, but if you remain quiet they will usually return and allow you to photograph them.

Diver and wreck photography are the most difficult. Even with apparently clear water and wide-angle lenses there will be backscatter, and you need to use flash if you are going to get a diver's mask to light up.

Underwater night photography introduces you to another world. Many creatures appear only at night, and some fish are more approachable because half-asleep. However, focusing quickly in dim light is difficult, and many subjects disappear as soon as they are lit up, so you need to preset the controls.

On the Shoot – Tips

- Underwater photography starts before you enter the water. If you have a clear idea of what you wish to photograph, you are likely to get better results. And, remember, you can't change films or prime lenses underwater.
- Autofocus systems that work on contrast (not infrared) are good underwater but only for high-contrast subjects.
- When you are balancing flash with daylight, cameras with faster flash-synchronization speeds – 1/125sec or 1/250sec – give sharper results with fast-moving fish. The lens aperture will be smaller, so you must be accurate in your focusing.
- Masks keep your eyes distant from the viewfinder. Buy the smallest-volume mask you can wear.
- Cameras fitted with optical action finders or eye-piece magnifiers are useful in housings but not so important with autofocus systems.
- Coloured filters can give surrealistic results, as do starburst filters when photographing divers with shiny equipment, lit torches or flashguns set to slave.
- Entering the water overweight makes it easier to steady yourself. Wearing an adjustable buoyancy lifejacket enables you to maintain neutral buoyancy.
- Remember not to touch coral and do not wear fins over sandy bottoms – they stir up the sand.

- Wear a wetsuit for warmth.
- Refraction through your mask and the camera lens makes objects appear one-third closer and larger than in air. Reflex focusing and visual estimates of distances are unaffected but, if you measure a distance, compensate by reducing the resultant figure by one-third when setting the lens focus.
- When there is a flat port (window) in front of the lens, the focal length is increased and the image sharpness decreased due to differential refraction. Most pronounced with wide-angle lenses, this should be compensated using a convex dome port. Dome ports need lenses that can focus on a virtual image at about 30cm (12in), so you may have to fit supplementary +1 or +2 dioptre lenses.

A major problem for travelling photographers and videographers is battery charging. Most mainland towns have stockists for AA or D cell batteries, though they may be old or have been badly stored – if the weight does not preclude this, it is best to carry your own spares. Despite their memory problems, rechargeable nickel–cadmium batteries have advantages in cold weather, recharge flashguns much more quickly and, even if flooded, can usually be used again. Make sure you carry spares and that your chargers are of the appropriate voltage for your destination. Quick chargers are useful so long as the electric current available is strong enough. Most video cameras and many flashguns have dedicated battery packs, so carry at least one spare and keep it charged.

Video

Underwater video photography is easier. Macro subjects require extra lighting but other shots can be taken using available light with, if necessary, electronic improvement afterwards. Backscatter is much less of a problem. You can play the results back on site and, if unhappy, have another try – or, at the very least, use the tape again somewhere else.

Health and Safety for Divers

The information in this section is intended as a guide only, it is no substitute for thorough training or professional medical advice. The information is based on currently accepted health and safety information but it is certainly not meant to be a substitute for a comprehensive manual on the subject. We strongly advise that the reader obtains a recognised manual on diving safety and medicine before embarking on a trip.

- Divers who have suffered any injury or symptom of an injury, no matter how minor, related to diving, should consult a doctor, preferably a specialist in diving medicine, as soon as possible after the symptom or injury occurs.

- No matter how confident you are in formulating your own diagnosis remember that you remain an amateur diver and an amateur doctor.
- If you yourself are the victim of a diving injury do not be shy to reveal your symptoms at the expense of ridicule. Mild symptoms can later develop into a major illness with life threatening consequences. It is better to be honest with yourself and live to dive another day.
- Always err on the conservative side when considering your ailment, if you discover you only have a minor illness both you and the doctor will be relieved.

GENERAL PRINCIPLES OF FIRST AID

The basic principles of first aid are:
- doing no harm
- sustaining life
- preventing deterioration
- promoting recovery

In the event of any illness or injury a simple sequence of patient assessment and management can be followed. The sequence first involves assessment and definition of any life threatening conditions followed by management of the problems found.

The first thing to do is to ensure both the patient's and your own safety by removing yourselves from the threatening environment. Make sure that whatever your actions, they in no way further endanger the patient or yourself.

Then the first things to check are:
- A: for AIRWAY (with care of the neck)
- B: for BREATHING
- C: for CIRCULATION
- D: for DECREASED level of consciousness
- E: for EXPOSURE (the patient must be adequately exposed in order to examine them properly)

- **Airway (with attention to the neck):** - is there a neck injury? Is the mouth and nose free of obstruction? Noisy breathing is a sign of airway obstruction.
- **Breathing:** Look at the chest to see if it is rising and falling. Listen for air movement at the nose and mouth. Feel for the movement of air against your cheek.
- **Circulation:** Feel for a pulse next to the wind pipe (carotid artery)
- **Decreased level of consciousness:** Does the patient respond in any of the following ways:
  - A - Awake, Aware, Spontaneous speech
  - V - Verbal Stimuli, does he answer to 'Wake up!'
  - P - Painful Stimuli, does he respond to a pinch
  - U - Unresponsive
- **Exposure:** Preserve the dignity of the patient as far as possible but remove clothes as necessary to adequately effect your treatment.

Now, send for help

If you think the condition of the patient is serious following your assessment, you need to send or call for help from the emergency services (ambulance, paramedics). Whoever you send for help must come back and tell you that help is on its way.

Recovery Position

If the patient is unconscious but breathing normally there is a risk of vomiting and subsequent choking on their own vomit. It is therefore critical that the patient be turned onto his/her side in the recovery position. If you suspect a spinal or neck injury, be sure to immobilize the patient in a straight line before you turn him/her on his/her side.

Cardiopulmonary Resuscitation (CPR)

Cardiopulmonary Resuscitation is required when the patient is found to have no pulse. It consists of techniques to:
- ventilate the patient's lungs - expired air resuscitation
- pump the patient's heart - external cardiac compression

Once you have checked the ABC's you need to do the following:

Airway

Open the airway by gently extending the head (head tilt) and lifting the chin with two fingers (chin lift). This will lift the tongue away from the back of the throat and open the airway. If you suspect a foreign body in the airway sweep your finger across the back of the tongue from one side to the other. If one is found, remove it. Do not attempt this is in a conscious or semi-conscious patient as they will either bite your finger off or vomit.

Breathing
- If the patient is not breathing you need to give expired air resuscitation, in other words you need to breath air into their lungs.
- Pinch the patient's nose closed.
- Place your mouth, open, fully over the patient's mouth, making as good a seal as possible.
- Exhale into the patient's mouth hard enough to cause the patient's chest to rise and fall.
- If the patient's chest fails to rise you need to adjust the position of the airway.
- The 16% of oxygen in your expired air is adequate to sustain life.
- Initially you need to give two full slow breaths.
- If the patient is found to have a pulse, in the next step continue breathing for the patient once every five seconds, checking for a pulse after every ten breaths.
- If the patient begins breathing on his own you can turn him/her into the recovery position.

Circulation

After giving the two breaths as above you now need to give external cardiac compression.
- Kneel next to the patient's chest
- Measure two finger breadths above the notch at the point where the ribs meet the lower end of the breast bone
- Place the heel of your left hand just above your two fingers in the centre of the breast bone
- Place heel of your right hand on your left hand
- Straighten your elbows
- Place your shoulders perpendicularly above the patient's breast bone
- Compress the breast bone 4 to 5cm to a rhythm

of 'one, two, three . . .'
• Give fifteen compressions
Continue giving cycles of two breaths and fifteen compressions checking for a pulse after every five cycles. The aim of CPR is to keep the patient alive until more sophisticated help arrives in the form of paramedics or a doctor with the necessary equipment. Make sure that you and your buddy are trained in CPR. It could mean the difference between life and death.

DIVING DISEASES AND ILLNESS
Acute Decompression Illness
Acute decompression illness means any illness arising out of the decompression of a diver, in other words, by the diver moving from an area of high ambient pressure to an area of low pressure. It is divided into two groups:
• Decompression Sickness
• Barotrauma with Arterial Gas Embolism
It is not important for the diver or first aider to differentiate between the two conditions because both are serious and both require the same emergency treatment. The important thing is to recognise Acute Decompression Illness and to initiate emergency treatment. For reasons of recognition and completeness a brief discussion on each condition follows:

Decompression Sickness
Decompression sickness or 'the bends' arises following inadequate decompression by the diver. Exposure to higher ambient pressure underwater causes nitrogen to dissolve in increasing amounts in the body tissues. If this pressure is released gradually during correct and adequate decompression procedures the nitrogen escapes naturally into the blood and is exhaled through the lungs. If this release of pressure is too rapid the nitrogen cannot escape quickly enough and physical nitrogen bubbles form in the tissues.

The symptoms and signs of the disease are related to the tissues in which these bubbles form and the disease is described by the tissues affected, e.g. joint bend.

Symptoms and signs of decompression sickness include:
• Nausea and vomiting
• Dizziness
• Malaise
• Weakness
• Joint pains
• Paralysis
• Numbness
• Itching of skin
• Incontinence

Barotrauma with Arterial Gas Embolism
Barotrauma refers to the damage that occurs when the tissue surrounding a gaseous space is injured followed a change in the volume or air in that space. An arterial gas embolism refers to a gas bubble that moves in a blood vessel usually leading to obstruction of that blood vessel or a vessel further downstream.
Barotrauma can therefore occur to any tissue that surrounds a gas filled space, most commonly the:
• Ears • middle ear squeeze • burst ear drum
• Sinuses • sinus squeeze • sinus pain, nose bleeds
• Lungs • lung squeeze • burst lung
• Face • mask squeeze • swollen, bloodshot eyes
• Teeth • tooth squeeze • toothache
Burst lung is the most serious of these and can result in arterial gas embolism. It occurs following a rapid ascent during which the diver does not exhale adequately. The rising pressure of expanding air in the lungs bursts the delicate alveoli of lung sacs and forces air into the blood vessels that carry blood back to the heart and ultimately the brain. In the brain these bubbles of air block blood vessels and obstruct the supply of blood and oxygen to the brain, resulting in brain damage.
The symptoms and signs of lung barotrauma and arterial gas embolism include:
• shortness of breath • chest pain • unconsciousness

Treatment of Acute Decompression Illness
• ABC's and CPR as necessary
• Position the patient in the recovery position with no tilt or raising of the legs
• Administer 100% Oxygen by mask (or demand valve)
• Keep the patient warm
• Remove to the nearest hospital as soon a possible
• The hospital or emergency services will arrange the recompression treatment required

Carbon Dioxide or Monoxide Poisoning
Carbon dioxide poisoning can occur as a result of contaminated air cylinder fill, skip breathing (diver holds his breath on SCUBA); heavy exercise on SCUBA or malfunctioning rebreather systems. Carbon monoxide poisoning occurs as a result of: exhaust gases being pumped into cylinders; inferior systems; air intake too close to exhaust fumes. Symptoms and signs would be: Blue colour of the skin; shortness of breath; loss of consciousness.

ROUGH AND READY NONSPECIALIST TESTS FOR THE BENDS

A Does the diver know:
- who he or she is?
- where he or she is?
- what the time is?

B Can the diver see and count the number of fingers you hold up?

Place your hand 50cm (20in) in front of the diver's face and ask him/her to follow your hand with his/her eyes as you move it from side to side and up and down. Be sure that both eyes follow in each direction, and look out for any rapid oscillation or jerky movements of the eyeballs.

C Ask the diver to smile, and check that both sides of the face bear the same expression. Run the back of a finger across each side of the diver's forehead, cheeks and chin, and confirm that the diver feels it.

D Check that the diver can hear you whisper when his/her eyes are closed.

E Ask the diver to shrug his/her shoulders. Both sides should move equally.

F Ask the diver to swallow. Check the Adam's apple moves up and down.

G Ask the diver to stick out the tongue at the centre of the mouth — deviation to either side indicates a problem.

H Check there is equal muscle strength on both sides of the body. You do this by pulling/pushing each of the diver's arms and legs away from and back towards the body, asking him/her to resist you.

I Run your finger lightly across the diver's shoulders, down the back, across the chest and abdomen, and along the arms and legs, both upper and lower and inside and out, and check the diver can feel this all the time.

J On firm ground (not on a boat) check the diver can walk in a straight line and, with eyes closed, stand upright with his/her feet together and arms outstretched.

If the results of any of these checks do not appear normal, the diver may be suffering from the bends, so take appropriate action (see previous page).

Treatment: Safety, ABC's as necessary; CPR if required; 100% oxygen through a mask or demand valve; remove to nearest hospital

Head Injury All head injuries should be regarded as potentially serious.

Treatment: The diver should come to the surface, the wound should be disinfected, and there should be no more diving until a doctor has been consulted. If the diver is unconscious, of course the emergency services should be contacted; if breathing and/or pulse has stopped, CPR (page 168) should be administered. If the diver is breathing and has a pulse, check for bleeding and other injuries and treat for shock; if wounds permit, put sufferer into recovery position and administer 100% oxygen (if possible). Keep him or her warm and comfortable, and monitor pulse and respiration constantly. **DO NOT** administer fluids to unconscious or semi-conscious divers.

Hyperthermia (increased body temperature) A rise in body temperature results from a combination of overheating, normally due to exercise, and inadequate fluid intake. The diver will progress through heat exhaustion to heat stroke with eventual collapse. Heat stroke is an emergency and if the diver is not cooled and rehydrated he will die.

Treatment: Remove the diver from the hot environment and remove all clothes. Sponge with a damp cloth and fan either manually or with an electric fan. Conscious divers can be given oral rehydration salts. If unconscious, place the patient in the recovery position and monitor the ABC's. Always seek advanced medical help.

Hypothermia Normal internal body temperature is just under 37°C (98.4°F). If for any reason it is pushed much below this – usually, in diving, through inadequate protective clothing – progressively more serious symptoms may occur, with death as the ultimate endpoint. A drop of 1°C (2°F) leads to shivering and discomfort. A 2°C (3°F) drop induces the body's self-heating mechanisms to react: blood flow to the peripheries is reduced and shivering becomes extreme. A 3°C (5°F) drop leads to amnesia, confusion, disorientation, heartbeat and breathing irregularities, and possibly rigor.

Treatment: Take the sufferer to sheltered warmth or otherwise prevent further heat-loss: use an exposure bag, surround the diver with buddies' bodies, and cover the diver's head and neck with a woolly hat, warm towels or anything else suitable.

In sheltered warmth, re-dress the diver in warm, dry clothing and then put him/her in an exposure bag; in the open the diver is best left in existing garments. If the diver is conscious and coherent, a warm shower or bath and a warm, sweet drink should be enough; otherwise call the emergency services and meanwhile treat for shock, while deploying the other warming measures noted. Never give alcohol.

Near Drowning Near drowning refers to a situation where the diver has inhaled some water. He or she may be conscious or unconscious. Water in the lungs interferes with the normal transport of oxygen from the lungs into the blood.

Treatment: Remove the diver from the water and check the ABC's. Depending on your findings commence EAR or CPR where appropriate. If possible, administer oxygen by mask or demand valve. All near drowning victims may later develop secondary drowning, a condition where fluid oozes into the lungs causing the diver to drown in his own secretions, therefore all near drowning victims should be observed for 24 hours in a hospital.

Nitrogen Narcosis The air we breathe is about 80% nitrogen; breathing the standard mixture under compression, as divers do, can lead to symptoms very much like those of drunkenness - the condition is popularly called 'rapture of the deep'. Some divers experience nitrogen narcosis at depths of 30-40m (100-130ft). Up to a depth of about 60m (200ft) - that is, beyond the legal maximum depth for sport diving in both the UK and USA -

the symptoms need not (but may) be serious; beyond about 80m (260ft) the diver may become unconscious. The onset of symptoms can be sudden and unheralded. The condition itself is not harmful: dangers arise through secondary effects, notably the diver doing something foolish.

Treatment: The sole treatment required is to return to a shallower depth but do not skip any necessary decompression stops.

Shock Shock refers not to the emotional trauma of a frightening experience but to a physiological state in the body resulting from poor blood and oxygen delivery to the tissues. As a result of oxygen and blood deprivation the tissues cannot perform their functions. There are many causes of shock, the most common being the loss of blood.

Treatment: Treatment is directed as restoring blood and oxygen delivery to the tissues, therefore maintain the ABC's and administer 100% oxygen. Control all external bleeding by direct pressure, pressure on pressure points and elevation of the affected limb. Tourniquet should only be used as a last resort and only then on the arms and legs. Conscious victims should be laid on their backs with their legs raised and head on one side. Unconscious, shocked victims should be placed on their left side in the recovery position.

GENERAL MARINE RELATED AILMENTS

Apart from the specific diving related illnesses, the commonest divers' ailments include sunburn, coral cuts, fire-coral stings, swimmers' ear, sea sickness and various biting insects.

Cuts and Abrasions

Divers should wear appropriate abrasive protection for the environment. Hands, knees, elbows and feet are the commonest areas affected. The danger with abrasions is that they become infected so all wounds should be thoroughly rinsed with fresh water and an antiseptic as soon as possible. Infection may progress to a stage where antibiotics are necessary. Spreading inflamed areas should prompt the diver to seek medical advice.

Swimmer's Ear

Swimmer's ear is an infection of the external ear canal resulting from constantly wet ears. The infection is often a combination of a fungal and bacterial one. To prevent this condition, always dry the ears thoroughly after diving and, if you are susceptible to the condition, insert:
• 5% acetic acid in isopropyl alcohol *or*
• aluminium acetate/acetic acid solution

drops after diving. Once infected, the best possible treatment is to stop diving or swimming for a few days and apply anti-fungal or antibiotic ear drops.

Sea or Motion Sickness

Motion sickness can be an annoying complication on a diving holiday involving boat dives. If you are susceptible to motion sickness, get medical advice prior to boarding the boat. A cautionary note must be made that the antihistamine in some preventative drugs may make you drowsy and impair your ability to think while diving.

Biting Insects

Some areas are notorious for biting insects. Take a good insect repellent and some antihistamine cream for the bites.

Sunburn

Take precautions against sunburn and use high protection factor creams.

Tropical diseases

Visit the doctor before your trip and make sure you have the appropriate vaccinations for the country you are visiting.

Fish that Bite
• **Barracuda**

Barracuda are usually seen in large safe shoals of several hundred fish, each up to 80cm (30in) long. Lone individuals about twice this size have attacked divers, usually in turbid or murky shallow water, where sunlight flashing on a knife blade, camera lens or jewellery has confused the fish into thinking they are attacking their normal prey, such as sardines.

Treatment: Thoroughly clean the wounds and use antiseptic or antibiotic cream. Bad bites will also need antibiotic and anti-tetanus treatment.

• **Moray Eels**

Probably more divers are bitten by morays than by all other sea creatures added together – usually through putting their hands into holes to collect shells or lobsters, remove anchors or hide baitfish. Often a moray refuses to let go, so, unless you can persuade it to do so with your knife, you can make the wound worse by tearing your flesh as you pull the fish off.

Treatment: Thorough cleaning and usually stitching. The bites always go septic, so have antibiotics and anti-tetanus available.

• **Sharks**

Sharks rarely attack divers, but should always be treated with respect. Attacks are usually connected with speared or hooked fish, fish or meat set up as bait, lobsters rattling when picked up, or certain types of vibration such as that produced by helicopters. The decomposition products of dead fish (even several days old) seem much more attractive to most sharks than fresh blood. The main exception is the Great White Shark, whose normal prey is sea lion or seal and which may mistake a diver for one of these. You are very unlikely to see a Great White when diving in Southeast Asian waters, but you might encounter another dangerous species, the Tiger Shark, which sometimes comes into shallow water to feed at night. Grey Reef Sharks can be territorial; they often warn of an attack by arching their backs and pointing their pectoral fins downwards. Other sharks often give warning by bumping into you first. If you are frightened, a shark will detect this from the vibrations given off by your body. Calmly back up to the reef or boat and get out of the water.

Treatment: Victims usually have severe injuries and shock. Where possible, stop the bleeding with tourniquets or pressure bandages and stabilize the sufferer with blood or plasma transfusions **before** transporting to hospital. Even minor wounds are likely to become infected, requiring antibiotic and antitetanus treatment.

- **Triggerfish** Large triggerfish – usually males guarding eggs in 'nests' – are particularly aggressive, and will attack divers who get too close. Their teeth are very strong, and can go through rubber fins and draw blood through a 4mm (1/6 in) wetsuit.
Treatment: Clean the wound and treat it with antiseptic cream.

Venomous Sea Creatures

Many venomous sea creatures are bottom-dwellers, hiding among coral or resting on or burrowing into sand. If you need to move along the sea bottom, do so in a shuffle, so that you push such creatures out of the way and minimize your risk of stepping directly onto sharp venomous spines, many of which can pierce rubber fins. Antivenins require specialist medical supervision, do not work for all species and need refrigerated storage, so

they are rarely available when required. Most of the venoms are high-molecular-weight proteins that break down under heat. Apply a broad ligature between the limb and the body — remember to release it every 15 minutes. Immerse the limb in hot water (e.g., the cooling water from an outboard motor, if no other supply is available) at 50°C (120°F) for 2 hours, until the pain stops. Several injections around the wound of local anaesthetic (e.g., procaine hydrochloride), if available, will ease the pain. Younger or weaker victims may need CPR (page 168). Remember that venoms may still be active in fish that have been dead for 48 hours.

- **Cone Shells** Live cone shells should never be handled without gloves: the animal has a mobil tube-like organ that shoots a poison dart. The result is initial numbness followed by local muscular paralysis, which may extend to respiratory paralysis and heart failure. *You should not be collecting shells anyway!*
Treatment: Apply a broad ligature between the wound and the body. CPR may be necessary.
- **Crown-of-Thorns Starfish** The Crown-of-Thorns Starfish has spines that can pierce gloves and break off under the skin, causing pain and sometimes nausea lasting several days.
Treatment: The hot-water treatment (30min) helps the pain. Septic wounds require antibotics.
- **Fire Coral** Fire corals (*Millepora* spp) are not true corals but members of the class Hydrozoa – i.e., they are more closely related to the stinging hydroids. Many people react violently from the slightest brush with them, and the resulting blisters may be 15cm (6in) across.
Treatment: As for stinging hydroids .
- **Jellyfish** Most jellyfish sting, but few are dangerous. As a general rule, those with the longest tentacles tend to have the most painful stings. The Box Jellyfish or Sea Wasp (*Chironex fleckeri*) of Northern Australia is the most venomous creature known, having caused twice as many fatalities in those waters as have sharks; it has yet to be found in Asian waters but its appearance one day cannot be precluded. Its occurrence is seasonal, and in calmer weather it invades shallow-water beaches; it is difficult to see in murky water. It sticks to the skin by its many tentacles, causing extreme pain and leaving lasting scars. The victim often stops breathing, and young children may even die.
Treatment: Whenever the conditions are favourable for the Box Jellyfish, wear protection such as a wetsuit, lycra bodysuit, old clothes or a leotard and tights. In the event of a sting, there is an antivenin, but it needs to be injected within three minutes. The recommended treatment is to pour acetic acid (vinegar) over animal and wounds alike and then to remove the animal with forceps or gloves. CPR may be required.
- **Lionfish/Turkeyfish** These are slow-moving

except when swallowing prey. They hang around on reefs and wrecks and pack a heavy sting in their beautiful spines.
Treatment: As for stonefish.

- **Rabbitfish** These have venomous spines in their fins, and should on no account be handled.
Treatment: Use the hot-water treatment.

- **Scorpionfish** Other scorpionfish are less camouflaged and less dangerous than the stonefish, but are more common and dangerous enough.
Treatment: As for stonefish.

- **Sea Snakes** Sea snakes have venom 10 times more powerful than a cobra's, but luckily they are rarely aggressive and their short fangs usually cannot pierce a wetsuit.
Treatment: Apply a broad ligature between the injury and the body and wash the wound. CPR may be necessary. Antivenins are available but need skilled medical supervision.

- **Sea Urchins** The spines of sea urchins can be poisonous. Even if not, they can puncture the skin – even through gloves – and break off, leaving painful wounds that often go septic.
Treatment: For bad cases give the hot-water treatment; this also softens the spines, helping the body reject them. Soothing creams or a magnesium-sulphate compress will help reduce the pain. Septic wounds require antibiotics.

- **Stinging Hydroids** Stinging hydroids often go unnoticed on wrecks, old anchor ropes and chains until you put your hand on them, when their nematocysts are fired into your skin. The wounds are not serious but are very painful, and large blisters can be raised on sensitive skin.
Treatment: Bathe the affected part in methylated spirit or vinegar (acetic acid). Local anaesthetic may be required to ease the pain, though antihistamine cream is usually enough.

- **Stinging Plankton** You cannot see stinging plankton, and so cannot take evasive measures. If there are reports of any in the area keep as much of your body covered as possible.
Treatment: As for stinging hydroids.

- **Sting Rays** Sting rays vary from a few centimetres to several metres across. The sting consists of one or more spines on top of the tail; though these point backwards they can sting in any direction. The rays thrash out and sting when trodden on or caught. Wounds may be large and severely lacerated.
Treatment: Clean the wound and remove any spines. Give the hot-water treatment and local anaesthetic if available; follow up with antibiotics and anti-tetanus.

- **Stonefish** Stonefish are the most feared, best camouflaged and most dangerous of the scorpionfish family. The venom is contained in the spines of the dorsal fin, which is raised when the fish is agitated.
Treatment: There is usually intense pain and swelling. Clean the wound, give the hot-water treatment and follow up with antibiotic and anti-tetanus.

- **Others** Venoms occur also in soft corals, the anemones associated with Clownfish and the nudibranchs that feed on stinging hydroids; if you have sensitive skin, do not touch any of them. Electric (torpedo) rays can give a severe electric shock (200–2000 volts); the main problem here is that the victim may be knocked unconscious in the water and drown.

Cuts

Underwater cuts and scrapes – especially from coral, barnacles or sharp metal – will usually, if not cleaned out and treated quickly, go septic; absorption of the resulting poisons into the body can cause bigger problems. After every dive, clean and disinfect any wounds, no matter how small. Larger wounds will often refuse to heal unless you stay out of seawater for a couple of days. Surgeonfish have sharp fins on each side of the caudal peduncle; they use these against other fish, lashing out with a sweep of the tail, and occasionally may do likewise when defending territory against a trespassing diver. These 'scalpels' are often covered in toxic mucus, so wounds should be cleaned and treated with antibiotic cream. As a preventative measure against cuts in general, the golden rule is do not touch! Learn good buoyancy control so that you can avoid touching anything unnecessarily - remember, anyway, that every area of the coral you touch will be killed.

Fish-feeding

You should definitely not feed fish: you can harm them and their ecosystem. Not only that, it is dangerous to you, too. Sharks' feeding frenzies are uncontrollable, and sharks and groupers often bite light-coloured fins. Triggerfish can come at you very fast, and groupers and moray eels have nasty teeth. Napoleon Wrasse have strong mouth suction and can bite. Even little Sergeant Majors can give your fingers or hair a nasty nip.

Bryson, Dr P.J.: *Underwater Diving Accident Manual* (3rd edn 1993), Diving Diseases Research Centre, Plymouth, UK

Chou Loke Ming, and Porfirio, M. Alino: *An Underwater Guide to the South China Sea* (1992), Times Editions, Singapore

Dawood, Dr Richard: *Travellers' Health – How to Stay Healthy Abroad* (3rd edn 1992), Oxford University Press, Oxford, UK

Debelius, Helmut: *Southeast Asia Tropical Fish Guide* (1994), Ikan, Frankfurt, Germany

Eichler, Dieter and Lieske, Ewald (1994) *Korrallenfische Indischer Ozean*, Tauchen, Jahr Verlag Hamburg, Germany

Eliot, Joshua, Bickersteth, Jane, Miller, Jonathan, and Matthews, Georgina (eds): *Indonesia, Malaysia & Singapore Handbook* (1993 edn), Trade & Travel Publications, Bath, UK

George, J., and George, J. David: *Marine Life – An Illustrated Encyclopedia of Invertebrates in the Sea* (1979), Harrap, London, UK

Ho Soon Lin: *Coral Reefs of Malaysia* (1992), Tropical Press, Kuala Lumpur, Malaysia

Kuiter, Rudie H.: *Tropical Reef Fishes of the Western Pacific – Indonesia and Adjacent Waters* (1992), Gramedia, Jakarta

Lieske, Ewald and Myers, Robert (1994) *Collins Pocket Guide to Coral Reef Fishes of the Indo-Pacific and Caribbean*, Harper Collins, London

Myers, Robert F.: *Micronesian Reef Fishes* (2nd edn 1991), Coral Graphics, Barrigada, Guam

Oon, Helen: *Globetrotter Travel Guide Malaysia* (1995), New Holland, London

Sim Yong Wah, Captain: *Malaysia's Undersea Heritage* (1993), Discovery Editions, Kuala Lumpur, Malaysia

Stafford-Deitsch, Jeremy: *Reef – A Safari through the Coral World* (1991), Headline, London, UK

Stafford-Deitsch, Jeremy: *Shark – A Photographer's Story* (1987), Headline, London, UK

Veron, John Edward Norwood: *Corals of Australia and the Indo-Pacific* (1993), University of Hawaii Press, Hawaii

Wells, Sue, and Hanna, Nick: *The Greenpeace Book of Coral Reefs* (1992), Blandford, London, UK

Wells, Sue, et al.: *Coral Reefs of the World* (3 vols, 1988), United Nations Environmental Program/International Union for Conservation of Nature and Natural Resources, Gland, Switzerland

Wheeler, Tony, Finlay, Hugh, Turner, Peter, and Crowther, Geoff: *Malaysia, Singapore & Brunei – A Travel Survival Kit* (4th edn 1991), Lonely Planet Publications, Hawthorn, Victoria, Australia

White, Alan: *Philippine Coral Reefs – A Natural History Guide* (1987), New Day Publishers, Quezon City, Philippines

Wong, Michael Patrick: *Sipadan - Borneo's Underwater Paradise* (1991), Odyssey Publishing, Singapore

Wood, Elizabeth M.: *Corals of the World* (1983), T.F.H. Publications, Neptune, NJ, USA

Index